MW00861701

Harmonious Healing

& The Immortal's Way

Jasmuheen

Harmonious Healing

& The Immortal's Way

Jasmuheen

Light Technology Publishing

Copyright © 2006 by Jasmuheen
All rights reserved.

All rights reserved. No part of this publication may be
reproduced, stored in a retrieval system, or transmitted,
in any form or by any means, electronic, mechanical,
photocopying, recording or otherwise, without the prior
written permission of the publishers.

ISBN 1-891824-59-7

Published by

3॰LIGHT
Technology
PUBLISHING

800-450-0985
www.lighttechnology.com

Printed by

GraphTech
DIGITAL & PRINTING

PO Box 3540
Flagstaff, AZ 86003

Disclaimer: The author fully recognizes and accepts the value of the traditional medical
profession. The ideas, suggestions, and healing techniques in this book are not indicated as a
substitute for proper medical attention. Any application of these ideas, suggestions,
and techniques is at the reader's sole discretion.

For
Arnie
and
Brigitte

Part 1
The Personal Journey

Part 2
The Magical Medicine of Mind Mastery and Meditation

Part 3
Harmonious Healing Help: An Alternative View Diagnostic, Cleansing and Healing Tools and New Technologies

PART 1

THE PERSONAL
JOURNEY

Introduction

At the end of 2004, as I completed my Law of Love tour with its freedom agenda, I found myself back in Australia, confronted with an immediate need to have surgery to remove a very deadly carcinoma. Shocked at having manifested such a situation, I began an extremely interesting journey into the reality of harmonious healing, a path that turned into the immortal's way.

As the weeks unfolded, I noticed a rapid deterioration and aging of my biological and physical system that I seemed to lack the energy or motivation to stop. It seemed impossible that only weeks before, I had been fighting fit with great calibration levels and testing, with kinesiology, a biological age of seventeen. I had sailed through the 2004 tour high on divine love, riding a wave of grace and completely unaware that I was also opening a doorway to my own demise.

With my life spirit withdrawing and my system showing very obvious signs that it was literally moving into the death process, I stepped into the world of harmonious healing while a few thousand miles away a dearly loved friend struggled with this same journey. "How could she have created this?" someone had asked upon learning of my friend's cancer-in-her-lung-and-bone-marrow diagnosis. "She meditates, she is conscious of what she eats and treats her body like a temple, and she's doing positive and meaningful work in the world. How can this happen to her?" Everyone was shocked, confused or saddened by the occurrence.

The reasons for the part we play in the creation of such things are multifaceted and always provide us with powerful learning, and although I have always focused on preventive medicine through lifestyle, here I was finally being confronted with a need to address not just the above question but much more that so few ever touch on: the need for compassion and care for ourselves and others in the healing process, the ability to recognize when it is our time to die and being able to do so with dignity and the ability to die without even succumbing to one of the seven deadly diseases now rampant on our planet.

And there were so many more questions. What about information overload, where people get so overwhelmed with advice regarding how to handle their health care that they simply shut down even further and lethargically surrender to their prognosis? What about the power of prognosis and the power of statements like, "You only have a few months left to live," statements that are made by those whose opinions we may respect? Just how damaging and how self-fulfilling can these statements be?

What about our physical, mental, emotional and spiritual nutrition and its role in the healing process? What about causative factors and the problem that surgically removed cancers often grow back? What about the role of holistic education as a tool for preventive medicine where people understand the true nature of their being and hence adopt lifestyles that prevent illness? And how much suffering will this prevent? What about the growing percentage of people who are now striding into their one hundreds full of health and vitality for life, radiant, fulfilled and positive? How do they achieve this example of harmonious health? What exactly is harmonious health, and how does it relate to the journey of those seeking to be filled with light? Does the journey of enlightenment demand harmony and health within before it can successfully complete its cycle in time?

All of these questions and more began to bounce off the walls of my mind during the early hours of each morning as I awoke to face another dawn, confronted again by my own mortality.

So many questions that I had heard over time now came back and seemed to be demanding answers, and for every question, stories would flow and research would magically manifest itself at my disposal. I had no idea where my journey would lead me or if I would even choose to stay—all I knew was that the warning had come and I was standing at the crossroads of choice. I knew that even nonaction was a choice, as allowing a potentially fatal disease to run unchecked through a body will bring a definite result.

Motivated by the desire to save my own life, more and more questions arose until it felt as if I was being prompted to research and find answers to so many questions. For example: Can a person become too detached and spend too much time in silence as the watcher of the worlds, even though the yogi's espouse that desirelessness and nonattachment are required states for the journey of enlightenment? What happens when a person loses her passion for life and what happens if a person chooses to leave her body, knowing her work is complete, via the process of bilocation? Will there be someone on the other side waiting there to meet her?

Is it okay for a spiritual teacher to leave this plane via the creation of a deadly disease rather than by sitting quietly in meditation and leaving a healthy body and not coming back, just like the lamas can do? What right, if any, do any of us have to judge how a person chooses to leave, and are all death scenarios chosen or determined by unresolved past issues?

What drives a person and gives him passion for life? Is it just the need to survive, or is it a higher calling to contribute something to the evolutionary process of life? What happens if passions are fulfilled so that there is no longer any real drive in life? Can a person buy time and stay even though his work is done? Is there a formula to create such a flow in life that the struggle and questioning ceases, and if so, then what? What happens when it becomes too easy so there are no desires or goals left in life?

And so, armed with a mountain of questions, I began to walk a new journey, feeling sidetracked, away from my focus on the freedom agenda and its law of love and yet realizing that it was all part of the same game. All I knew was that time was no longer on my side and the choice before me was critical.

The journey into harmonious healing is a complex one at best, and the months soon unfolded for me in my journey of discovery. I needed to discover why I had created such a thing; I needed to discover the bigger picture behind it; and I needed to discover how to move back into, and permanently maintain, a state of optimal health.

All of it was also to lead me into such an amazing journey of merging deeper with my DOW—the Divine One Within—the One who loves me enough to give me life. Yet as the months moved on, my journey ended up branching completely into a new direction, a direction that allowed me to discover the door to the immortal's way.

So the first part of this book details my personal journey, beginning with the discovery that I had created a potentially terminal disease within my system, which, if left unchecked, would allow me perhaps another eight or nine months of Earth time. It was a journey that culminated in my discovery of how to reset our exit choices, how to choose to die in the most dignified way—when we are ready and not before. Beyond that I also discovered how we can repattern ourselves into the immortal's way. The second part of this book reveals the magic of meditation plus pragmatic tools to reenergize and find the perfect healing program to heal ourselves. The last part offers research on alternative diagnostic and treatment systems.

Compassion and Care:
Experiencing Empathy

Christmas Eve 2004

C lose your eyes," the doctor said. "Most people get squeamish when they see scalpels and needles. I don't think you'd like to witness this."

Directly above me hung a huge overhead light, and as I lay on the operating table, I could see my image in its reflective casing. No matter how deeply I breathed, all I could feel was the beating of my heart.

Walking into a clinic, as I had done, and offering my face for mutilation seemed such an absurd thing to do, yet, according to the doctor, if I didn't, then the cancer would quickly spread and reach into my lymphatic system. Hopefully we had caught it just in time.

Slowly the needle penetrated into my mouth and, stinging sharply, began to release the numbing liquid that would allow the surgeon to cut out a large section of my mouth, to excise the cancer that had so silently been growing there.

A byproduct of childhood sun baking in the virulent Australian sun whose seed was planted while roasting myself, the cancer had first appeared as a small, scaly, brown spot just above my top lip that I had eventually burnt off using the usual dry-ice method. Fifteen years later, it returned as a pimple-like apparition that refused to heal and began to quickly grow. I had no idea what it was until a small inner voice told me to investigate it further, for no matter what I tried, the sore on my upper lip simply would not recede.

As I never get sick, I have no need of a regular doctor, so I made an appointment to see a lovely woman who had doctored my daughter throughout her pregnancy. Concerned by what she saw, she phoned the local plastic surgeon and asked him to rearrange his busy schedule to take me in immediately.

"It could be fine," she said reassuringly, "but if it's not, then at least he'll excise it neatly and the scarring will be minimal. He does this all the time. Unfortunately, it looks to me like a squamous cell carcinoma, and although it's not quite as deadly as a melanoma, if left untreated, you will die. So the sooner it's removed, the better."

The next day, I found myself in his clinic, nervous and yet relieved as I remembered the scaly brown spot that had first appeared so long ago and listened to stories of cancers whose roots had grown spreading like wildfire to fatally disable so many. "Once it's in the lymphatic system . . ." they'd say with a knowing look of helplessness and concern.

The initial diagnosis was not good, and surgery for removal of the growth was booked without delay. A second opinion and my research on the Internet confirmed that the growth was potentially fatal, and if it was not removed immediately, huge problems could follow. Through kinesiology my body confirmed that the right course of action was the quickest—and the scar would be a reminder of a lesson that needed to be learnt. After six weeks of looking at the spreading growth, I was silently relieved that it could be removed so quickly and effectively.

As I sat in the stillness of my meditation the day before surgery, my mind drifted to France and my close friend Brigitte now surrounded by loving friends and healers. A few days before our retreat in November, when my own growth had first appeared, Brigitte had been diagnosed as having dark shadows in the X-ray of her lungs, and a biopsy performed suspiciously looked like cancer. By the time of my scheduled operation, it had entered her bone marrow, and her family was pressuring her to begin chemotherapy. Most days she spent lying in a morphine-induced semi-coma, unsure of her desire to go or to stay.

Having had cancer once before, I knew what she was confronting and I wished that I could wave a magic wand and save her from her pain. Confusion, doubt, anger, disbelief, courage, questioning, surrender, compliance, acceptance—all of it reveals itself along with a heavy dose of sadness when someone is told she has cancer. I had felt it all, and so I watched as Brigitte journeyed through the pathways of her own emotions. As reports about her progress continued to flood in via email from our mutual friends, all I could do for her, as I now sat thousands of miles away, was pray and trust that I would see my friend again.

"You need to write more on this," an inner voice said as I contemplated it all at that moment. "So many are suffering, and there is more you can do and discover to ease their pain."

There are times when I dislike my job as a writer, for I can only write about things that I live through, and living through this again was not on my most-sought-after-experiences agenda. It was enough to deal with the last time, when I had manifested a cancerous growth on my liver in the early nineties, at a time when I felt that I could deal more easily with whatever I was destined to encounter.

Now, after eleven years on the road sharing the Divine Nutrition agenda under the scrutiny of the media, all I was interested in was peace and quiet. Writing another controversial book and one that could challenge traditional medicine was not appealing at all; still, intuitively I knew that it needed to be done.

Reliving my creation of cancer so long ago, I recalled how it took months to lovingly rebalance my system into health, to deal with the emotions behind the creation of the cancer and to transmute the cellular damage and clear the pathways so it would not return to my liver.

Eleven years later I looked in the mirror at the growth upon my lip and sought again the revelation of a higher meaning. The answer remained the same: "Write about this, write about it all as you live through it." And I knew that Brigitte and countless more deserved the tribute, for in the past five years, so many loved ones exited this world via the creation of cancer. As I lay on the operating table waiting for the anesthetic to take effect, their names and stories flashed before me, and I knew that once more I would have to write.

I close my eyes and neither see nor feel the sharp scalpel begin to cut through my flesh, making an incision from just under my right nostril down into the lip. Nor do I see the large section the surgeon is intent on removing just to make sure he takes it all, for this type of cancer is deadly, and taking more now may later literally save my life. But I do feel the blood begin to flow and fill my nostrils as the nurse works to sponge away the excess.

A red river of warmth flows into my eyes and down my throat as the surgeon begins to slowly sew a complex pattern of stitches after cauterizing the vessels still exposed. The smell of the burning flesh is pungent. I can only trust that he has removed enough of my mouth to stop the spread of the tumor and prevent its carnivorous cells from reaching my lymph system. My heart beats faster as he weaves layer upon layer, and my face lifts up with the pull of the needle as the stitching thread lightly pulls up and rests to then caress my chin. It's as if all my senses are alert, absorbing the scene to record what my eyes are choosing not to see. The nurse touches my wrist and whispers, "Nearly finished now," as she mops up the last of the blood. She is as kind and compassionate as the surgeon is, thankfully, skilled.

My face is tender and swollen; the stitches hold together the blood-red, raw wound. I feel as though I have been in a boxing ring and received an unrelenting stream of blows to my mouth. My inner child feels vulnerable. My physical body is in shock.

My daughter greets me in sympathy, and the baby stares at my mouth and then looks deeply into my eyes as if to acknowledge my pain. For once my granddaughter does not smile at me and instead reaches her tiny hand out to lovingly touch my cheek. I feel I am in the presence of a sage, and the words resurface in my mind about speaking of the poison of the world and the vulnerability of our mouth when we do so. It has been a warning seen and accepted that will leave its permanent, visible mark.

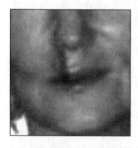

As the anesthetic wears off, the pain is amazingly quite bearable, managed by regular low doses of painkilling drugs. I think of how open-heart surgery and pharmaceuticals prolonged my father's life so long ago now, giving me his presence for an extra thirty years, and although I recognize the benefit of all these things in a modern-day world, I still hold on to the vision of a world no longer requiring such things as education eliminates the eventual need. Still I give thanks to it all.

Later people's stares change from disdain for the growth that they had seen to sympathy about the stitches that have taken its place. The change in their reactions is interesting, and the obviously wounded seem to elicit more compassion. Family file in to celebrate Christmas Eve at my house, and their awareness as they see me morphs from shock to tender concern as all had no idea of the drama; they had no idea that the small spot they had seen could grow so quickly and be so potentially deadly.

Christmas celebrations unfold, and I feel my postsurgery limitations. There are words I can't say, as their pronunciation requires particular mouth movements; I cannot laugh or smile, and if this spontaneously happens, it feels as if I will burst all the stitches. By the end of the night, I have learnt to hold my mouth with my hand to contain any laughing movement, since it's impossible to be with loved ones and not laugh or smile.

Sucking a Christmas drink through a straw, it feels weird to be the center of attention, and yet it is sweet to see how much everyone genuinely cares since I rarely give them cause for concern.

But I feel sadness; it's as if my body is traumatized at how quickly it all came to pass and has had no time for adjustment. I long for silence and solitude to make sense of it all, to seal the weakness in my field where seeds were sown so long ago for this manifestation. Once again I realize that by having this experience, my empathy levels have deepened; once again I realize how important it is to live through it all and be able to write from this point firsthand.

I remember how, when I was diagnosed with the cancerous growth on my liver, using the words "I have cancer" instantly seemed to download all the sadness of that reality. And I feel how real death by this silent parasite can be as cancer cells devour healthy cells to break down the body's ability to function.

During my long, silent walks along the beach in the days that follow, I remember how last time it took me four months to heal what I had created. I remember how the universal field of intelligence seemed to download the perfect data that I needed to do so. And I remember how, once the healing was done, so many seemed to cross my path to learn the secrets of self-healing.

I think of the confusion and horror of those who feel that the lifestyle and attitude of "spiritually aware" people should preclude them from such creations, yet deep self-analysis would always reveal when they had begun to weaken their field and planted a silent seed of destruction. Anger swallowed goes to the liver and sadness to the lungs, so our bodies reveal the emotions that we bury later in form of disease.

Most of all I think of Brigitte and all those who are rallying to help her. I long to pick up the phone and call her and talk as we have always done, yet my mouth is too sore and numb to form words. All I can manage are a few basic sentences, and so the silence becomes my friend. In silence I say my prayers and find her on the inner planes, a little disoriented as the morphine flows through her to keep her pain at bay.

Michael Newton's research on life between lives makes me feel comforted to know that even if it is Brigitte's time to go and she will no longer have a body, we can still connect on the inner planes. Death is just another door, and all the doors can be opened between the realms. Yet I also know that just as I now miss kissing, we all miss the physical comfort and closeness of those who move on.

And so I find myself waiting for the biopsy report, trusting that no further surgery will be done and that I do not need to dance this dance of looking at my own mortality further.

Days pass and the world is rocked with a sadness that adds another layer to my own as I realize again the power of empathy in the healing game. Thousands of miles away, the tsunami claims the lives of over two hundred thousand people, injuring many more and displacing nearly a million. As the world moves from shock into a space of caring and compassion to organize aid and support for the suffering, a new year begins and our issues pale into insignificance. Regardless of our trials and tribulations, there is so much we have to be grateful for, and life always delivers amazing insights to our door. My own trials are no exception.

Experiencing something so personally gifts me with a deeper level of compassion for those suffering in our world and the fear and sadness many feel when confronted with the loss of loved ones. All whom I speak with agree that for the thousands who have moved on, there is rest between lives and the joy of returning to Spirit, and yet our sympathy reaches out to those left behind, who must begin again without the ones they love. In my experience, there are never adequate words to share when those we love leave us, and the only healer is the passing of time. Time delivers days when we take one small step and follow it with another; days filled with nostalgia and tears and the unreality of it all; days filled with grief and sorrow and anger and confusion at the injustice of the loss; and days filled with healing and support.

For those anchored in the reality of the immortality of the soul, there are days filled with clarity and insight, knowing that our loved ones rest in a place of peace, to assess the life just passed before they make plans to return again. And with this reality comes the soothing of a turbulent tide.

New beginnings, new lives, new insights come to us all in so many different ways. For some we are the watcher in the void, surrounded by a sea of forever, held in a state of grace that allows us to see the Isness of all life—and here there is no right, no wrong, no judgment and no need to change; here there is just a constant flow of moving cycles of time. In this state of awareness, all is born, and changes, and ebbs and flows, and moves on a wave that is seen as a breath behind life. In this state, all is perfect in its ability to provide growth, expansion and insight. And in this state, I face my own healing challenge.

Insights and Information

Immediately after my operation, with a mouth swollen and an upper lip full of stitches still congealed with blood, I quickly stopped off to pick up the final Christmas present I had ordered and found myself, while waiting to be served, standing next to an acquaintance well versed in the art of healing, someone whom I would periodically meet and share insights with. As we stood together, he glanced at my mouth and studied my auric field, and a look of concern crossed his face. He didn't talk much. I felt uncomfortable and sensed that there was something that he wanted to say. I briefly mentioned that I had just had surgery to remove a squamous cell carcinoma, and all he said was that I looked tired. As I could hardly talk, there was little to respond with, and so I paid for my purchase and left.

Next morning was Christmas, and a call came through from one of my surrogate sons, who now lives in London. My youngest daughter mentioned that I wouldn't be able to talk for long due to the surgery, and when he came on the phone, he said:

"What on Earth are you doing to yourself? I thought you were beyond such things!"

"Obviously I'm not," I replied with a faint chuckle, aware that I was being led through a maze of deeper learning, still looking for the pieces of the puzzle I was in. It seemed so strange for me, for I had just returned from tour where the focus had been on calibrating the human biosystem into a level where we no longer create disease, a tour where we had spoken so much of demonstrating things like freedom from human limitations.

A few days later, we gathered with my daughters and their families in the city to enjoy a belated Christmas, and when I returned home, there was a message on the answering machine from Einstein, the man I had met in the shop. He simply said: "We need to talk. How soon can you see me?"

A day later he arrived in my ashram and hopped off his bike. Removing his helmet, he followed me through the house to sit on the swinging rainbow chairs that adorn my back veranda.

"There are times when I feel like a naughty child in your presence."

"There are times when I feel like your father," he responded.

"A past life?" we concurred in unison, and I giggled.

We smiled at each other and he said, "Have you heard of a double bind?"

"Perhaps, if you use another term."

"Come inside and I'll demonstrate."

I followed.

"Stand about ten feet away from me. Now come here," he commanded as he held up his left hand in the stop position while his right hand beckoned me on. Seeing it all, I chose to ignore the stop signal and walked up close to stare at his face. It felt like a silly game.

"What did you see?" he asked. "What did you sense?"

"Well, your body language was inconclusive, not clear. One hand said go, as did your voice, and the other hand said stop."

"So let's try this again." He repeated the act.

"Okay," I responded before moving. "Let's get clear, what do you want me to do? Stop or come and how close?"

"Precisely," he said as he sat back down. "You need to be clear, to have more information and make sure there is no confusion, or else there are conflicting signals that create a double bind. It's the same with your body." Looking me squarely in the eye he said, "So I only have one question to ask you."

I waited and listened.

"Do you want to be here?"

I drew a deep breath and hesitated, knowing that on one level, I had reached a point where it no longer mattered—I had long been just a watcher in life. Detached. Fulfilled. No longer driven, no longer searching and finally free of questions.

"Let me get straight to the point then," he added. "I have worked with people in the healing industry for more than thirty years, and I went through a space some time ago where over a period of thirteen months, I watched thirteen people die, taking themselves off this planet through the creation of cancer. I began to recognize the signs, and I have understood that with them and many others, the system seems to shut down over a period of trimesters.

"First a grayness develops in the aura, and I can see that person's system beginning to shut down. At any point in these trimesters, these individuals can stop the process and heal themselves. But many go through a familiar pattern until at the end of the third trimester, their body has broken down, and they die." He paused for effect and I remained silent.

"You have entered into the first trimester of this same pattern, and unless you decide what you want and address and move beyond whatever your double bind is, I give you nine months to live. So if you are preparing to leave, are your affairs in order? You know that you have a legacy with your work to maintain and to make sure it's all still accessible to the world if you choose to go."

I listened quietly, a little surprised at what he was saying but knowing the rightness of it all. On one level, I could accept his reality, and yet I also knew that, now clearly warned, I would not accept it as a reality for myself.

On the drive back from the city, I had asked to meet with wisdom and clarity and knew that this was how the universe had responded, that it had sent me Einstein to give me this insight. I also knew that double binds can create confusion in the human biosystem and that for so long, my body had been listening to me say that I had completed my work here, that I had fulfilled all my goals and all my dreams and wishes.

I had also come to realize that the world is perfect exactly as it is and that as a school, for teaching us limitation and giving us the desire to move beyond it, the Earth is doing her job superbly; that the Divine One Within, the DOW, is really in charge, whether we all acknowledge this or not; and that everyone is quite beautifully guided through each phase in his or her own evolution and is always given all the insights needed at any given time. I had also come to realize that all of it is part of the grander design that will unfold with or without our spiritual teachers; spiritual teachers can just speed this up a little. Knowing all of this, I had become complacent and amazingly detached.

My body had also heard me say so often that the world had been presented with all my research and findings and that now it was all done, now it was up to the world to do with it all what it would regarding the Divine Nutrition program.

And so I had taken more and more of the role of watcher and decided to just be in each moment, to radiate only the love and the wisdom of my own divinity and to go where grace delivered me. At the same time that I had become desireless, I had also become passionless.

All of this my body had listened to for more than three years, and it had finally begun to shut my system down, assuming that if I had completed my work here, then it must be time to go.

As Einstein and I sat and talked in depth about things that I hadn't shared with anyone for so long, the more we shared, the more I realized that there were a number of issues that I was living in a double bind with.

Einstein looked at me and smiled. "Perhaps it's time to move beyond what's safe and comfortable and into the unknown? When you move into the unknown, passion and excitement and potential can flow. And you really need to regain your passion for life right now if you want to stay. Do you?"

Still I had no answer, so I asked him: "How do you ground yourself here? How do you commit to being here?"

"I fall in love," he responded. "All the time—with everyone, with everything. Every day I fall in love. It keeps me passionate about life."

When Einstein said that he maintained his passion for life by falling in love every day, I asked him how he did this.

"It's simple," he replied, smiling. "I look for something special in that person or thing. Maybe it's the color of the eyes or the shirt the person is wearing. When I can see the special, it opens me up to the possibility of falling in love, because that person has something special. There is always something special to be seen in every person or situation—if we are willing to look."

"Then what do you do?" I asked further, curious. "Do you pursue the person? Make yourself known?"

"No, often it never goes anywhere; it's just a constant moment-by-moment feeling of potential, of the possibility of being able to fall in love in every moment, with everyone and everything."

"So you have moments of 'falling in love potential' strung together, of 'appreciation potential' strung together, of 'specialness' strung together, to form a chain that keeps your passion for life?"

He nodded and smiled as I thought to myself what an interesting insight it all was.

"But you haven't finished your work here, have you?" I asked.

"No, I am still recording all my stories and insights. It will be a while before I am done."

"Well, that's another double bind for me," I said and began to tell him the story of how this bind had come into being. I did so perhaps to clarify it more for myself, although I had already spent so much time thinking it all through. Still I realized, as I shared with him, that I had settled for comfortable choices that gave my body conflicting signals, choices that removed the passion from my life. I saw as we spoke that I needed a passion that would light up my auric field with color and brightness and song, allowing it to stay healthy and strong.

"I guess it was three, maybe four years ago now," I began. "I was in Germany, in a concert listening to Nina Hagen . . . have you heard of her?"

Einstein shook his head.

"She does amazing sacred music, bhajans. Anyway, I was there with a few friends and my husband, and the evening was full of magic. There were sounds being created of such love and sacredness and holiness that the most incredibly powerful energy vortexes were being revealed. And so I alchemically joined Nina in her song, weaving her sound waves with rays of light to open up the fields even further. It was the first time I had experienced a musical orgasm. I was so uplifted and amazed, I had no idea that sacred songs could be performed in such a powerful way as to transport an audience so far. I don't know what happened, I can't explain it, but I found myself melting, disappearing into a stream of such sweet, sweet love. It was as if I had magnetically risen out of my body, lured and seduced by such love until the 'I' of me just disappeared.

"The only reason I can talk of it and even understand what had happened is that my husband was sitting beside me and he sensed that something was happening, so he squeezed my hand, which brought me back into an awareness of my body. Reorienting myself I stopped the love pull and looked at what was going on, and I found myself in the light-filled presence of the holy ones who had been with me for so long. Sensing my need for answers, I received the telepathic imprint of an understanding that was something like: 'Your work is complete. If you want, you may dissolve into this love and go.'

"All I felt in that moment was so much love, so much acceptance, so complete, so whole. It was a feeling that was so alluring, so melting . . . it's so inadequate to describe it with words . . ." I stopped for a moment and thought about my life. I understood that I had come to anchor the Divine Nutrition program in the western sphere of the morphogenetic field and that this had been done and that my part in it all was complete.

Images began to flow into my mind—images of choice, of a crossroads of choice. Moving into a future time when I had chosen death and had allowed the love flow to take me, I saw my children and their grief at the choice I had made; I saw that they would miss me and yet accepted that I had gone on. I saw myself relaxing in a field of bliss, enjoying life between lives and then volunteering to come back into some other planetary system and continue the service agenda, as we do. There was so much flashing before me, it was as if the universe was revealing so many pathways and choices and agendas, all in the blink of an eye as the holy ones held the space for it all to flow. Somewhere through it all I scanned for the presence of my granddaughter, and I felt that for her I wanted to stay—not that she would need me; I wanted to stay just for the fun and the play.

And so I asked, "If I have finished my work here, maybe there is more I can do?" And I felt as if the universe smiled and I chose to stay.

Einstein sat there gaining insights into how my first major double bind had begun.

"You know, I was confused for a week, even more," I said. "Wordless, speechless. I know that everything is perfect, and if I was really complete and meant to move on, my husband would not have squeezed my hand and the love would have just melted me entirely. There would have been no discussion, for all is perfect, and it was just a cosmic play reminding me I have choice. And yet I felt that perhaps I had cheated time, that when your time is complete, it is complete, for a week later we were coming into an Italian tunnel, traveling much too fast, and I lost control of the car and missed crashing into the wall by inches. We were nearly killed, and so I thought that perhaps I had tempted fate, that if it is time to go and the love comes for you like that and you turn away, the fields of time will close for you anyway, in another way.

"I also knew, with every fiber of my being, that at least the main chapter, if not all, of my work was complete. I knew that if I never said or did anything with it again, it still would be complete—the seeds had been planted and an evolutionary path had been recorded in history, ridiculed but recorded."

We both laughed and then Einstein stayed silent, allowing me to unravel the double bind I had been in.

"I also remember thinking, how could I go when I hadn't gone through the ascension process, when I still had questions? And then about a year later, that too was fulfilled." We sat in silence as I tried to find words to describe what I could not, realizing I didn't even want to try.

"All I can say is that the experience I had in deep meditation left me knowing the perfection of everything, really knowing it, seeing it, filled with the beauty and the feel of it. It left me with no more questions and also with no more voice, as it had fulfilled all my realities about the ascension process, freeing me again from any last spiritual desire to be here. For a long time after my time in this light, I felt I had seen too much and had nothing left to either do or say. It felt weird to teach people how to create their paradise when it is here all along, when I know that all people will come into this paradise state and that they are already in the state that is currently perfect for them.

"Then another year or so later, I found myself in the presence of the Christ as I sought to find something to do here, something of meaning and worth, something that would ground me again in purpose and passion to this life. Although I was given a new project, I still feel as though I am in a state of nothingness—in a state of just watching, radiating, being passionless, not striving or trying to create or transform, just allowing and being. No highs, no lows.

"And so I continue to travel to share of the wonder of the DOW, an intelligence that is woven through us all, that guides and loves all, an intelligence that needs no voice for It already weaves through all and reveals Itself in time when called. And yet I am here, rudderless, in a state of stillness, aware of the perfection, yet it is as if the air has gone out of my balloon, for there is no drive."

"No passion," Einstein said. "What I would like you to do is write out all your double binds and seek resolution, for until you get congruency, you will continue to give your body conflicting signals. Your energy patterns are stagnating and your body is taking the dominant signals and is shutting itself down."

Perhaps those weren't his exact words, but that was my understanding at the end of our conversation. It felt so good to talk so openly and honestly, for it is rare to even meet someone with whom we can discuss such matters. Einstein went on to discuss Patanjali and the sutras and how what I was experiencing was normal in a certain level in human consciousness and how it was important not to get stuck there and how falling in love every day with life had been so helpful to him and later, just as he rode off on his bike, we agreed to meet again soon.

"Thank you," I said as I hugged him.

"Remember, the cause of all illness is to do with ethics—perceptions and attitudes that create double binds. Just fill your life with things that fill you with passion, fall in love with life again, don't feel just appreciation; allow yourself to fall in love," he said as he waved his goodbye.

I had a lot to think about and yet, as the days passed, I realized that I had already thought so much about it all and had already made my choices. Now all I needed to do was to clearly reprogram my body and then support it back into a state of harmonious health. I also realized that decades of meditation had not just given me detachment but also a dangerous level of indifference and that I truly had no passion for life.

Einstein had also shared his belief that the base emotion behind all cancers is resentment, which can come in many forms, including manifesting as the energy of frustration. I have experienced a lot of resentment in my life, in various degrees. Originally, I held huge resentment at having to raise my children on my own without any emotional or financial support. Later I held, albeit at a much smaller level, resentment at being targeted by the media because I dared to share some of the gifts of my DOW. As I assessed my life again, I could see how the seeds of my cancers could easily have been fertilized by resentment, and I wondered at the deeper causes of the cancer I had now.

As I later spoke with a friend about Einstein's insights and the understandings I had gained, I saw how dangerous sharing this type of information could be. I realized that Einstein knew that I had the strength to accept it all as a warning and not to succumb to a foretold early demise; he knew that I knew that the nine months he foresaw of my time left here were real only if I didn't adjust my current pattern. I had seen so many whose doctors had given them three months to live, and on the last day of the third month, like clockwork, they had died. I had also seen many others who had lived long beyond the time their doctors had told them they'd have.

All I knew was that if I chose to go, it would not be through the ravages of cancer; cancer was definitely not how I wanted to exit. And I still felt I had choice. I didn't doubt what Einstein had foreseen or the things that he had to share, as my inner being confirmed it all as we spoke. What I doubted still was the depth of my own desire to stay.

Brigitte lay in her bed in France, with the morphine to kill her pain, and her doctors gave her three to six months to live. Yet both of us knew that she too still had choice, that all she had to do was to decide to stay. Concerned friends continued to bring a seemingly endless stream of healers to help her, and yet she knew—and I knew—that the healing power now depended solely on her wish to remain.

With the assumption that no news is good news, I had been putting off inquiring on the results of my biopsy. When I finally did ring the doctor's clinic, the receptionist told me that she could not reveal the results to me and that no news was not necessarily good news. No news was simply due to the fact that both the nurse and the doctor were on holidays and still out of town.

Strangely nonchalant I let Einstein's insights slowly settle as complacency once more became the ruler of my day. More people around me began to share their insights and advice on self-healing and the creation of disease, and I began to feel the problem of information overload—how easy it is to feel overwhelmed, do nothing and then simply fade away!

The need for discernment and the ability to choose the right course of self-healing, to be responsibly active in our own healing path and to also find and trust the appropriate course of treatment began to gain importance in my mind, and yet I felt also that before we can begin to heal, we need to know if it is our destined time to go or if we can choose to overcome the challenge and stay.

As the days unfolded after my meeting with Einstein, the telepathic message to write about it all intensified in regularity, and so I asked for a title to be downloaded. Although the words "Harmonious Healing" flooded in, I felt that they were incomplete, that the journey before me would take some surprising twists and become more than a project on healing something like cancer. It was strange to begin to record an unfolding journey, with no clarity as to the outcome, and yet I knew that this was one book that I could not write retrospectively; I knew that I was about to record my journey back to health—or the journey of my dying.

Dignity and Dying

Toward the end of May 2003, going into June, I was in Europe attending one of our retreats and, after six days of working with everyone to create a very beautiful energy field, we all gathered for our usual cabaret night. This is an evening where we share songs, jokes or skits and just have fun. Toward the end of the evening, a beautiful young belly dancer began to entertain the group. Young, fit and a sensuously good dancer, she soon had the crowd enthralled.

As I sat at the back of the room enjoying it all, I started to feel another presence by me, as if someone was watching the scene through my eyes. I sensed immediately that it was the presence of my father, Arnie. I asked him if he had finally left his body and crossed over and died, for he had been hovering between life and death for the past month. He telepathically confirmed that he had, so I asked if it would be better if we left the room to connect deeper in silent meditation. He laughed and said no, that he had come for the entertainment, for he had always liked a pretty girl and loved the belly dance.

My initial feeling was one of sadness, yet I was also pleased that he had finally let go and died. (Although, for myself and many others, there is no such thing as death but simply the changing of forms where we are body-less for a while.) And so I sat and felt him watch and experienced his emotions—joy that he had finally let go and was free from pain, happiness that we could maintain contact in this way. When I rang home the following day, they confirmed he had been in a deep coma the night before with little breath to his body, but no, he was still holding on. Something had pulled him back, and I realized that he was experiencing what I had come to call "morphine meandering."

Morphine meandering is that state of confusion that happens when a body is close to death and is given morphine to ease the pain, so that the person is more comfortable as he or she leaves. My sister had reported that during the past few weeks, he had constantly been pulling the drip out; he didn't seem to want the morphine.

Two weeks later, during a weekend workshop in Zurich, I awoke in the middle of the night after a dream and with full recollection of where I had just been. Within half an hour of my waking, the phone rang—my sister called to tell me that our father had finally let go, that as she had sat by his bedside reading the last psalm of the Lord's Prayer, he had finally sighed his last sigh and slipped away. I already knew, as I had just spent what seemed to be an eternity with him in the dreamtime and was recalling the details when she rang.

Filled with love over every moment of our dream contact, I relived how we had just sat together in another dimension on a wall outside my hotel, where he described to me in detail the agony of morphine meandering and the confusion that it caused, how he felt that somehow it dimmed the light of his exit way, making his death transition difficult. He shared of how often he had thought he had finally died, only to be brought back into his body and how, frustrated, he would have to unhook again. It was not, he said, a dignified way of dying and one he would rather have avoided.

After my mother had died from a massive heart attack, my father went through many stages. My parents had always thought that they were twin flames, and when she left, he missed her dearly. On the road, I have shared many stories about the relationship between my father and me after her passing as he learnt to work with the angels to brighten up his life and later used the Cosmic Dating Agency to find a new wife. But part of him always longed to be with my mother, and as he approached the middle of his eighties, I could see how impatient he was to leave his body. He had often said how unfair it all was, for it had taken my mother all of five minutes to leave her body and he had been praying and asking God to take him and to let him die quickly and with dignity and grace. With no more interest in being here and no more passion for life, all he longed for was rest and time away from the human state.

We had many discussions about this before he finally manifested a breakdown in his body so that he could fulfill this deep desire. Once I offered to teach him tools he could use to leave his body and come and go at will, until he could then one day choose simply not to return, just as the lamas do when they know that their work is complete. However, he was living with his new wife, a staunch Christian who kept reminding him not to play such games, that it really was up to God as to when it was his time to go—an answer that he graciously accepted but didn't really believe.

And so the more he focused on his desire to die and fed his annoyance at being here, the more his body listened to his plea until finally, in January of 2003, he called us all to him and said: "I've got some bad news. It seems I have a cancerous growth in my stomach; it's big, it's growing, and they say that there is nothing they can do. At eighty-six I'm too old to survive an operation. They say that it's easier for me to just allow it to grow and leave this way; they say they can adjust my medication so I don't suffer. I wouldn't want an operation even if I was stronger; I've made it clear that I am ready to go."

We spoke a lot over the next few months, and he set the intention then that he wanted to die before I went on tour, so it could all be dealt with before I was gone, but it didn't happen. I said my final goodbyes to him before I went overseas, for he would not let me cancel my plans, and I knew, as we held each other, that it would be our last touch and that I would never physically see him again.

But we had agreed that he could find me in my dreams. True to his word, we have had many visitations. He has come at times when I have not expected it and at times when I have been in deep meditation and sensed both my mother and father standing before me on the inner plane, happy to connect with me and happy to be together, and happy too that I could sense and acknowledge them and they could share more about their life between life. These visits always bring us joy, with the communication pure and telepathic, coming from a joyous place within our hearts. Most of the time when my father comes, he tells me how he understands it all now from such a different point of view. In the beginning, he'd apologize for not really understanding what I had been doing in this world, for not seeing the bigger picture and giving me the credence that he now knew I deserved. He'd say how he understands that so much more now and would help me where he could, just coming in from time to time and holding me in love.

For me his passing has created no separation, just a missing of the physical contact and the hugs. Yet this is not the point of my sharing this story. Rather, it is about the right to choose with dignity our method of death, but not through euthanasia as we know it.

I have always felt that the most dignified way to go was like the lamas, who, knowing when their work was complete and sensing and feeling intuitively that the time was right for them to move on, would sit in meditation and leave their body by taking their consciousness to another plane. They would then either allow the body to dissolve, unattended, into death or send a beam of love back to the body, dissolve it and take it with them back up into pure light.

I shared the story of my experience at Nina Hagen's concert with a friend of mine who is a leading proponent in the field of physical immortality. When I came to the part about being given the opportunity to leave and moving into a future time and seeing my husband having to ship my body back home, she was horrified and said: "Why on Earth wouldn't you just dissolve it and take it up into light?"

"At the time, with the dissolving into love, there was no thinking anymore," I responded. "It was just what was occurring, without thought. It was a dissolving and perhaps, if I had allowed the process to continue, I would have dissolved the body as well. I do not know—it was not consciously planned; it was just a spontaneous combustion into a melting space of love, beyond mind and conscious awareness, until that combustion was halted by my husband squeezing my hand."

It seems to me that there are so many ways that we can leave this physical body, and because we are so unaware of the practice of bilocation and other ways of exiting the body, we usually leave via an accident or a disease, choices that are made due to our lack of holistic education.

My father and I had had various conversations regarding his upcoming death and he asked many questions regarding my research with prana, especially about the difference between getting nourishment from prana and depriving the body of food via fasting and starvation. I explained as much as I could until he realized that prana prolongs life, whereas conscious starvation terminates it and that the two are completely different.

Before I left to go on tour, he said that when he had had enough, he would simply stop eating and drinking and this action would determine the timing of a preset course, one that the doctors had agreed was inevitable. It was true that as the cancerous growth formed in his stomach, blocking the entry to it from the esophagus, he could still maintain some semblance of life through the ingestion of nourishing liquids, until this too became too difficult, and so he eventually did as he said he would and stopped taking even liquid. For him it was a painful form of self-euthanasia, but it was still preferable to trying to prolong his life.

Although it was not to be my destiny to be with my father at this final time, my sister and his wife were there to provide for him, along with a contingent of palliative home-care nurses. We had all of these bases covered, and so my father and I were at peace when we said our final goodbyes. He knew that he could be with me on the inner realms, that he could always find me and be with me there, regardless where I was in the world. This knowledge gave him peace, and yet the confusion of the morphine meandering, while it allowed him to move in and out of his body easily to be with me, also added a little chaos in his mind, dragging him back through his memories to lay his life journey's ghost to rest. He told me in the dreamtime we had just after he died that this was not a dignified way to go and that he wished that he had accepted my offer to teach him the lamas' exit way. He told me that it would be good if I could teach others so that they could leave with dignity and grace and shut down the body when they were ready, rather than be overcome with disease and numbed with drugs to ease their pain. He said that the crossover would then be easier, with less confusion to deal with on the other side. "Although," he added, "all eventually find their way to the light again."

I filed his request in the back of my mind with a sense that healing also needs to happen in our own hearts as our loved ones move on—either leaving with dignity in their dying or being taken from us savagely by natural disasters or other means, like fading away with bodies ravaged with their cancers. Everyone confronts death at some point, and being holistically educated regarding it all helps somehow, although only time can lessen the pain of our loss.

I thought a lot about what Einstein had shared with me and the potentiality of what he had seen, and I thought about that I had decided to stay. Now all I needed was to let my body know and find more passion for life, yet I knew that I could do this only when I was free of double binds. However, when I looked deeper within, I felt that a small part of me was actually very happy to go. Strangely enough, I also realized at this time how magnificent the freedom is that we can gain by the very act of dying.

The withdrawing of the life spirit from a human biosystem is an interesting phenomena and one that can be both witnessed and experienced in a myriad of ways. In Australia 47 percent of people experience this withdrawal and their death via heart disease or cancer; across the globe, one in four adults finds the biosystem shutting down via the destruction caused by diseases that are preventable with holistic education.

The human life spirit withdraws from a body due to numerous reasons, one of these being that it is simply time to move on. It is the belief system of many metaphysicians that agreements are made prior to taking embodiment, not just of things we agree to learn here in each life, but also on the actual length of time we give ourselves to do this before we can leave the Earth plane to rest and maybe come back again later.

The lessons we choose to learn reflect our personal calibration levels, which are set via the journey of expansion of our own consciousness, a process that can confine us to a particular planetary system for at times hundreds and thousands of years.

Another reason why the life spirit chooses to leave a body is when we have completed not just the learning but also the service work that we have come to do in this life. A few years ago, an old friend of mine came to the conclusion that his work here in this life was done, and so he organized his worldly affairs, told everyone important to him that he was leaving in a week and, on the day declared, manifested a massive overload of energy into his heart causing it to shut down, and so he left.

Most people don't do this with so much awareness. Rarely do we realize on a conscious level when it is our time to go, although when we know how to recognize them, the signs are always obvious via the unconscious actions of the one who is preparing to exit and die.

The last time I physically saw my mother was in 1994. As I was leaving after a visit, she enfolded me in her arms in a very tender and loving embrace and told me how deeply she loved me, that she always had and always would. During her final week, she managed to put all of her affairs in order, see or talk to all those she had loved in her life and spend intense, poignant time reminiscing with my father about their life together. On the day before she died, they spent the time together making love and looking back over their fifty plus years as a couple and all their shared experiences. They talked of how much they loved all of their children and each other and how different we all were. She also told him how she felt that she should be the first to die, as she knew that he was strong enough to cope without her, whereas she felt that she wouldn't have the strength to cope without him.

Early the next day, she suffered a massive heart attack in her sleep and died within minutes.

Having also made an agreement that whoever died first would make contact from the other side and to do so within days of passing, she came to him the night before her funeral and filled his whole body with light and healing energy. She left him with an intense feeling of love and well-being that left no doubt in his mind that she had just fulfilled their agreement.

A week or so before my twenty-five-year-old niece died in a car accident, she began to indulge in various conversations regarding her path in life and the choice she felt she was facing, which was to either focus 100 percent on her ascension process or to open up to the possibility of being a wife and a mother. For some reason, she felt it was a choice she needed to make and that at this point, she couldn't split her energies to do both. During that week, she came into a deep state of peace that seemed to emanate from her and, just like my mother, she seemed to literally pulse with a radiant and a healthy love of life. She organized a huge party to be with all her friends, and when many asked her if she was going somewhere, she responded that she just felt inspired to gather them all to celebrate life. A few days later, on a straight, open road with no traffic, in the middle of a clear, sunny day, she lost control of her car, and moments before its impact into a tree, she left her body so it could die. Intuitively she must have known that it was her time to leave.

It's true that her passing, like my brother's a few decades before, seemed to further weaken my mother's heart, leaving wounds of sorrow that would block the energy flow through it and allow her own passing two years later to be easier, for when we die in this way, via a disease, it will always manifest itself in our weakest organs. If the body is too young and strong for enough disease to take hold to release the spirit, then, like my niece and brother, a person will manifest an "accident."

There are anomalies to this process as well, one of which I was now personally exploring.

Sometimes when a person has completed her work here and had the opportunity to leave her body but had chosen to stay, as I had, then a whole new game applies—the conscious choosing of life when there is perhaps no higher drive to go on. It seemed to me, as I looked at it deeper, that our drive or passion for life is stronger when we have something we previously agreed to do that is still unfulfilled.

For those who have completed their work and whose body appears to be manifesting their exit through a disease, a few things need to be decided. Not all disease is a death sentence, and there are countless stories of miraculous and spontaneous healings where people have brought themselves back into harmony enough to keep the life force with them.

How do we know which applies to us? This is an important question, for when we know, how we act is quite different.

As I received more and more information for this book, I realized that knowing if it is our time to die or just a challenge was one of the most crucial, initial questions we need to have answered. Three meditations can reveal the answers to this question (for guides through these meditations, go to "Meditation Magic" on page 123):

The first meditation is for people who are currently faced with a life-threatening illness or who may find themselves dealing with this in the future. It allows us to determine if it is our time to die or if what we are facing is simply a challenge. Our path to harmonious healing will differ, depending on the answers we gain. If it is our time to go, then, although we cannot provide quantity, we can still do things to improve the quality of our life.

The second is a meditation to energize our biosystem with life-feeding and affirming energy and hence helps prevent disease—now or in the future. It also improves the quality—if not the quantity—of life for those who are affected by dis-ease.

The third meditation is an ancient metaphysical method of safe self-euthanasia. Based on the lamas' way, this is perhaps one of the most controversial topics in this book and also perhaps one of the most necessary ones for those who get a yes, that it is their time to die. For many, being able to leave their bodies in dignity and when they choose, is a birthright, and having an ancient tool to do this will provide great emotional relief. Knowing the pathway and being practiced at coming and going from our physical form is a worthy skill to have for all of us, regardless of the quantity of time we may have here and our current state of health.

I never realized, when my father died, that I had the skills to possibly prevent others suffering in the same way. Offering to teach a family member self-euthanasia, the lamas' way, is very different from releasing this information to the masses, and yet I suddenly began to feel called to do so. Already being controversial in my work with the Divine Nutrition program, I realized that to share information like this was important, as people need holistic education and information that allows them to broaden their choices and to learn how they can heal hearts by being better informed.

A few days after the December 2004 tsunami hit, I overheard a conversation in a coffee shop in the village where I live. A woman was saying how incredible it was that a few hundred thousand souls had given the world the gift of compassion as we begin a new year. She pointed out how their mass death was part of a soul-group game that would switch the world into another energy level that it so needed and what an incredible service this was.

There are so many stories regarding the reasons for mass disasters, whether they are classified as Earth changes, such as the shifting of tectonic plates, or whether we see it from an esoteric viewpoint, yet none of these explanations really matter. What matters is the outcome.

The outcome of the tsunami was one of shifting our world into an energy space of unity, caring and compassion, and in that there is a gift and purpose. It is the same with our personal health challenges.

One of the most beautiful things that we can be given on this planet is education, and in order to create harmony as we move through life and into the death process, we need the choices that education brings. As some would say, from the moment we are born, we begin the journey to our death, unless we find and choose the immortal's way.

One of the interesting things with the tsunami were the help lines set up on the Internet to keep people up-to-date and help them find their missing loved ones. Here was something that was organized within hours that proved to be most effective. The Internet is also an incredible tool to offer education in the world so that we have more choice when dealing with issues like dying with dignity or understanding the destructive nature of double binds that cause a body to perhaps shut down before our time.

This then allows us to ask another question: "Is there such a thing as dying before our time?"

In metaphysics we know that we choose the time of both our entry into and our exit from this world. The details of what we do in between, as we learn and grow, are for us to fill in, yet even then, there are previously agreed to things we have come to learn and share.

Do we come in with a time frame to do the work we have come to do? And once it's done, do we then simply move on? Can we also repattern our exit path and die in a manner of our choosing? Dying, like living, is either a conscious or an unconscious choice, but it is a choice nonetheless—and it is a choice that can be dignified or a struggle.

Passion and Positivity

17 January 2005

Days flow on, and my insights and my work continue. Doing the final edit of my first book in the *Enchanted Kingdom* series makes me begin to feel a little passion again for life. The story excites me, and I am pleased at what I have written. As I close the book, determined to take a much-needed walk upon my favorite beach, the phone rings and grabs my attention.

"Hello?"

"It's Dr. Brown's surgery here."

"Ah, you have the results of my biopsy? I assume that since it's been over three weeks now, the results are all clear? I'm sure you would have called me earlier if they weren't."

"Well . . . no," the nurse said as she interrupted my happy chatter. "I am sorry, but the doctor wants you to come in for further surgery. The biopsy confirmed that it was definitely a squamous cell carcinoma, and since it was so fast growing and since the biopsy reveals that the cells were so close to the perimeter, he really would like to remove some more of your mouth, just to make sure."

Immediately I started to cry, feeling a dam burst within me. I had been so brave going through it all, and the healing was taking place so nicely, with minimum scarring and my lopsided grin only noticeable if I wore a darker shade of lipstick or if someone really stared. But it was more than that; the surgery itself, the cutting, the blood, the trauma, all of it was too fresh in my body's memory. Every cell within me just said, "No, I can't; I won't do it again."

Sensing my silent rejection and my tears, the doctor's assistant softly persisted. "We can see you this Friday morning; the sooner you do it, the better."

"I'll come and talk to him," I agreed. "11 o'clock? Okay, but I don't know if I can redo the surgery. How much does he need to remove this time?"

"Not as much as before, but he won't know till he sees you. If you come in here earlier, we can give you something to relax you . . ."

"What, so I'll be asleep through the surgery?"

"No, but you'll be a lot more relaxed."

"I'll see you at 11 o'clock. We'll talk, but I don't know if I want it done."

Both shock and emotions overwhelmed me. A few days earlier I had received an email letting me know that it looked as if Brigitte was ready to leave and that her system was failing fast. All the sadness I felt for her now flowed freely through my body as I picked up the phone to arrange for my daughter to take me back to the clinic and, if I decided to do the surgery, drive me home.

Within the hour I had seen my local kinesiologist, who'd found my body too emotional to give clear answers as to whether further surgery was the right path to take. Other testing systems revealed no further insights. The interesting lesson for me was watching my body's initial response to questioning, for when the therapist asked if more surgery was appropriate, my body's answer was a definite "Yes!" This surprised me, and yet something within me dawned, and so I asked my body if it felt that surgery right now was the right action simply because it had no confidence in my ability to heal it naturally. To this question, we also received a clear "Yes!" Again I realized that my body's response was very natural as I—its master—was, in that moment, much too emotional to have the strength to do anything with clarity and focus.

Clarity and focus are essential in the self-healing game. The body's consciousness is like our inner child, only confident in the divine power and its healing ability when we are acting as divine beings. Physical body consciousness is like the youngest child in the family, emotional body consciousness is like the middle child, mental body consciousness is like the eldest child, and the consciousness of the Divine One Within (DOW) is like the confident parent. A child feels secure and trusting of the parent when the parent is strong, committed and focused, and my physical, emotional and even my mental bodies were feeling the trauma of it all.

Regardless of my body's lack of confidence in my ability to self-heal, undergoing further surgery was unfathomable to me.

After our session, my kinesiologist told me about a Dr. Holt in Perth, who treats cancer with radio waves, and he recommended that I call him.

I was aware that if the cancer was as fast growing as the surgeon had said, it meant that in the three weeks since my surgery, chances were that any cancerous cells he had missed had already entered into my lymph system. I resolved not just to see my surgeon and listen, but also to wait at least another week before contemplating more surgery.

Emotionally raw and overwhelmed, I know I need time to go within, to scan my own body, to do some further research. Intuitively I feel that another battle has begun and that the cancer cells have already entered my lymph system. (Later, when I am finally at peace, I confirm this in my meditation.) I am aware of how quickly my beliefs can be made reality and how important clarity is for me right now, so I continue to meditate deeply to access my next step of action, yet all I feel is a new turbulence of emotion. I am not scared of dying; instead, I am being confronted with the very real opportunity that I am at choice now and that within this year, I could pass on from this world. My husband is distraught and wants to join me right away, although I know he has work to do in the city. So I tell him to wait for a few days so I can settle myself and become a little more informed.

With a day to go before I see the surgeon, I feel again the enormity of information overload and understand how people just shut down when they are bombarded by all of our choices, filled with overwhelming questions like: Why do we create it? What is the best treatment, alternative or traditional medicine? Is it my time to go or do I want to stay? If I do want to stay, is it for me or for my family? Where is my passion in life? Is my desire for rest time in other realms now greater?

Later a small, inner voice told me that even after I had that first surgery, I was beginning again to become too complacent, but this was not something I could ignore; the choices I had to make would bring very obvious, inescapable consequences. The problem was that I didn't feel like doing anything, and for the past few weeks, I had begun to act as if everything was okay and yes, I had become much too complacent. Over the past week, that same small voice had been reminding me to redo my will and make sure that all the loose ends were tied up. Yet I was still passionless and indifferent.

Since the first surgery and Einstein's visit, I had learnt so much and confirmed that yes, I was beginning to manifest my death. Yet even with the idea of leaving potentially riddled with cancer, I still had remained relatively inactive, writing about the journey, excited that I had a new project that was beneficial to the world but lethargic regarding my own healing until, with the biopsy news, I decided to finally act.

The real reason for my inaction was that I still had no strong, definite desire to stay. Without that passion for life and the wish to be here for me and not just for my family, I knew my days were numbered; I could drift into the path of my own demise as easily as a sailboat glides across a calm, blue ocean.

Slowly passion and being positive became my daily focus, as well as gaining both the clarity and motivation to discern the perfect healing course, so I could then take the appropriate action. Unfortunately, it would still take time to discover the main reason why I had lost my passion and to reignite it all again, for although I knew some of the reasons why my system had begun to shut down, I still had not seen it all.

Pieces of a puzzle were revealing themselves slowly, and while searching to understand the causes, I also had to begin instigating my cure. With limited time at my disposal and feeling overloaded with information, I needed dependable methods of discernment so that I could find and quickly implement a cure before my physical deterioration grew.

Dependable Discernment and Information Overload

Although we do have to look at the causes for what we have created and the reasons why it has come into being, we must also begin to apply the appropriate cure. Whether the cure lies in changing our thinking patterns, our feeling patterns or our dietary, exercise and life-style patterns, finding the right course of action can be completely overwhelming. One of the problems on this path is the overload of information, for as soon as others are aware of what we are undergoing, they all wish to share their stories.

Offered with various degrees of sensitivity or insistence, everyone has a story to tell, something he or she wishes to share. In their compassion, in their love, in their caring and concern, they say, "I had a friend who had this, and he cured himself from doing this. You should see this person!" "That therapist is wonderful!" "Have you heard about this healer?" ". . . that doctor?" "So-and-so specializes in this; she knows everything! Why don't you go and see her?" "What about this? You should do this course of treatment. And how about that course?"

And so it goes on, becoming so overwhelming that, as one of my healer friends said, "Many people simply tell everyone to go away, to leave them alone, and then they withdraw quietly and eventually die, confused and unsure of which direction to take."

Becoming more overwhelmed myself, I soon began to long for more dependable discernment mechanisms, tools that allow us to understand exactly what the right course of action is for us, as my usual methods of inner guidance had become unclear.

In one of my conversations with Brigitte, we talked a lot about this. She shared how she was feeling so overloaded with information, having tried so many different healers, plus the pressure coming from the hospital staff and the doctors telling her that she had to begin chemotherapy and radiation before it was too late, because she would move into a stage with the cancer where none of this would be helpful anymore. "I feel as though it is all so self-created," she said, "it's all coming from my mind. It is the power of my mind that has brought this into being, and therefore the shifts have to happen there."

"I don't know," she contemplated later. "Sometimes I feel that I should go for radiation, and then I muscle test the body, and it says no. Other times, when I am weak, it feels okay; it feels that yes, radiation is something I should do. I am getting conflicting signals. I keep asking the Divine One Within for clarity as to my course of action, but as the pain worsens and I have to take the morphine just to deal with it, all my clarity goes . . . it's all so confusing . . ." I understood exactly how she felt.

There is often so much information from all the well-wishers and the researchers that we don't know where to begin. We know we need to look at the cause, but what is the perfect cure? And how do we later discern what is right for us? For some people the answer lies in immediate surgery, which gives the body the help it needs to get rid of the virulence of the cancerous growth. Provided that they then take the time to address the cause of its creation and take future preventive measures, surgery can be the perfect option for them.

When I first manifested the tumor on my liver over a decade ago, I had time on my side, for I knew that I could cut out part of the liver if every alternative treatment failed and that the liver could even regrow itself, because that is what livers can do. I didn't feel pushed for time—the growth was small and the cancer was on the liver, not in it, so surgery could be the last option, when everything else had been tried.

With this new cancer on the mouth, I didn't have the luxury of time. Within days, within a week, it could spread into the lymph system, and a whole new reality with this would begin. Therefore, I took the quickest path of cancer removal, which was by surgery—an intrusive choice that sends the body into shock, as it feels mutilated and violated, yet also a choice that can buy us more time to heal.

The possibility of dying often stimulates deep reflection and appropriate action. I realize that on one level, I needed to go through the experience of surgery, for this is something that many undergo, and it has given me great empathy. My choice for surgery came as I succumbed to fear, prompted by statistics given and my doctor's warnings. In addition, I felt that the cancer's growth had advanced too quickly and left me with minimal choice. When I asked my inner being regarding all of this, I felt that I was also being given my scar like a badge of honor, to remind me of the poisons of the world and the cancerous power of my and others' thought forms. I have seen the power of the thought forms in my own being and witnessed how well trained all the cells in my body are now, how they listen to what I say as the master who I am, and how these cells have responded so quickly to my repetitive thoughts. There is medicine to be found in the mastery of our minds.

Whether we choose surgery and/or the traditional treatment of chemotherapy or one of the more noninvasive, alternative methods depends on each of us individually, and we need to have methods of discernment available to us to ensure that we make the perfect choices in our healing path.

For many years, I have been sharing with people about our Divine One Within, our DOW, who is the true teacher, the one guru we all have, and whose advice to us is pure and incorruptible, whose voice is our sense of intuition and knowing. And yet as I travel the world, so many people say, "How can I tell the difference between my mind, my ego and this voice?" so over the years, I have developed a three-level system of dependable discernment methods.

Apart from using kinesiology and asking the divine self to express its wishes through the muscle responses of the body, the best method is to meditate and ask your DOW directly for guidance. We can also liaise with the universal field of intelligence, the UFI, to receive confirmative information, which then comes through people, books, meetings and coincidences that capture our attention. All of these are dependable methods of discernment that help us work our way through the minefield of information overload, no matter what choices are confronting us in life.

Personally, I feel that our dependable discernment methods need to be developed more thoroughly. I am convinced that this is one of the reasons why the universal field arranged my "coincidental" meeting with Einstein, who has developed, and later shared with me, further methods. He has also graded them according to their effectiveness and their freedom from outside influences. For example, many use the pendulum to obtain information, but the pendulum can be manipulated by other forces, thus giving us incorrect or incomplete answers. Similarly, kinesiology also has its restrictions.

Nonetheless, whether we are gaining information to make the perfect choices for our journey through life or understanding the perfect path for us to bring our healing into a more harmonious state, all of us need to develop completely incorruptible, dependable sources of discernment, so that we can make the right choices and don't succumb to information overload and move into a state of lethargy and inaction.

I discussed the need for clear discernment with an alternative healer friend, and she reminded me of a story. "Remember," she said, "years ago when I was at a retreat that was filled with healers and people completely aware of emotional causes behind disease? Remember how I got something in my foot and how everybody gave me advice on what it was related to, on the emotional symbology of damaging one's heel?"

"I remember," I replied. "But I don't recall the outcome."

"Well, after the retreat, I went back to where I was living, and I was at the markets the following week, still limping, when I bumped into a friend who was amazed that my foot was not better. Anyway, before I could react, she had bundled me into her car and took me to the local hospital where they did an x-ray that revealed a two-centimeter piece of metal that was lodged in my heel. You know, not one of the healers at the retreat picked up that there was a physical reason for this irritation. I accept that perhaps I had an emotional issue that created a weakness in the field of that area that attracted it all in the first place, yet sometimes I think we get so sidetracked with emotional causes that we overlook the simplicity of the physical."

After a moment's comfortable silence, I replied, "Maybe we also need to experience things this way so that we have stories to remind us later. Anyway, we still need to look at all levels. You know, I just read a story in a magazine about a yoga teacher's journey with breast cancer. It took all of her focus to go through the surgery to remove her breast and attend to the healing process afterward, and so she had no energy or interest to even look at the deeper causative factors. I hate to think that it will return as it tends to do unless we address these things, because her story was so sad and unsettling. Like many she couldn't believe it could happen to her, since she meditated, had a great diet and did regular exercise."

"Yes, but what about self-nurturing?" my friend added, aware of how so many givers fail to give to themselves and knowing how manifesting cancer in the breasts was often indicative of a lack of feeling nurtured. "That's the beauty of holistic medicine, that we get to look at all levels and integrate everything back into balance. Unfortunately, it can be very time-consuming, and many just want to get it over with and move on. Anyway, sometimes we need to do the cure before we can address the cause."

"I agree, but surely, the perfect cure is dependent on understanding the initial causes, no?"

"Catch-22! I guess it depends on what disease someone has and how fatal it can be in the time frame the person has to deal with it all."

"You know, the real interest for me in the yoga woman's story was that she intuitively had felt that something was wrong. She said she went to three different doctors, who all examined her and said she was fine, yet she persisted. There was no lump; she just felt a difference in the energy flow. The fourth doctor ordered different tests at her insistence, and that's when they found a very virulent form of cancer deep inside the tissue and ordered the surgery without delay. Her intuition and insistence saved her. She said that the gift the journey gave her, as she opened to receive love and help from her friends, was the gift of greater compassion and empathy, which allowed her to dive deeper into her own spiritual practices, plus the gift of accepting being truly nurtured."

As we spoke, I realized yet again the importance of following my own intuition, for although many will surround you and give you their advice, perhaps their insights are not right for you.

When a person is strong, connected and focused, it's easy to get clear inner guidance or guidance from the fields of life. But when one is weak or confused, particularly when a person has received life-threatening news, the clarity can disappear and one can become vulnerable and unsure.

In such a situation, our first challenge is in discerning the *perfect, personalized, step-by-step healing program.* As I already mentioned, one of the greatest problems with self-healing is getting the right guidance regarding the correct course to follow to support our body back into health. We know that the causative factors in dis-ease are as varied as we all are as individuals and that there is literally no one path that everyone can follow.

It helps when we accept the fact that if the disease was created in our own body, then only our own body has the answers as to how to heal or *un*-create it.

A three-level information access and confirmation system helps us figure out a clear, step-by-step, perfect and personalized healing process (see page 117). It is important, again, to really understand that the physical body has an independent consciousness, as do our emotional and mental bodies, and that all bodies often work in disharmony with our spiritual objective of being in perfect health on all levels. Being harmoniously integrated within all our bodies creates and sustains our health. So the body needs us to select a healing course, and it then needs us to trust that this course will work and that we will not deviate here and there, chasing all sorts of options, which are often a waste of time and money. People with a deadly-disease prognosis often clutch at straws and will do anything in the hope of finding a cure to save or prolong their life.

Although there are many standard things that we can do to provide a better quality of life, like change of diet and other things we will discuss in later chapters, prolonging the quantity of life can occur only if it is not our time to die yet and if we follow the course of healing that our being requires on a physical, emotional, mental and spiritual level.

Thus it is imperative that we have access to dependable discernment methods. Part of this requires us to ascertain on which level—emotional or mental—the dis-ease originated before it flowed into the physical body. We also need to realign and heal the etheric schism that is providing the space for the disease to be anchored into. Again, only the body can know all of this, for our DOW stores all Its knowing and life-experience memory in our body's cells.

For example, for the past few years, I suffered from an intense pain in my right knee, which I knew from kinesiology was anchored in the emotional plane; chiropractic testing showed no physical problem. Through using a system of holographic kinetics, I was later able to discover that my knee problem was due to both an emotional and physical memory pattern and that my physical knee had actually sustained acute damage in my last life, when I fell onto a rock as my legs collapsed underneath me due to a huge emotional shock. For years I had been addressing this weak-knee problem—first as an issue of an old yoga injury and then as an emotional matter of too much independence and pride, along with a touch of being reluctant at times to freely stride into my future. This analysis had not come directly from my body's own memory, and hence I had been unable to effectively clear it until I discovered the true cause of this weakness in my knee.

I share this story to stress again that only your body knows when and why we have created our dis-ease; and only our body knows how to heal it. Continual dis-ease can often lead to disease.

In my own harmonious healing journey, in the beginning, I mainly utilized the universal field of infinite intelligence, or UFI, to gain my information. Once I had established, in meditation, that it was not my time to die yet, I asked the UFI to bring me the perfect therapists and tools and methodologies required for my healing. I also asked that I be able to recognize these clearly by feeling either at peace with what was presented or agitated if what was presented was incorrect, so I could use my intuition to screen out what was not the right path for me. I also asked to find clearer and more perfect methods for discernment.

The energy that is the Divine One Within is the same loving and infinitely intelligent energy that drives the universal field, and It has a way of presenting circumstances and synchronicities that are impossible not to recognize. People, information, situations come our way with such ease and grace and a knowingness that they hold something for us, that it is easy to trust that if it is not our time to die, life itself will bring us the support we need to overcome this temporary challenge, especially when we tune in to the UFI and ask. This belief in itself is very placating.

Being prepared to accept that we have created our disease and that if we can create it, we can also un-create it is a basic step on this path. Trusting that we will be given the tools to do so is another basic step, and asking for these tools to come to us is yet another. Harmonious healing is a step-by-step process where our own being needs to guide us, for only it knows the answer to undoing what we have done. Healing generally happens in reverse, with the last thing we created being healed first.

It is so important that we do not get sidetracked by others' concerns and insisting that they have all the answers we need, whether this be family or well-meaning friends and therapists. It is also important that we don't get too caught up in the why-have-I-created-this or I-refuse-to-believe-that-I-have-created-this game while understanding that unless we address the causative issues, no healing pattern will hold. Cancers can be surgically removed, but they often return if the underlying issues are not addressed. We need to know that our body knows all about the underlying issues and that all we need to do is to find what they are and then address them. We also need to find what the physical body's immediate support requirements are.

There are so many issues that we may need to address and gain confirmation about. For example, to facilitate our perfect, permanent healing, we may need to detoxify ourselves physically, emotionally, mentally and/or spiritually. I elaborate on how to do this in more detail later in this book, in Part 2.

Just what else do you need to check for and attend to so you can heal? Exactly what is your perfect step-by-step healing program? Your body requires answers to these questions, regardless of what your doctor or alternative therapist or family may think. Remember, only you have the answers, and so setting in place dependable discernment methods is crucial.

Here I want to add something very important that I have found over the years of working closely with the physical body consciousness, particularly when we want the body to provide clear answers regarding its needs or to release information that we need that it has stored in cellular memory. The key to understanding your body is love, to gently bombard the body every day with love, for when it feels truly loved by its master, it is more than happy to comply with the fulfillment of any requests we may have. (To help you with this, there are some additional meditations and tools in the "Dependable Discernment" section starting on page 117 in Part 2.)

I always know when the path I'm on is perfect for me, as I am lovingly and powerfully supported by the universal field. Circumstances present themselves and information flows to me, almost overwhelming me with their consistency and common theme, until they are impossible to ignore. It's as if a path opens before me that I just have to walk, and when I do, every step is confirmed to be perfect due to the levels of surrounding support. For years I have walked freedom's way, often ignoring both tradition and convention as I learnt to listen to an inner call. Always the focus and learning have come back to the power and gifts of the DOW. Comfortable with challenging the status quo, I feel as if there is an inner-plane network that holds solutions to all our problems on Earth, a network that can deliver these solutions to any seeker. All we need to do is ask and recognize the reality of why we need the help.

David Hawkins shares: "The individual human mind is like a computer terminal connected to a giant database. The database is human consciousness itself, of which our own cognizance is merely an individual expression, but with its roots in the common consciousness of all mankind. This database is the realm of genius; because to be human is to participate in the database, everyone, by virtue of his birth, has access to genius. The unlimited information contained in the database has now been shown to be readily available to anyone in a few seconds, at any time, in any place. This is indeed an astonishing discovery, bearing the power to change lives, both individually and collectively, to a degree never yet anticipated.

"The database transcends time, space, and all limitations of individual consciousness. This distinguishes it as a unique tool for future research, and opens as yet undreamed-of areas for possible investigation."

He is, of course, talking about accessing the universal field of intelligence that is within and around us all, and the dependable discernment tools shared in this manual will help us do this.

I find that as the days go by, there is so much to contemplate, and yet every day, the universal field of intelligence presents me with another layer of understanding so that I can write with greater insight and depth. The statistics that I find and am guided to add to Part 2 of this manual have shocked me, yet all of it is confirmed as I find myself surrounded almost daily by people in the grips of one of these diseases. It's like being pregnant and suddenly seeing pregnant women everywhere, except now I keep meeting people suffering from various stages of cancer, some who have surrendered to dying and some who are seeking to be reborn. My own search for answers continues.

Causes

1 knew that once I had become calm and centered enough to ascertain my perfect healing program and begin it, I also needed to continue to address the cause of it all so that the cure would be permanent and not a temporary solution. I knew that it is not enough to just cut out diseases using surgery and hope that the body will heal with minimum scar tissue, nor is it enough to heal it naturally through willpower and thought and visualization or changes of diet and lifestyle and thinking patterns.

A short time ago, I met with a childhood friend who told me of a mutual friend who had just undergone a biopsy to remove another lump, which was a different form of cancer than the one she had removed surgically a year before. The new lump was a virulent cancer that her doctor said only a mastectomy and chemotherapy could stem. As my childhood friend sat there with tears running down her face, I knew that she felt so raw from the loss of her own mother, who had died of heart disease only some weeks before. Now she was being confronted with the loss of one of her oldest and dearest friends, and the pain was too much for her.

"What did she do last time to eliminate the cause?" I asked my friend gently.

"I don't think she did anything," she responded.

"So it's back?"

"Not in exactly the same place but close."

"And this time? Is she looking at the underlying factors?"

"I think she's just doing as her doctor suggests. Recovering from her mastectomy, healing, being brave, worrying about her kids in case the chemotherapy fails and she dies. Trying to be positive and feeling up, then down. I can't believe that it's back with her again."

"Some sources say that it will keep coming back until we look at what caused it in the first place. Even when we eliminate the causative factors in one area, sometimes it manifests somewhere else, a different area with different causes and learning. You know, a woman I met recently was telling me how her husband died of cancer; he had it three different times, in three different places. She said that she's just come out of a seven-year mourning period."

"What happened to him?" my friend asked.

"First he had a melanoma in his leg that went into his bone. The doctor wanted to amputate, but he cured it through a juice diet, mind mastery and meditation. Five years later, he found a tumor in his stomach, which he shrunk and eliminated by the same methods. Finally, after another five years, they found cancer had gone into the fluid of his brain. He gave up then, didn't want to fight anymore, just surrendered to it and died."

And so we talked of our experiences, first- and second-hand, in dealing with and understanding the reasons behind dis-ease.

Seeing and hearing all of this I knew that I was receiving further confirmation from the universal field of the need for me to complete and then share this research, as I seemed to be constantly magnetizing people who were suffering in one way or another. We gain confirmation from so many sources—from the friends the universe sends us to give us warnings and insights and trigger deeper understanding when perhaps we are blindly missing the point, to the books we find or experiences we have daily. Still I sensed that for me personally, all of it was just a warning so that I would look more deeply at the matter of choice. I knew that not all diagnoses of cancer or heart disease are a door to our death or dying, that they often are simply warnings. And although the woman's husband died, the experience prompted her to change her own lifestyle and adopt much healthier habits.

Every day I gently massage the scar tissue that runs like a red river beneath my nose and into my mouth, lovingly applying rose hip oil to minimize the visible damage and facilitate the healing. For the first few weeks, it is too tender to touch, and I miss being able to laugh, till finally I can smile without feeling any pain. The shape of my mouth has changed and so has the way I smile. All of this seems so inconsequential in the scheme of greater things as every day I hear more stories and gather more research, for I know that when we bring anything like this into effect, we need to look deeply at, and then eliminate, the cause, which I am now being driven to do.

Using my higher senses, I sit in meditation and scan the fields for an understanding and clarity of how I could so quickly have gone from running my system at a biological age of seventeen, feeling so fit and fantastic, so energized, so full of life, getting younger and younger every day to, within a month or so, feeling as if I have aged a hundred years, listening to my bones literally creak as I walk, feeling pain in so many places in my body as if I am an old lady on a rapid decline, sailing into the arms of my death. As I scan further, I find that my life force is continuing to slowly leave and that my body is feeling this profoundly and is beginning to shut itself down. By demonstrating the symptoms of aging, my body is giving me a warning and the chance to refute what I have begun. All of this I find confirmed by the intelligent universal field around me as circumstance after circumstance presents itself to give me data to support this new project of writing about this sudden change and to support my own process of healing.

Going even deeper into my meditation, I begin to clearly piece together all the different causes and layers and influences in the creation of this cancer game and to find the medicine in my mind. I go back in time and observe myself lying in meditation, semiasleep on a pillow that I now see is filled with the chemical formaldehyde, and I see how my body is beginning to react to it. Next I see a small pimple on my mouth, the skin disturbed and ruptured, and how it begins to absorb the poisons into the skin, preparing the field for what is to come. I look further back in time and see in my auric field schisms that have been born there from repetitive thinking patterns, weaknesses in my field that are of my own creation as I powerfully and repetitively stated, "I have completed all the work I have come to do in this life."

In my meditation I see that the more I have pronounced that my work is complete in my own mind and heart, the more detached I have felt about being here. I see how, slowly, all of this has given food to create the schisms and how now, combined with the contact with the chemical, something deadly is beginning to grow. As I scan the fields of my emotional body, I see that I am also full of sadness for the potential passing of my friend, having just been given the news of Brigitte's cancer, and I see how all of it has built up to weaken my fields.

Looking for more causative factors, I meditate deeper still, again going backward in time, scanning my body and energy fields through thousands of years as I assess my mortality patterns. Once I have a clearer picture, I then add the information I have gleaned through working with kinesiology and other ways of receiving confirmation from the universal field. Slowly, through all of this, I can see the weaving that has taken place to bring this into being.

I then look beyond it all to a higher level, and I see how it is all so perfect; I see that it is part of a future blueprint, for I now recall asking for a project of worth to regain a little passion in my life.

As I continue to piece together the causative patterns of my own journey so that I can make sure that I stop creating such physical manifestations, I find that I become excited again, fired up, and that I am beginning to regain a little of my passion for being here and to feel again more purpose, a feeling that I can contribute something that will aid others in a positive way. What I have asked for, I have received.

"But," I wonder, "how passionate will I still feel when I've completed this book, this project?" I sense intuitively that my lack of passion is due to a deeper reason.

My search for the answers in my own journey with harmonious healing have revealed so much to me and released within me a deeper knowing and understanding from the heart and mind of the Divine One who breathes me. Over time in my journey of enlightenment, all my questions have disappeared, and now I find that with this disappearance, I have allowed detachment and the art of being the watcher to dissipate my passion for being here, and I see how this has also contributed to my system shutting itself down. There is a destruction and aimlessness in too much Now time and, as long-term meditators, we can indulge too much in the silence so that we are no longer really participating in life.

All of this I see, and so I begin to understand the multiple levels involved in my cancer causation and that it is never as simple as diet or attitude, or lifestyle, or cosmic blueprints for completion of life patterns so that the soul can leave the body and rest.

I got together with another friend of mine who has been such a brilliant companion, who has given me so much valuable research data for the *Law of Love* manual and now for this. She seemed sad as we sat together. Eventually she told me how the night before, during a routine breast examination, she had found a lump and how the discovery spun her out completely, how she felt sad and overwhelmed with the potential of what this lump could mean. We talked about how as soon as we accept a possibility of something like breast cancer, the word itself or saying "I have cancer" opens us up to all the sadness held around this in the morphogenetic field.

Many years ago, on one of my travels, I asked members of the audiences in every city if they had had some personal experience with cancer. Surprisingly, 80 percent of them said they had, either personally, through a loved one or a friend. Hence the fear of it and the suffering it has caused is anchored in the emotional energy field around the planet and has become part of the morphogenetic field, and as soon as we relate to this in a personal way, such acknowledgment opens us up to experience all that is anchored there.

So of course my friend felt sad, as did I, and yes, it can overwhelm some.

Many years ago, shortly after I had self-healed my first cancer, I shared my experience with a group of women who had all been diagnosed with cancer. Somehow they had found their way to me to learn the art of destressing through meditation. It was interesting that of the four classes I was beginning that week, only this one class had anyone with health problems in it—and they were all women suffering from cancer who had arrived within a week of me having cured my own. It was also interesting to witness the various emotional stages they were in—denial, guilt, anger, grief and acceptance. Some were emotionally strong; others were feeling overwhelmed; and all needed clearer insight.

I discovered then that sometimes we manifest these types of disease realities as a service in the global agenda, and I remembered how relieved a friend of mine was when she understood this, for up to that point, she had kept feeling that she had been doing something wrong. A long-term meditator, someone aware of nutrition and diet and the power of positive thinking and a person with a loving soul and heart, she couldn't understand why she had manifested this in her life.

She relaxed so much when I shared that at this particular point in humanity's evolution, there are some souls who have chosen to come in and manifest a disease like cancer so that they can heal themselves through alternative methods. She saw how, in becoming healthy again, she could share with others the power of self-healing and alternative methods and so offer another option besides surgery and drugs. She saw how important this was, since so many in the Western world have lost the understanding of the power of self-healing, herbs and other therapies such as basic nutritional change. And she saw how too many still gave away their power to the limited gods of modern medicine and how others could re-create health but could not hold the new health pattern until they dealt with the causative issues holistically.

All of this dawned on her, and her confusion and self-recrimination left, as she felt intuitively that it was true. Armed with a different perspective, her cancer sentence became a positive challenge to which she could apply her skills, and so she lived to tell her tale.

I have also come to understand, watching the dying process of so many, how alternative methods work only with those who wish to tread the self-healing path, who are open to other ways. When my husband's father died many years ago, we saw clearly that it was a death that was preventable through nutritional change, yet every time we shared with him alternative ways of dealing with the problem, he would smile sweetly at us and say, "Sounds good, but unless my doctor tells me to do it, I'm afraid it's not my way. I really believe in my doctor, and I'm totally happy to follow his path of instruction." The doctor's path of instruction led my father-in-law to having multiple surgeries that eventually led to a collapse of his vascular system, and yet, perhaps it was just his time to go. Nonetheless, the feeling of helplessness and powerlessness that we can experience when we allow ourselves to get too involved with another's choice in the path of his or her healing can be quite destructive. It is good to remember that it is the other person's path and it is the other person's choice.

The field of healing was something I had been rather reluctant to be involved in as I traveled the globe this past decade, for although the healing game can be harmonious, the path can be as complex as the causes and cures are numerous. Harmony with healing comes only when we gain an understanding of the multiplicity of the human psyche, the holistic nature of the human biosystem and how everything is interconnected, for then we can see how the shutting down of the biosystem occurs through numerous influencing factors. Yet the truth is clear: We can track the original path of the creation of our disease and, thankfully, we can also discover how to un-create it.

Motivated now by the statistical data I had read and also by Brigitte's and my own situation, I resolved to find the perfect cure. The more data I gathered in the understanding of the cause of my own situation, the closer I felt to Brigitte, for I felt that I was gathering this information not just for my own journey but to be of aid to her as well as others. I knew there was a secret here that I was learning, a secret that would aid us both in our healing journey.

Two days later, I received an email from a mutual friend of ours in Paris, in which she told me that Brigitte had taken a turn for the worse; I also received an email from Brigitte's daughter, full of sadness and shock at how rapid her mother's deterioration had been. My friend prompted me to call Brigitte, as everybody feared that she would not live through the coming week. I was stunned—and yet I was not, for I could see and feel the rapid deterioration of my own body as I still hobbled around feeling like an old woman. Although I had begun dosing my body with intense nutritional and mineral support and high doses of oxygen, changes in my energy level still seemed slow to manifest. Lethargic and listless, I knew that I needed to do much more.

The Complexity of Cures

The phone rings and when I answer it, a good friend and healer is on the line: "Just rang to tell you that when I was meditating and doing some distant healing on you again today, I picked up something strange."

"What do you mean?"

"Well, I cleared your etheric web of some pretty heavy energy hook-ins the other day, and once I have done that, it usually stays done, but today I noticed that they're back."

"You mean I'm under some sort of psychic attack?"

"Well, something is draining your fields in a big way. I bet you feel listless and tired all the time."

"Sure do," I responded. "Still can't seem to get too motivated to do much even though nonaction is unacceptable, given my current situation."

"I'll do some more work on it, but I just wanted to let you know. Whatever is draining you seems too big for just me to handle, and I know you'll feel much better with it gone."

We talk a little more and say our goodbyes.

Later, in deep meditation, I begin to see and then unhook energy lines that seem to have moved through time to leach and drain my life force. I see how they represent thoughts and limiting energy lines of my own belief patterns, plus psychic lines from other beings that my friend had been dealing with, some of whom I knew I had unfinished karmic links with, and others, who wish to cripple my work in the world. I see how the energy webs around me and through me are complex and how some are now blending together to create a deadly stew. I see that although each one is not fatal in itself, when added together, they are draining my energy field.

Although I clear these lines, a day or so later they are back, stronger than ever. Other friends who are used to inner-plane alchemy join me to repair my field and unhook the psychic lines, but they too soon come under attack. The lines are relentless, like heat-seeking missiles that constantly aim to drain the life force from all of our fields. Though I have dealt with these types of energy lines for years without any problem, at this time they have hooked in too deeply to be further ignored. Reluctantly I add the words "psychic attack" to my list of cancer causes so that I can manifest and apply the perfect cure.

Days later I finally call Brigitte. Her lover puts her on the phone; he sounds weary, for they have just had a very rough night. His voice fills with emotion to hear me as he hands the phone to Brigitte. Tears begin to roll down my face as I feel the love that we have for each other. Knowing our bonds through so many lives, I share with her a little of my story and listen as she reveals her understandings with her own journey, her current need for morphine and the inner-plane meanderings she goes through when she leaves her body as the drug frees her from her pain.

She understands why she has created this rapid deterioration and that it comes from the loss of her passion and desire to be here, and like me she is a little amazed at how powerfully the body feels this and at how quickly the system is aging and shutting down. I feel like a husband who is having a sympathetic pregnancy, displaying all the symptoms for his loved one. Brigitte and I laugh at the comparison, and I share with her the need for passion again and her need for choice.

"Do you want to be here?" I ask her as we talk also of our double binds.

"I am looking at all of this," she says. "But if I do choose to stay, what will my life be like? I see that there are changes that I will need to make, but yes, I think I want to stay."

We talk of her grandchildren to come and of the joy that my granddaughter gives me, how she is my one link of passion in this world and how I too am seeing the need to find more passion for life.

It is good to talk and laugh and cry together and share our understandings. We plan for her to come and visit me and spend some time walking in the prana-charged air of my beautiful beach paradise. She lights up, feeling excitement and hope, a reward at the end of the next few months of her journey, assuming she chooses to stay. As we hang up the phone, the sadness of it all cuts through me, as does the warmth of our love, as does the excitement about the pact we made to both stay and rediscover our passion.

The focus on causes now moves itself to the focus on cures, and I promise to email Brigitte all the data I have found so far, the problem with double binds and lack of passion, the need to hit the system with oxygen and good nutrition, the need to have the body advise us of its perfect healing path so we can avoid information overload and make the perfect choices.

And yet I sense that there is still so much more to come, that I am standing on the verge of an important revelation. So the search for the perfect cure goes on . . .

There is a formula for preventive medicine, a lifestyle that we can adopt that will keep us healthy on all levels. Unfortunately, there is no set formula for the process of re-harmonizing our health once we have lost it. The more I am led to explore the different cures, the more I see how confusing it all can become.

So many doctors or even alternative practitioners feel like theirs is the best way, that by the time dis-ease manifests in the physical system, it's due to lack of nutrition or lack of oxygen or trapped toxic emotions or interdimensional interference or too much negative or too much limiting self-talk. The list goes on, with everyone having an input as to how to cure another of his or her diseases. No doubt there is truth to be found in every diagnosis, as disease creation is a multilayered game.

Still without energy and lethargic, unable to permanently unhook all the debilitating psychic ties and aware of things that I need to do while somehow still being unable to do them, I manage to gather enough strength, and the day after my biopsy diagnosis, I see a specialist in the field of holographic kinetics. John has spent years investigating the harmonious healing phenomena from a viewpoint of disengaging energy interference systems from both outer- and inner-plane sources, yet he was not someone whose work would normally hold appeal for me, as he is a little conspiracy-theory oriented. Although conspiracy theories are based in fact, the problem is that what we focus on we feed, so although it's great to be aware, it's also important to be conscious of what realities we feed by our attention.

Yet somehow, a week or so before, I had found myself synchronistically in John's presence and now, as the days wore on and my listlessness and inertia increased, his name would not leave my mind. So I went to see him, intuitively feeling that he had a part in my path of healing.

According to the founder of this system, Steve Richards of Dreamtime Healing, holographic kinetics looks at the body holistically, as all illness starts as an imbalance in the universal flow of energy within it. He says: "This imbalance is created from the individual thoughts or emotions. This energy becomes trapped as internal electromagnetic flux with no escape, forming into potential energy. This then aligns itself into plutonic geometry forming a crystal that becomes trapped into the stress point of the body, such as organs, bones, eyes, cranium, arms, legs, blood or muscles at that moment in its own separate dimension known as time. It then manifests in the visible as effect into pain, anxiety, fear, stress, anger, guilt, sexual problems, self-punishment, compulsive behaviour, emotional problems, confusion, or in many other ways. Using Holographic Kinetics it is possible to access internal hyperspace, these separate dimensions of time where all causes of the imbalance to the effect can be recalled and brought back into balance."

Although his literature sounded a little complex, all I knew was that for me, his system held a key. After an intense session releasing the psychic energies that were adding to my system shutdown, we managed to finally get a clear kinesiological response and arrive at a personalized healing course of action, something I had attempted to do with my usual kinesiologist the day I received my biopsy results. I knew that my emotional state at the idea of more surgery was creating interference with the muscle-testing system, yet intuitively I felt that there was something more that was aiding my inertia and that perhaps the astral-plane psychic energy lines were draining my life force more than I realized. Further, I needed to confirm my intuitive feeling that the cancer had already begun to progress deeper into my system, so I had John check all of this with my body.

We finally got a strong muscle response after having cleared the psychic lines, and it was good to confirm other things that I had already intuitively received. For example, I had felt like I needed to increase my daily intake of oxygen to at least sixty drops, but my body confirmed that the need was higher and to take eighty; it also confirmed that yes, I needed to do another in-depth analysis using the LISTEN system. And we determined that my body would benefit by sessions with some new DNA light technology plus the multiwave oscillation system run by a naturopath in Cairns. Intuitively, it all felt right.

Reenergized and armed with a step-by-step healing program, I left John's office, and later that afternoon, I sat and watched the LISTEN system go through its usual testing and diagnosis. As the system tested my meridian pressure points to diagnose the energy flows and show how everything was functioning, I could not believe how close my body was to total shutdown. Only three months before, all testing had confirmed me to be in a place of perfect health, energized and rejuvenating, and here I was, posttour, displaying near critical readings.

A healthy reading is between forty and fifty, and critical readings are under ten. My liver and spleen were struggling at thirteen and fourteen, displaying classic signs of the strong possibility of cancer moving through my body. Every joint and acupuncture meridian point ached to the touch, and as the therapist, Ingrid, stimulated each point, all I wanted to do was tell her to stop and go to sleep. Ingrid was amazed and couldn't believe I was the same person who had been so healthy such a short time ago; to her it seemed she was reading a completely different person's system.

Finally completing her diagnosis, Ingird looked at me and said: "This is strange. There's two main poisons currently bombarding your system, formaldehyde and the Simian monkey virus."

"I had already tuned in to the formaldehyde poisoning, as I think I picked it up when I was in France. But the Simian virus?"

"I don't know where it's come from, but it's there. It could have come in from a childhood polio vaccination and lain dormant in the system, but it's not dormant now," she responded. "No problem, though. We can reharmonize you energetically and rebalance both."

She scanned the results in her system further and said, "The great news is that since this has happened so quickly, you can shift it all back into health again just as quickly." She smiled optimistically, completely convinced that I could do this. "A few days of these," she said as she handed me the vibrational remedies, "and you'll have a much clearer mental state and greater energy levels to make the perfect decisions and take the perfect action." (Thankfully, she turned out to be right.)

"Oh, by the way," she added, "I know you live on prana, but for whatever reason, you're not getting enough right now, so you need to hit your system with a massive dose of colloidal minerals, nutrients and also juices." Her words only confirmed what my body had already told me. "Also, instinct tells me that you'd respond well to ganotherapy."

"Ganotherapy?"

"Yes, it's based on the ancient reishi gano mushrooms that the Japanese royal family used to take for immortality and health. Let's just check the system and see if you need it."

Confirming that it would be beneficial for me, she went on to explain how ganotherapy was being successfully used to not just treat and eliminate cancers but many other diseases as well. The literature she gave me shared how it can cleanse, regulate and rebuild the body internally by detoxification and by boosting the immune system.

The Bach flower clematis she prescribed shifted me out of despondency and out of that place of "polite suicide" that my system was engaged in due to my indifference to life, while a heavy dose of colloidal minerals and an even heavier dose of high-frequency carcinoma formula repatterned me back into feeling energetic enough to book myself on a flight to Cairns, a thousand kilometers away.

Now that I had checked that the cause of the system shutdown was currently anchored in the physical and free from any emotional influences, the course of action continued to reveal itself more clearly. Still I knew that no matter what I did next, the healing had to hold and not just provide a temporary reprieve—unless I was ready to leave, and this was a decision still waiting to be finalized. Yes, I wanted to stay, but that small part of me was still feeling ready to go and I couldn't ignore its presence.

I had the feeling that I was part of a group of woman shamans whose time was complete on Earth. These were strong, vital, active women who had come in on a wave to do particular things and who had earned a well-deserved break, yet I also knew that even accepting such a thought form added power to my checkout time door, particularly since I was still undecided as to whether or not I really wanted to stay. Strangely enough, all of it felt okay, and as I sat in my morning meditations enjoying the paradise of my Japanese-style garden, I began to really look at reasons to inspire me to choose to remain in my body. I felt like I could just move into a state of allowance and be gone by the end of the year, as Einstein had predicted. I was in my seventh year of a seven-times-seven-year cycle, so in this system, it was a year of maturity and completion. Though not yet fifty, all I kept hearing was an inner voice confirming that my major work here was done and that if I chose to stay, then I still needed to rediscover my passion.

There comes a point in the healing journey when we have to move on, when we have to let go of trying to pinpoint or understand the causes and concentrate instead on the cures. Although it is important to understand how we bring something like a disease into being so that we can learn and move on, clear it and not create it again, there is also a time in the journey to become fully focused on the healing path at hand.

Having discovered the challenge and having understood enough of the ways of its creation, having moved through the minefield of information overload and having ascertained a clear path that the body is happy to follow, we now need to come into a state of allowance and action. Allowance is the willingness to be healed, and action is what we do to achieve it.

Everyone's action path into harmonious healing will differ; my path was as follows:
1. A LISTEN-system diagnosis to determine the biosystem's general state of health and to rebalance it as required.
2. Kinesiology to determine the correct healing path that my being required.
3. Oxygen therapy to boost the immune system and its natural capacity to self-heal.
4. Ganoderma detox and reishi mushrooms to purify, boost and regenerate the system.
5. Nutrition and minerals, that is, colloidals and isotopes, to support the physical system, since for some reason, I was no longer fully on the pure prana beam.
6. Bach flowers and vibrational medicine to rebalance the emotional and physical systems.

7. Juices (carrot, beta-carotene) to alkalize and support the physical body.
8. An increase in my daily meditation program to restore, then maintain inner peace and clarity.
9. Light-wave DNA repatterning to eliminate all limiting emotional and genetic imprints and release and recalibrate the causative factors behind the creation of the cancer.
10. Sound therapy using Tesla and Lahkovsky's multiwave oscillator (MWO) to recharge the cellular voltage and boost it from the cancer-forming fifteen millivolts back to the healthier seventy millivolts.
11. Removal of energy interferences so I could get clear guidance and to check for, find and remove any blocks and/or negative attractor patterns that were adding to the causative cancer game using holographics kinetics and meditations.
12. Reprogramming the body and how it was behaving with new, clear instructions for regeneration and harmonious healing.
13. Lightower nanotechnology to reionize my external environment and free it from energy pollutants and thus create a more supportive external energy field. (This was something I added during my trip to Cairns.)
14. And most importantly, rediscovering my passion for life.

A note here: Although I have touched on some of the above modalities throughout telling my story, I have elaborated on all of them in Part 3 of this book, so that you may appreciate and understand these modalities in greater detail.

Having already come to the conclusion that although there is a set path of prevention, there is no set path for cure due to the complexity of each person and the reason we come into such disease-filled spaces. Nonetheless I realized that each of the therapies mentioned can offer so much to so many.

I began to incorporate more of my healing program, and the night before I was due to fly out to Cairns to begin the sound- and light-wave therapies, I found myself even more profoundly at the crossroads of choice, for intuitively I knew that no therapy or repatterning would hold unless the underlying core issues of my double binds were also soon addressed. This was my second time with the creation of cancer, and although the causative factors were different, in essence both were born from double binds. Try as I might, I could not recapture my passion or find the deeper reason why I no longer had it in my life, and so I sat down again to meditate and explore the pathways of my options.

The Crossroads of Choice

Being labeled with having one of the seven deadly diseases swimming through one's body places a person firmly at the crossroads of choice. Each thought, word and action has the power to place us on the track of either healing or exit. The paths are distinct and obvious, and both the decision process and consequent steps need to be clear, aware and also cautious and well advised.

Most people stand before one road. Perhaps it is more like a river with many tributaries, yet they have a future that seems like an unlimited stretch of time. For those of us with a potentially deadly disease, we have future either in a body or out of a body, and we have additional choices. We can choose the path that takes us out of the body via the disease and death and into a known and loved but forgotten existence that celebrates at our return, placing us, as Michael Newton shares in his research on life between lives, back into the most harmonious and nurturing and loving state with spirit beings whom we are close to. Free of a body, free of the density of the Earth plane, we can move throughout the inner-plane realms, resting and enjoying and holidaying before we begin new, exciting adventures. This path offers us the choice to drop the body, then enjoy some healing time of integration in our etheric form of light and to do it in a safe, loving, out-of-body environment.

Or we can choose another path, where harmonious healing brings us into a healthy space again as we overcome the disease challenge, get healthy and remain in the body and continue on, with various degrees and experiences of success. A little worse for wear or healthier than ever, we continue our journey through life, hopefully more compassionate and empathetic and generally thankful to be here. Many say that having chosen this path, everything becomes an experience to be savored; they say they now live with a sweet poignancy regarding life, an appreciation hitherto unknown. This path generally makes for a happier family, who can then avoid the game of having to deal with the emotions of personal loss, the missing that occurs and the anger and grieving a family feels when one of its members moves on through death.

The crossover point of choice is actually about great freedom, for here we make a conscious choice as to which road we will take and why. Some people go back and forth for a while between the roads while they assess their options and the outcomes as they perceive them. Some surrender into death willingly, tired of the struggle of life; they sail peacefully along the path feeling strangely, contentedly complete, rejecting treatment and happy to allow the disease full reign. They have made the choice of flowing into the energy stream of a life without maintaining a body, and the more aware their next decision is on how to die: "Do I want to exit due to the collapsing of my physical system or do I wish to exit with control by moving the consciousness out of my body when the time is right and simply not go back?"

Although both options were of interest to me, for they offered different gifts, I finally decided that it would be more masterful to leave when I am ready and not because my system breaks down into instability and can no longer house my spirit. Understanding this I then realized that I needed to override my current cellular functioning and, after connecting lovingly with my body, tell it clearly that it was my intense wish and command that it now enter into a process of perfect healing and regeneration and to maintain this status until I decided that I was ready to leave.

The next morning, as I began packing for what I hoped would only be a week-long journey, I had the realization that I needed to give the body an additional set of instructions. Perhaps it was being bombarded by poison from within and without—with formaldehyde, the Simian virus, squamous cell carcinoma plus other life inhibitors that were shutting down my system. Nonetheless, regardless of what had occurred, I was its master and the cells of my body needed a clear, new program to obey. "Body," I commanded in deep meditation, acting as the master who I am, "body, I love you. Cells of my body, rejuvenate now. Body, regenerate and bring yourself into a state of perfect healing now!"

As I tuned to it and did the necessary reprogramming, I felt from within a sensation of relief, as if my body was happy with this new, clearer command and was more than capable of doing as instructed. In my dialogue with the body consciousness, I thanked it for being so attentive in fulfilling my thought patterns and interpreting my feelings, and I gave it new instructions, basically telling it that I would let it know clearly when I was definitely ready to leave and that until I did, it was to get itself back into a holding pattern of regeneration and harmonious health.

As I prepared for my journey to experience and investigate the light-pulse systems of DNA realignment in Cairns, I called in to see and say goodbye to my daughter and grandchild. When I got to their house, they swam and played in their pool, and my nine-month-old granddaughter floated over to me as I sat with my feet dangling in the water.

She grabbed the moonstone crystal that I often wear around my neck and pulled it down into her mouth, an act that pulled my head to her until our foreheads rested together. I pulled her up and as she sat before me, happily chewing on the crystal necklace, I felt an energy of acceptance pass between us. It was as if her divine essence was acknowledging what was unfolding in my life and my status at the crossroads of choice. I felt as if whatever path I chose was okay for her, and yet she also seemed to be inviting me to stay on the Earth plane with her and play. It was a comfortable exchange on a spirit level between two lovers of love.

Having come so recently from the spirit realms, she knew how harmonious the healing there can be when we go back to being pure spirit, and yet she also was completely enamored with being here in her physical-plane life. She held an energy of being absolutely happy to be in her body, and she was fascinated with everything that was going on. Watching her commitment to life, her interest in it, her thirst for it and also her ability to just be the detached watcher in the field was a revelation and an inspiring experience for me, for somehow I had lost what she had.

Other family members reacted to my health challenge as if it was a drama in which somehow I was a victim, and yet all I felt was a deep calm, a peace and awe at times, an excitement of being able to research and experience such an adventure. Yes, I decided, it may be my last year of a seven-year cycle of seven lots of seven years, but slowly I realized deep down that I was just not ready yet to leave.

And so the decision was made.

Now a new challenge remained. Could I rebalance a system that I had begun shutting down years ago, that went into cancer mode three months ago? Could I heal it all within a period of the next three weeks? Was it possible for me to come back after my time in Cairns and be able to find, via the LISTEN system, that my body was back in a state of harmonious health? I truly believed I could do it. Armed with both desire and belief, I knew that my journey into a harmonious pattern of healing had begun, for I had taken that crucial step—I had made the choice and accepted the challenge to stay.

I checked my emails one more time before my flight, and I saw that a good friend had sent me a testimonial by a well-known healer called Ken Page. Ken had been diagnosed with Hodgkin's lymphoma in 1999, and his testimonial related his journey. As I came to the end of his story, I felt my being suddenly leap to attention. Here Ken revealed more data on the Simian virus, which was something that was currently wreaking havoc in my system, along with the chemical poison formaldehyde; both had shown up strongly during my recent LISTEN-system diagnostic.

Ken's research pointed to the National Immunization Program page on the Center for Disease Control's website (http://www.cdc.gov/nip/vacsafe/concerns/cancer): "SV40 is a virus found in some species of monkey. Soon after its discovery in 1960, SV40 was found in polio vaccine. Over 98 million Americans received one or more doses of polio vaccine during the period (1955-1963) when some of the vaccine was contaminated with SV40. SV40 has been found in certain types of human cancers, but it has not been determined that SV40 causes these cancers. The majority of evidence suggests there is no causal relationship between receipt of SV40-contaminated vaccine and cancer; however, some research results are conflicting and more studies are needed."

Had I been contaminated via my childhood vaccinations? Why was the Simian virus now active in my system?

And how did I collect so much formadehyde poison and how was I to now deal with it all?

Thankfully Ingrid, my LISTEN-system therapist, could offer vibrational medicines to bring it all back into balance. Armed with these and as much data as I could gather plus a powerful healing program, on January 22, four days after I had received the bad news of my biopsy, I confidently flew to the tropical paradise of Cairns.

"What do you know of this method of treatment?" my family had asked before I left.

"Not a lot at the moment, but it just feels right to go, and my body, when I asked through kinesiology, supports my choice."

Knowing they had faith in my intuitive insight, I had hugged them all goodbye, rung the surgeon to cancel our appointment to discuss further surgery and left to embrace a new adventure.

During the flight, I began to gently touch the healing scar tissue from the operation, but stopped when I felt another small growth on my mouth. Was it the carcinoma regrowing or was it just lumpy scar tissue? Had I done the right thing by refusing the second surgery? Only time would tell, and yet I had to also trust what I had come to know. I recalled the conversation with my husband as we lay entwined in each other's arms the night before.

"You'll be okay without me, won't you?" I asked knowing, trusting and confirming that he would.

"I don't even want to go there," he promptly replied, aware that I was talking about what would happen if I died.

"You mean, if we open that door as a possibility, we feed it?"

"Definitely. I won't even entertain the idea of it—you'll pull through this. I don't believe it's your time to leave yet."

"Nor do I, but I'm writing about it all and the crossover-of-choice reality has to be looked at. So many I talk to have lost their passion for life and many are choosing not to stay. We can't choose to stay because our family needs us; we have to choose to stay for us. I know you'll be okay, but the girls? I'm not too sure. I think they'd be devastated by it all."

"Look," he sighed, not really wanting to have the conversation, "I'm sure we would all do fine, and if you really need to look at it, then we can talk about it."

And so we addressed it further, and yet all the time I kept feeling that somehow I had already closed the door to that game and that dying for me was no longer even an option.

As the plane flew through banks of soft, cumulous clouds and the sun began to descend deeper into a still, clear, blue sky, I felt as if something new had begun and that my journey would gift me with something quite sublime, for out of the greatest confusion can finally shine the greatest light.

23 January 2005, Cairns, North Queensland

I awoke in a tropical paradise with the sound of waves lapping at the shore and cicadas shrilling all around. At the tail end of a dream instruction, all I caught of it was that if everyone creates three hundred cancer cells a day, which are dealt with naturally via our immune system, then all I had to do to halt the spread of the squamous cell carcinoma through the lymphatic flow was to boost the immune system. Supplying my body with carcinoma eradicators, additional nutrition, colloidal minerals and a high dose of stabilized oxygen was a great start that would form a base for the therapies I had come to Cairns to explore.

The investigative journalist within me was excited at the prospect of exposure to new technology, for there are only two of the DNA light systems in Australia, and yet the results are profound and promising. Still I knew that I needed to keep my mind focused—not on the dilemma of the cancerous cells now growing and roaming more freely through my system, but instead on my system coming into a more harmonious state of health, for whatever we focus on, we feed, and mind power is potent, for there is medicine in the mind.

As I prepared for my first early-morning treatment session, I received an image in my mind of a being whom some would portray as the Grim Reaper waiting patiently beside me. I imagined that it now spoke and said, "Perhaps it is your time to leave this year." And I heard myself responding, "Not this year, for I am just not ready." I knew that if I could choose my entry time, then surely I could be totally conscious enough to choose my exit, both the time when and the manner in which it would occur, and so the image of the reaper faded away.

It's true that surrendering to this potentially fatal process would be so easy; it would be so easy to stick my head in the sand and act as if I haven't received the warnings, to just get on with life and allow the cancer exit-train to take me to its obvious destination. However, I feel I have choice, and muscle testing my body reconfirms that I have options. Intuitively I feel that I have created this path to research and write about and share my experience and findings so that others can gain tools and solace. Yet I also know that the journey holds great danger; I know that the focus must be clear, that all issues must be looked at and that all my double binds must disappear. Again I remind myself that diagnosis and treatment depend on dealing with both symptoms and causes, and yet for now, all I can focus on is the path of my cure.

Sacred Synchronicities and the Universal Field

had taken my laptop computer to Cairns, so I completed my last book, *The Law of Love and Its Fabulous Frequency of Freedom* by offering a synopsis of David Hawkins' calibration system, which uses kinesiology as a diagnostic tool—a system that has many potential flaws, which Hawkins also recognizes.

In his book *I: Reality and Subjectivity,* Hawkins also recognizes entity interference, for in the case of schizophrenia, the kinesiological response depends on which force is dominant in the body. Apart from external or internal interference, to gain clear answers, there is also the need to look at the calibration of the person testing us and at the questions being asked. Knowing the correct questions to ask the body is also an art.

In that synopsis, I offered a testing system using the following three approaches:

- Guidance from the Divine One Within, DOW, who knows all.
- Kinesiology or something similar, or the north-sway tool, which I was to discover in Cairns, to get confirmation from the body, or other discernment tools.
- The universal field of intelligence (UFI), which delivers sacred synchronicities to confirm or trigger what we need to know.

As I shared earlier, although the above system is great for gaining clear insights regarding life choices, unfortunately, when people are suddenly overwhelmed with the potential exit time and confronted with their own mortality or just tired and emotionally drained from being on the I-have-cancer or I-have-heart-disease train, then it is often impossible for them to gain any clear insight from within, as their emotional patterns overwhelm the more quiet, intuitive voice.

Nonetheless, the UFI will always provide clear guidance, signposts and warning signs, provided we train ourselves to see, as sacred synchronicities can be common in our world.

To me the UFI has become, over the years, like a friend—the type who always brings interesting news. It was no coincidence that I met Einstein on the day of my surgery; nor was it coincidence that we met later so he could say what I needed to hear to recognize my double bind and its debilitating energy. It was no coincidence that I found myself attending John's evening lecture so that I could later free myself of energy interferences and finally gain clarity as to the correct course of action that I needed to shift me from complacency. It was no coincidence that John had just discovered the new DNA light-wave healing technology and could connect me in this way. It was no coincidence that information came to me, the day after my own discovery of its destructive process within me, on the SV40 Simian virus and its effect in stimulating carcinomas. It was also no coincidence that I found myself in Cairns.

All the doors around me were opening so freely, and so many pieces to an amazing puzzle in the game of harmonious healing gracefully slotted into place. Flights to Cairns were incredibly cheap, as the airline carriers were currently indulging in a price war. It was a similar situation with the hotels there, and so obtaining the perfect place to stay and even procuring an inexpensive rental car, all happened easily with one phone call. So far I had encountered absolutely no obstacles in my way.

David Highman, the naturopath at the Inn Harmony Centre, who was to provide me with the sound and light technology over the next ten days, was a font of information, and I found myself being fascinated by him as I asked him questions during our first session. Having healed himself from two deadly diseases and survived a plane crash, David is calm yet strong in his convictions as he explains how the new GenMed system uses harmonics of both light and sound to restore the natural blueprint in our DNA and how it removes emotional and disease signatures from our DNA. This is done via violet-light rays that pulse through 180 quartz crystals, at the same frequency as our original DNA blueprint. Thus it repatterns us, for as we know, our DNA is altered by our internal and external environment and, over time, can be imprinted by limiting patterns.

The violet-light rays pulse through me as I sit before the system and reprogram myself with the chant: "Body, perfect health now. Body, self-sustaining, self-regenerating, now!" These are the words that seem to intuitively flow. After fifteen minutes, we move on to the multiwave oscillator (MWO) system.

Coming through the Thomas Brown Borderland Institute, the multi-wave oscillator is a Tesla-Lahkovsky invention that sends radio waves into the body to produce ozone and recharge and restore the natural capacitants of the cells to 77 millivolts of electrical charge, which gives the cells power to heal. Again, as the electrical violet light and sound waves for the MWO work their magic, I hold an intense reprogramming focus, visualizing the sound that is carrying my new codes of instruction deep into my system.

Later, when the sound and light work is done for the day, I mention to David that I am not sure if the carcinoma is regrowing itself under the scar tissue, as it's hard to feel the difference between a possible regrowth and the normal scarring that comes as my mouth heals.

"No problem," he tells me, "we can put some black salve, Cansema, on it. If it's cancer free, there will be no reaction. If it's not cancer free, then you'll definitely feel it." He then shows me photos of a woman with breast cancer who applied the salve and the way the ointment drew the cancers from her body, bringing complete healing in a matter of weeks. The photos are horrific but document an obvious process of release and eventual healing. "First she used ganotherapy to identify the cancer and draw it out of her system, then she applied the black salve to eliminate it further," David later shares.

"It's a mixture of herbs and bloodroot plus a few herbal carrier chemicals to draw the salve deep into the body and track the carcinoma to its roots, " explains David as he applies the salve to the scar tissue on my mouth. Immediately it begins to pulse and sting, and by the next morning, my mouth is so swollen I can hardly talk. The salve has revealed a four centimeter by two centimeter large area of cancer cells that seem to be at war with the salve. The pain is relentless, but I know it's doing me good.

To be able to see the complete area that is affected is a blessing, as my greatest shock came when David told me how when a surgeon cuts open a cancer, as soon as it is exposed to oxygen, it flees immediately into adjacent areas of the body, as contact with oxygen kills it. For the surgeon to remove what is there now, my whole top lip and the area under my nose would have had to be cut away, and later extensive reconstructive surgery would have been required.

As I stare at the blackish-green, puss-filled, infested mass that now sits on my top lip, I feel so grateful that I came. I also know that if I had known exactly what it was when the growth was still at the small-pimple stage and if I had had access to and knowledge of the bloodroot salve, so much discomfort, from surgery and the cancer's consequent spread, would easily have been avoided.

Yet "if onlys" are a waste of energy, for what is, is, and I feel even more deeply the need to write my story and share these findings with the world. I imagine a world where every skin cancer clinic has the black salve at its disposal, and then I imagine a world where we know enough to never create cancer in the first place.

Trusting that all is perfect, the next day I return for my second session, an intense facial bath of the violet light. Temperature rising and face tingling, I ask David if all the herbs and vitamins and concoctions I am taking are overwhelming my system, to which he replies: "When dealing with cancer in its early stages, you have to hit it with everything you've got. It literally is a battle for life, and only by bombarding the system in this way do you have a chance to reverse the game."

I think I prefer Ken Page's mindset where he lovingly told the cancer in his body to go back to sleep.

David confirms that in the game of harmonious healing, mental attitude decides whether our healing patterns will hold or give us just a temporary reprieve, and so I begin to wonder if in the cancer game there is room for the battles or fear that support states of separation. Cancer cells are in us all, kept in check by our immune systems; they are part of us and part of life. To try to eliminate them from within us is a waste of time when we can use our energy instead to boost the immune system and support the body's own innate intelligence to bring everything back into health and balance.

David tests my PH levels and confirms them as being dangerously low. "Much too acidic," he declares. "Anything under 7—and yours is 5.2—is a perfect breeding ground for cancer and disease."

For thirty-six hours, the salve pulses its magic through my mouth as I visualize it lovingly drawing the carcinoma from my cells. When the pain stops, I can feel the healing begin as the black disappears and is replaced by a green-white covering and bubbled cells that sting if I accidentally bump them. The healing process is so powerful, and after three days on the machines, I earn a day of rest. All I feel is being tired, and so I sleep and sleep.

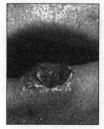
Here are a few photos of my journey. Although I don't have a photo of my mouth from before the surgery, there is an image from the Skin Cancer Foundation's website (http://www.skincancer.org/squamous/index.php) of a typical squamous cell carcinoma that has grown on someone else's mouth. The photos below show my mouth the day of the surgery with its incision from just under my nose.

The other photos show my mouth nearly three weeks later, when I began the Cansema black salve treatment to combat the spreading cancer cells that were not removed by the surgery.

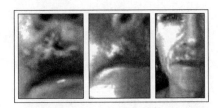

Surgery day.   Treatment with black salve: day 2, mouth swollen; day 3, healing begins.

The second row of photos shows the bloodroot/black salve solution working to eliminate a mole on my daughter's back. Photo 1 is the 0.5-centimeter-sized mole before treatment, then the black salve does its work. Although the bloodroot mixture for treating moles is different than the Cansema salve, both seek and destroy any cells that are dangerous. It was amazing to see the changes, the drawing out and the healing. The final picture of my daughter's mole shows it next to an Australian ten-cent coin, which is 2.7 centimeters in diameter.

The Changing Game

27 January 2005

have started to notice some interesting occurrences as I continue to undergo my repatterning process via the GenMed and multiwave oscillator (MWO) systems. As I sit in meditation and focus on programming to direct the repatterning process rather than just indulge in random thinking, I am beginning to glimpse another level to the current reality I have created.

After doing the love-breath and body-love tuning techniques (see Part 2, pages 144 and 146, respectively), I find my words "Body, perfect health now" expanded to "Body, perfect health now; perfect rejuvenation now; self-sustaining, physically immortal now." No matter how much I try to just program "Perfect health and perfect regeneration and rejuvenation," the other words keep coming. It's as if the repatterning systems are providing me with an opportunity to not just harmoniously heal but to go to another level.

Physical immortality has never interested me and yet, when I have checked in previous meditations, I always get that "Yes, this is part of my blueprint this life." It seems strange that someone who is so good at manifesting such extremes, including cancer in my system, has such a choice, yet why not? I can imagine physical immortality when I am in the state of health that I was in three months ago, but now, as I focus on just bringing my spleen, liver and total system out of their collapsing tailspin and back into harmony and health, the idea of immortality seems a little far-reaching and ill timed. And yet . . .

Is this just a path of healing or also an opportunity for immortality?

I am now taking eleven of each of the reishi gano mushroom tablets a day and am experiencing no side effects. Many people have a huge reaction to just one tablet a day, and when I tested my body, it said I need fourteen of each a day. I asked—using kinesiology—if these were needed for healing, and I got a no; so I asked if it was for immortality repatterning, and I got a yes.

It's interesting that the *Ganoderma lucidum* mushroom has long been known in Japan as the trigger for immortality and that I am currently taking a total of twenty-two tablets a day.

I have just completed another session with the MWO and light-pulse systems when my phone rings and my daughter tells me that Brigitte is now comatose again and in hospital. Appearing to be in the final stages of her death process, she is at peace and no longer conscious. I hang up the phone, go into a deep state of prayer and meditation and find Brigitte on the inner planes so that we can say our goodbyes. I pray for a team of angels to make her journey easy and light and for more angels to be with her daughter and partner, to give them the comfort they may need. Earth will be a little less sweet without her.

It still feels strange to be in a time when so many around me are shutting down their systems and leaving, exiting via the weakest part of their being, creating a fatal illness or overloading the heart with excess electricity. It seems the choice to take the body up into light is not high on the list. Perhaps the schism in the field attracts the disease and then, when they are aware of the choice before them, many decide to just surrender to it and go. Brigitte and I had so many discussions about the need for passion to ground us here, and I know the last time we talked that the call for her to go was stronger than the call to stay.

It seems strange to meet with Brigitte on the inner planes and to connect in love and say our goodbyes, for she'll never be farther away than a thought in my mind. She knows this and so do I, but I'll miss seeing her smiling face and her bright, brown button eyes. I'll miss the grace of her and seeing how efficiently she would organize what we would do and how loved she is by her team. I'll miss hugging her and laughing with her and sharing of all our journeys in the months between the times that we would meet each year. It seems we've been friends forever and in other lives we have, and I know that to find her again is only a journey of an open heart and mind. Still, there's a part of me that wishes she would stay.

I think of her daughter who, although grown, will miss her mother so, and I think of my own daughters and how much they would hate for me to leave, how I know that in time they both would feel cheated somehow, wishing I was there to share the myriad of special times that are ahead for them. It seems the process of dying can be just as complex as the process of living, and I wonder when—if ever—we are really prepared to let our loved ones go.

Each morning I return for my light sessions and leave feeling exhausted and in need of sleep, that is, until the day when David's new shipment of nanotech lightowers arrives.

"This one has the capacity to influence a field in a 120- to 150-kilometer radius," he says smiling like a kid with a new toy. "They say it can even divert cyclones. People have been placing them throughout major cities and reducing all the air pollution and even water pollution. Plant and animal life in those areas just thrives. They're amazing. I just love these things." And setting it to the north to activate it, he places it under the chair where I receive my light-wave treatments. "See if you feel a difference today."

He's right; I do feel a difference, and I'm not half as tired at the end of the session as I was the other days. Impressed, I buy a small one that has the capacity to reionize the atmosphere within a ninety-kilometer radius. Sleeping with it beside my bed I can feel the difference immediately—it's as if I am lying in a highly charged pranic environment. It's the same feeling I get when I walk each day on the beach as the wind blows its pranic forces through my auric field, somehow recharging and energizing me.

Based on plasmonics, which is said to be the next big thing in nanotechnology, the lightower, which acts as an antenna, changes positive ions into more healing negative ions that support us when it is aligned from the magnetic north to the south. It does this by harmonizing the surrounding energy field and by rebalancing any disturbances from the electromagnetic field radiation (EMR) of appliances that surround us and bombard us daily. Using plasmonics, lightowers restore the delicate balance of light in both the external and internal environments of our bodies. Over twenty years of research have linked EMR with causing a range of health problems, from headaches to leukemia and cancer—and I had just spent ten years and nearly 75 percent of my time each year traveling through the most intensely EMR-polluted areas of the world.

It seems as if the universal field is providing me with ways to retune not just my internal energy flow but also my external one. As I ask within, I am told that at this point in time, I need all the support I can get, for although my system has been recalibrated, it is still nowhere near as strong as it was, and holding this new delicate pattern of healing is crucial. Gone are the days when I could travel the world and be in any energy environment and remain unaffected. From now on, with the new levels of chaos arising in the world, plasmonic-based technology would be my constant companion—at least for a while.

People in Europe, particularly in Germany, have been bombarding me with these types of ionization products for years, but I never needed them, preferring to use my own light bioshield to screen out or transmute any external energy interference. It seems that the game has changed.

"Remember," an inner voice says, "you are writing and researching all of this for others, not just yourself, and many have need of these things in this world today. The new scientists in these light fields also need more support and proof of the power of their inventions."

When I receive my usual copy of the *Ode* magazine, I find an article on electromagnetic field radiation that is fascinating and further supports the need for such fine-tuning.

Back in the 1970s, the American physician Robert O. Becker, now Professor Emeritus of Orthopedic Surgery at the State University of New York, warned that our health would be affected by artificially generated electromagnetic frequencies. Becker, who was twice nominated for the Nobel Prize for medicine, is convinced that the increase in these frequencies is directly linked to the rise in rates of cancer, birth defects, depression, learning disabilities, chronic fatigue and Alzheimer's. "All matter living and non-living is an electromagnetic phenomenon. The material world, at least as far as physics has penetrated, is an atomic structure held together by electromagnetic forces," he argues and is concerned that the "human species has changed its electromagnetic background more than any other aspect of the environment." . . . "How damaging is it," Becker wonders, "that the density of radio waves around us is now 100 million or 200 million times the natural level reaching us from the sun. The question is, how exactly are these waves affecting us?" (I am so fascinated that I add more of the article in Part 3 of this manual.)

In meditation I asked for the source of the GenMed technology to be revealed to me, and I was told that it was being downloaded through the universal mind via the higher-light scientists anchored in the Arcturius field. They were the same ones who had given me all the dimensional biofield technology with its support of the Divine Nutrition program. How to attract and hold and expand the pranic flow so that we can nourish ourselves and also use it globally, to eliminate health and hunger problems, is also part of inner-plane higher-light science. No wonder it all felt so familiar and right! I was finally beginning to understand on yet another level as to why I had been taken out of the prana beam and manifested the game of cancer.

With my current situation of being held in a more fragile and delicate body, I began to reexperience what it felt like to be "normal," particularly with having to support my biosystem with external nutrition and minerals, having colonics to stimulate my digestive system with herbs as it learnt to deal with external supplements, having to rely on external aids such as reionization products to purify the environment around me, having to spend time and effort and money on my health, having to seek further information and help, having to learn to sort through the overwhelming mountains of information that abound in the healing game!

For eleven years, I had been shielded from it all, held in a healthy field of my own creation, my frequency keeping me free from all disease. I didn't realize just how much I had taken it all for granted until it disappeared. Someone had once said to me that the pure prana nourishers were like the spiritual elite, never sick—and also no longer empathetic for the trials and tribulations of the many who had not yet anchored themselves permanently in the disease-free prana band. I didn't realize that perhaps I needed more compassion; I didn't realize how when we are out of the chaos game, in time we can forget just how difficult it is to survive there.

I also knew that it was all good, that it was just like when I first learned how to be fed by prana and how to stabilize my system in that field, and then how to take food from time to time and transmute even things like coffee or chocolate into pure light. Always experimenting, always expanding my personal knowledge through living experience . . . Surely all of this was no different.

Since I had been in that healthy, pure pranic flow for so long, then once I stabilized my system and finalized my path to self-heal, written this book and learnt all I needed, all I had to do was magnetize myself back into that pure pranic beam again and stay there—it was all just resonance, after all.

After having tasted over a decade of a pill-free life, having to take the ganotherapy tablets plus antioxidants and multiminerals in pill form seemed to me a chore. Yes, it was all helping me to stabilize my system, but it was also definitely something I would tune myself back to being without as soon as I could. My body confirmed that it would take two more months before I could be pill-free again, and so I shifted my attitude and got back into gratitude for it all.

I walk along the boulevard watching the sunset over the bay, and I have gotten used to the myriads of tourists who, seeing the mass of dead, green, puss-filled cancerous cells above my top lip, turn their horrified gaze away, pitying and thankful that it's not them or wondering what has befallen me. All I feel is happiness that the cancerous cells have died and that my body is expelling them this way.

David says that my healing is miraculous, that no one has ever healed so fast with him before—what usually takes weeks has taken only a few days. Yet I know that the journey has just begun and that I need to keep my focus if I am to hold the new pattern of health I am creating so that I can stay. Too busy with the healing sessions, I have given little further thought to my double binds.

I awoke this morning feeling clearer than I have for a while, energized and understanding that many in the world can't find the funds to come and sit in front of an MWO or GenMed system or afford the lightowers. Therefore, if I research them all, maybe I can then channel from the UFI the perfect meditations to do the same job. Relying on mind power and DOW power and using the rejuvenating, regenerating violet light spectrum, we can hook into the morphogenetic field to the original researchers and receivers of these devices and, through our DOW, download from these devices exactly what we need to attain and maintain our harmonious healing state. By adding this download as an etheric template into our bioshields, we can bypass the availability problem by going straight to the source from which the inventors originally received their data. All I needed to do was channel the perfect meditation to achieve this or, better still, to trust that the aware ones would know what to do once the suggestion of this possibility was made.

As I realized this, my heart smiled, and I thought of the thousands of people I could reach who have neither the time nor the money to seek and enjoy the remedies I have found. All it would take, once the recipes were tuned into and downloaded, was focus and faith—focus on the meditations and faith that they would work.

Then I thought, "What about the nutritional mineral level? Could we do something there?" I was taking nearly sixty tablets a day of high-quality, pure-potency supplements that many people couldn't afford, or even find in such quality.

We had a decade of experimental research behind us regarding the Divine Nutrition program, where for eleven years I had needed no external vitamin/mineral supplements and where I had maintained perfect health in the most trying of circumstances. Could we do the same there? Couldn't anyone just download the knowledge needed on these issues directly from the universal field? Surely all that anyone had to do was tune in to it and ask?

Yes, it was true that I had recently weakened my field and tuned myself out of the pure prana nourishment flow, and yet I felt that all of it was part of a bigger game to motivate me to find, meet and report on some of the cutting-edge technicians in the healing field. It was also a lesson to teach me to be more compassionate toward those still in need of, and searching for, harmonious healing, for although the ideal pattern is to not create disharmony in the first place by applying a preventive-medicine program, this will remain only an ideal until we have sufficient holistic education on our planet.

I remember a conversation I had on an airplane a few months ago with a family returning from collecting two sisters they had adopted in India. The children came with no birth background records, and so their new parents gave them the day of their formal adoption as their birthdays.

When I gently shared that they could use kinesiology to muscle test the children and find out their correct birth time and date, the father, not understanding what I was implying, shook his head and said, "You can't test these girls' bodies for anything as they haven't had proper nutrition, so they are totally underdeveloped." Intuitively I felt that he wasn't meant to hear me or understand what I had suggested, and so I let it go.

My ideas for these things are based on the fact that as we are all cells in the one body of a divine being, we are all interconnected and therefore can download any data from this living energy field that we need. Using intention and meditation or tools like kinesiology, we can access valuable tools and data without restriction. We just need to know how, and to ask.

Many people in our world are creating one of the seven deadly diseases. Some will find a cure, whereas others will surrender to it and drop the body and die and then move on to rest awhile in another plane. Some will read this book and absorb the message and turn their life around. Some will gain temporary relief and re-create it all again, failing to look at the causative factors and treating only the symptoms. There are so many new diseases that will come due to our constant exposure to the negative effects of electromagnetic field radiation. As yet unnamed and unidentified, they will bring havoc for many. On one level, all of it is perfect, for it teaches us so much, and as our life spirit is eternal, we get to play the games again until we finally come into, and stay in, a space of harmonious healing where we no longer create disease.

When she finally leaves her body, Brigitte will rest awhile in the etheric realms and regenerate herself there, and in time perhaps she will rejoin us on the wheel of life, if not on this planet then perhaps on another, if not in this dimension then perhaps in another.

Yet right here, right now, new technologies abound, and so I sit in the chair in David's office in Cairns and hold my moonstone crystal in my hand, the one I often wear as a pendulum around my neck. Sending it a beam of pure love I make contact with the elemental within it and ask it to tune to the GenMed and MWO systems and to copy, record and store, for later transmission, the signature harmonics of the sound wave and light rays that I am now being immersed in—for crystals love to record and amplify what they can. Later I instruct it to download in perfect doses what I need of these light and sound rays to keep the electrical charge around my cells in perfect equilibrium and to maintain my DNA pattern in its original harmonic state.

So far, so good; the learning and the healing are all unfolding nicely.

The Immortal's Way

28 January 2005

The reishi gano mushroom was taken for centuries by Japanese royalty for its healing, life-sustaining and regenerating powers. Grown in templelike conditions and revered by its growers, it is known to deliver the food of immortality to its users and is referred to as the King of Herbs. Although many feel the effects of taking one tablet a day, within five days I was on twenty-two tablets a day and showing no side effects; I could feel my body still able to accept and utilize more.

Today is my husbands' birthday. I meet his flight, then we settle him into my beachside apartment at Yorkey's Knob and take to the beach to share of our past week's journeys. Later we sit in silence at the river mouth and enjoy the setting of the sun, and I see again two paths clearly etched out before me—except this time, it is not a crossroads of choice about staying or going but rather a choice as to how to view the Now. I realize that I can see my current time as a "healing of my being" or as "the immortal's way." There have been enough opportunities within the path so far for me to choose either one and build on it to make it real.

For years I have been using the mantra "I have forever," and like any statement that we say consciously and regularly, it gets us looking at its implications. "I have forever" is the immortalist's mantra, and it confronts us on many levels, as we all *do* have forever. Whether we keep our bodies for long or finite periods of time, our consciousness flows on—in and out of form, always growing and expanding and reawakening to the potential of All That Is.

A possible problem with this I-have-forever mantra is that we can become complacent, knowing that there is no rush, for we have all the time in the world. It also gets us thinking that we may outlive all our loved ones, especially those who are not consciously embracing the immortal's way. This in itself is kind of sad, as we realize that we will see our children die before us. Most parents feel that they should die before their children and that this is the more natural, logical order of life and is another interesting concept to deal with.

When we embrace the I-have-forever reality—as in, we have a forever of physical time—we see everything so differently. For example, do we need to work forever to support ourselves? We also tend to become more of the watcher and observer as we pace our journey differently, no longer in a rush to bring anything into being. How does it feel to see eternity stretched out before us?

Exciting?

Endless?

Manifesting a new reality requires believing in and acting as if the intention we are setting and the programming we are using are powerful enough to make our vision real.

And so I walked along the sunset beach in the tropics of northern Australia, halfway through a program of light repatterning that was resetting my DNA back into its original program of perfect. And I realized that a new beginning was being handed to me, that the game was changing, as I had suspected, for megadoses of the reishi mushroom were floating through my system, with their gift of immortality ready to break free. Anchored deep within me was the resolve that it was not my exit time, nor would I exit via the cause of cancer. And so with each step I began to feel the power of the choice of a new way, the immortal's way. And with it I began to see so much more.

For years I had been so focused on being here to fulfill the work I had come to do: to find the frequency that was receptive to the Divine Nutrition program and to be the frequency where I could demonstrate it in action, which meant, in essence, demonstrating a life that was filled with grace. And when the work was done, the grace shifted and called me to move with it to stay in its flow, and so I became the watcher and the one who was to wait for a new game to bring a new level of passion into life.

"Trust you," a good friend laughed. "You always thrive on a challenge! Wouldn't surprise me if you created all this just to have something beneficial and challenging to do." Perhaps she is right, I thought, and yet, for any game to have depth, it has to be real so that we can explore the crossroads of choice and live through and learn from our choices.

Years ago I read that every four seconds, an adult dies unnecessarily of health-related problems, and every two seconds, a child dies from health and hunger problems. After a decade with the Divine Nutrition program, we had found how to eliminate the children-dying-of-hunger reality, so it made sense to now start on the adults-dying-unnecessarily-from-health-related-problems project. What better way to do this than to unhook myself from the prana game, so that I had to rely on normal nutrition as I created a life-threatening cancer that had a myriad of causes, so that I could discover how to harmonize it all back into health?

Immortality and harmonious health all relate to our Divine One Within's, our DOW's, radiation levels as we release It from within us and allow It to flow through us and out into the world. Our research over the past three decades has proven that we can control our DOW's radiation levels via our attitudes and lifestyle. Diet, nutrition and the oxygenation of our physical system, plus exercise and service provide a powerful template for our DOW to be anchored in. Positive emotional and mental attractor patterns also increase Its radiation capacity, as does time spent in silence and meditation where we make ourselves available to experience more consciously Its presence. When radiant and connected with our DOW, It consciously links us to the DOW of all and lights up pathways through the universal field of intelligence that bring clarity, tools and support for whatever we need, exactly how we need it and until we need it no more. It's easy to be overwhelmed by more dominant field energies, especially when we are feeling vulnerable and unsure. (In hindsight surgery had not been the best option for me, as it only spread the cancer cells further, and yet without it and the scare of the biopsy result, I probably would not have discovered the light machines and the bloodroot salve and flown to Cairns to spend my time in the tropics and rediscover the immortal's way.)

31 January 2005

A few days ago, I began to feel nauseous from my herb/vitamin/oxygen mix, which means I have to decrease the dosage. So I have booked myself in for a session with a local Cairns kinesiologist to check what my body now needs and confirm what I am receiving intuitively. Am feeling wonderful levels of clarity again and receiving much clearer guidance.

This morning, as I sat receiving the light pulses from the GenMed system, I heard very clearly, "Your time with this is complete; any more may create damage." It was a very clear voice that said the same thing over and over, until I told David to shut it down. When I asked about the MWO, I also received the answer that it was to be the final session.

I thanked David for all his help, left and soon found myself in the presence of a young, local Aboriginal woman who was the kinesiologist I had intuitively selected from the phone book. As we talked, we realized that I was not a candidate for her usual way of working and so we exchanged further information, tested my body and received my next month's program so that I could hold my new health pattern. It was as I was leaving that she delivered a wonderful gift. "Have you tried the self-testing methods?" she asked, showing me the two common finger methods.

"Yes, but they don't seem to work for me."

"Nor me," she laughed, "but I do like the north one."

"The north one?"

"Yes, all you do is find north on the compass and face it. Breathe deeply and relax and then ask your body to confirm a truth, like 'I am in a female body.' And if you are, you will automatically fall forward—it's as if truth calls the body to lean to the north. If it's not true, your body will fall or sway backward. Try it. It may work for you; it does for me." And with a huge smile, she shook my hand and closed the door.

She's right. It does work for me.

Focus and faith are imperative ingredients in our journey into harmonious health and its end result of embracing the immortal's way: maintaining the focus of doing what is required to fine-tune our system and having the faith that what we are doing will deliver the outcome that we seek; having the faith to trust and know that when we surrender to our DOW, It will deliver what we need to attain our preprogrammed goals.

Using the north-sway body testing technique, I have verified my maintenance program and that my mouth area is now totally free of damaging cancer cells. My body tells me that it requires more of the reishi gano to stabilize itself into its new patterns and that I still have a few mental-plane adjustments to make plus a little emotional fine-tuning, as the body still holds a little residue of sadness and shock at confronting again its own mortality. Even within an integrated system, the physical body consciousness and the emotional body's inner child still require tenderness and care, for they operate on, and within, slightly denser levels than the master of our system, our DOW.

Coming into a state of harmonious health is about coming into a state of loving integration and weaving our systems into a supportive and loving web of light that nourishes us on all levels.

It's eleven years since my last confrontation with cancer, a time and test that have delivered so much on so many levels and that was then closely followed by an amazing initiation where I learnt to live solely on the nourishment of the divine. I can't help but think that after this intense period of cleansing and retuning with the light- and sound-wave systems, another intense initiation will be offered as I step into the next month.

Confronting any fears regarding our own mortality and the things we have looked at in this book, like the dignity of dying, for instance, is so beneficial to us all, as it allows us to clear so many limited patterns. There are many layers and realities regarding the existence we call our life that we can uncover and also weave, and many of us need our time of assimilation and integration before we can move on.

It is so good to have regained my clarity of thought and intuition and to have also been given the north-sway testing tool for easy confirmation. It has been so good to spend these ten days in the tropical north. It has been so good to journey through the oldest rainforest in the world and weave some of the magic of the past forty-five thousand years of Aboriginal tradition through my field during the time I took to sail and feel the ancient essence of the Daintree river. All of it has been such a blessing in so many ways.

Now that I had bombarded my physical system with the type of support it needed, I was soon ready to return from my adventure in Cairns—with its experience of the black salve and the MWO and GenMed systems—and to continue to address additional causative factors so that I would no longer imprint my newly reset DNA with any emotional limitations. So far I had discovered that the roots of my cancer creation came from the need to understand even deeper the poisonous power as well as the healing power of words; limited thinking and repetitively telling my body that my work here was complete; lack of cellular oxygen and nutritional support; formaldehyde and Simian virus poisoning; heavy and constant psychic attack; constant, heavy exposure to electromagnetic field radiation (EMR), which finally penetrated my field and led me to discover plasmonics; the need to gain greater compassion and empathy and the sadness schism from Brigitte's situation; the need to address the impact of the seven deadly diseases globally and, as a researcher/writer, offer alternative solutions; the need to discover and share more dependable discernment tools; and the need to discover and then choose the immortal's way.

As I got ready to leave for the airport, David asked me if I had heard about the Cairns nightclub that had recently closed down.

"No. Why?"

"It's just an interesting story that confirms some of the work Steve Richards and John are doing with holographic kinetics."

"Go on, what happened?"

"Well, I think it was the week before you arrived, all the backpackers and locals were partying in one of Cairns' most famous nightclubs when there appeared to be a massive energy crackle or spark in the field. When everyone turned around to look, there was a huge, twelve-foot high, gray, reptilian-looking creature standing there. Apparently, the frequency of the field drew it through a doorway in time."

"You're joking!" I said, not sure whether to believe him.

"No, seriously, everyone just ran and the club has been closed ever since. People think it's haunted. Locals say it scared everyone out of their wits!"

"You know, I remember meeting some people in Europe who'd developed an energy reader that could pick up disembodied spirits. They said when they took it to pubs and nightclubs, the rooms were full of them, all swirling around the drinkers and dancers."

"No doubt the energy field in nightclubs and pubs is perfect for them to feed off and attach themselves. All that alcohol and drugs and full-on heavy music! That seems to be the majority of Steve's work these days, clearing interdimensional interference. That plus the work he's been doing with youth suicides, particularly among the Aborigines. I'm told that it all has had great results, but then the Aborigines are big believers in the disembodied spirit world."

"Personally, I find it all hard to relate to," I answered. "It's not that I doubt the possibility, it's just that what we focus on grows and I would just rather not focus on such things. I prefer the quantum explanation to Steve's work."

"That holographic kinetics is about freeing trapped emotions caught in weaker energy fields in the body? I guess it sounds a little more plausible than psychic and or disembodied spirit attack. Anyway, whatever gets results, eh?"

I laughed and asked him, "So you're sure it's okay to write about you and the technologies you have here?"

"Sure," he responded. "The GenMed people are keeping a low profile, as many of the traditionalists seem to like the expensive, more complex route of healing that lines their pockets with more money, but I'm happy to liaise with anyone about it all. Works a treat, doesn't it?"

"Time will tell, David; only time will tell. Anyway, just how many people can afford to spend the time or money to fly in to see you? What about people in Third-World countries? I would like to be able to set up a system where we can just download all the new healing light technologies and their benefits directly into our biofields from the morphogenetic field. It's already anchored there, so surely we can access it via meditation and the right commands." Used to my ideas after our days together, David looked at me as if perhaps it was an idea that was valid.

After eight sessions on the DNA GenMed system and six on the MWO, I was feeling both energized and elated. Convinced that there were no more cancer cells in my mouth and lip area and that any others in my system were now peacefully asleep, I stepped onto the tarmac and boarded my plane, leaving the humidity of the tropics and their Aboriginal dreamtime magic behind me.

As the plane veered south, I thought of the young Aboriginal woman whom I had just met and who had taught me the north-sway tool, handing it to me as if it were just a throwaway line, unaware of what a perfect tool it would turn out to be for me. As the sun shone its potent rays across a cloud-filled sky, I gave thanks again for all I had met and all I had so recently come to know. Life was an adventure after all.

I scribbled the following summation note and general procedure, then sat back to enjoy both the flight and my constantly changing journey.

1. Deactivate all of my self-destruct programs, emotional and mental and past life; more to do on this.
2. Continue to support my systems with a strong nutritional and mineral base, etherically with more prana and also physically.
3. Continue to oxygenate my physical body to boost the immune system's innate healing ability. Keep taking ganotherapy.
4. Rediscover and expand my passion and my purpose in life; still to discover how.
5. Do more meditation; is always beneficial.

Walking the immortal's way has become such a gift that my healing challenge highlighted and enticed me into. I love how it all has happened so naturally and with such ease and grace and obviousness regarding the power we have of choices and of our focus. The immortal's way requires us to begin with the knowing and acceptance that we create it all and that if we don't like what we create, we can refine it into something healthy and harmonious for all, whether we do this personally or on a global level, for when we heal personally, we also heal our world. The immortal's way requires us to choose to let go of our death urge, to choose to exit with dignity when we complete all that we have come to do and when the time is right—and to intuitively know when it is. The immortal's way requires smooth-flowing rivers of energy, free of crystalline blocks and negative attractor patterns that promote dis-ease. The immortal's way requires a pure and compassionate, love-filled heart and a mind open to our divine potential, a mind harmonized to the universal field of intelligence and its love. The immortal's way requires an understanding of the oneness of the fields of life, of the weaves between time and of the ancient power of dreaming, of seeing new futures and new fields in our dreams and doing whatever reweaving is needed to alter outcomes, knowing that if it is our time, then the fields will reveal the way, simply because it is the path of our own evolution.

All of this I have come to understand as I walked the northern beaches in Cairns, surrounded by tropical bird song, held in a humid flow of tropical heat and embraced in the loving presence of my DOW. With the Aboriginal dreamtime energy now more awake and pulsing within me, I step off the plane as it lands and, reborn somehow, I embrace a light-filled day. Still, after all of this, I feel as if there is so much more to come. Choices have been made, action has been taken and yet something else is now intuitively calling me on.

Trust and Triumph, Focus and Faith

1 have never been big on the trust game; for me, it's too nebulous and unscientific. I like formulas and templates and a science that is able to ascertain specific outcomes. Thus is my baser nature: inquisitive and appreciative of an order that can deliver an outcome of my choosing. For more than thirty years, my constant guidance from the universal field of intelligence (UFI) has been to have more faith and trust; that my life, with its journey of enlightenment, would unfold more fluidly if I had more faith and trust.

Back in my hometown on the beach, with my light- and sound-wave repatterning complete, I booked myself to see both John and Ingrid again and to continue to rebalance any remaining cancer-causative factors. I knew that clearing these causative factors was crucial to holding my new health pattern and that I still had more to clear. Even though my DNA had been reset and had dumped its genetic and emotional limitations, it was still only a reprieve in time, giving me a clean slate that I decided not to pollute again. And even though I had checked using intuitive tools that the area around my mouth and lip was clear of cancer, I wanted to double-check that the cancer cells were again asleep throughout my body, controlled naturally once again by my immune system.

Although I had dealt in depth with the emotional cause for creating the first cancer, on my liver, which was due to a buildup of frustration and anger and my reluctance to let go and forgive, dealing with the emotional issues this second time was a little more complex. The first time I used vibrational medicines such as Bach flowers and homeopathy to support the system, as I did again this time. I also used deep meditations to let go of stored emotions, particularly the anger and frustration that had been held in my liver.

This time, I knew, I needed to go even deeper still, back through past timelines, to review the life where this destructive pattern had begun and, through neuro-linguistic programming (NLP) and reimaging tools, release the triggers of the cycle. My next session with John brought into focus my mortality patterns and revealed that I had an attractor pattern to violent endings as scene after scene revealed the way I had died so many countless times before. Sadness and shock and then death walked hand in hand, setting up repetitive fields to be fulfilled until the cycle was broken. As the session and memory fields unfolded, John and I finally released the need for it all and in doing so eliminated the last of the cancer-causative factors.

As I continued to research and write, I realized once more that the power of our emotions and the way they can create disharmony and disease needed to be covered in depth, not just for my journey but also for the journeys of those reading about it who may also be seeking to heal. Hence I have taken the chapter on this from my book *In Resonance* and added it to Part 2 of this manual to benefit our harmonious healing discussion.

Regardless of who we are today and how aware we are, we still store within our cellular memory attractor patterns based on past experiences that can create both dis-ease and limitation. These are held in check by radiation from our Divine One Within (DOW), which, when strong, keeps us healthy, but when weakened or ignored, these limiting attractor patterns can dominate our fields and create various degrees of chaos. And we all have set mortality patterns until we clear them to walk the immortal's way.

On February 4, I sat in my local Chinese doctor's office and listened to his interpretation of my biopsy report and his traditional treatment recommendations.

"They discovered the squamous cell carcinoma in deep tissue, on the borders of what was cut out. The risk is too great to ignore, so you need further surgery."

"Can't do," I replied. "The biopsy was done five weeks ago now, and I've addressed a lot since then. You know that they did the surgery the day before Christmas, and then they closed their clinic for a few weeks?"

"That's common for the Christmas break."

"I know, still, even though the biopsy report had come back to them, it took another two weeks to let me know, by which time the cancer had spread. I am glad in a way, as it made me seek alternative options, but it's still negligent.

"Anyway, Doctor, by the time I finally got the biopsy news, I knew intuitively that it had moved deeper into my system. The surgeon would have needed to remove most of the area above and including my top lip to eliminate all the cancer. On one level, I am grateful they waited so long before giving me the biopsy results, for if they had told me much sooner, I may have consented to more surgery and never learnt what I now know."

"How do you know that it had spread that far? Perhaps he needs to remove just a little."

As I told him of my journey to the north, Dr. Zhan's eyes opened with interest at the mention of the multiwave oscillator (MWO) and the GenMed system and the beauty and the pain of the black salve with its bloodroot magic. He admitted that whenever he got sick, his wife sent him to the Chinese herbalist.

"Fixes me all the time. My grandmother used to use the black salve and bandage it like a poultice. Hurt like crazy, but it worked. Perhaps I need to understand more of my own culture's medicine!"

We laughed.

After a continued discussion during which he realized that I would not submit to further surgery, he told me to at least immediately begin chemotherapy.

"Regardless of what you've been doing, have the chemo just to be safe. I can refer you to a good local oncologist."

I shook my head and said, "I just came in for a blood test, some way of medically confirming that all that I have been doing has worked. I know you can do a blood test to track prostrate cancer, surely there is something to track this as well?"

"Sorry, there's nothing we can do, no way to tell. By the time it's in the lymph system, it usually first attacks the liver before moving into the bone marrow. The liver defends itself so well that by the time it displays a weakness via the tests we use, the cancer is usually well advanced. If you won't have chemo, then I ask that you monitor yourself closely."

I remembered David, the Cairns naturopath, telling me how important it was to discern the right course of action and then to trust that it will deliver the outcome and not to deviate or allow in confusion. It was the mind-power placebo principle that was based on a sound understanding and action plan that would address causative issues and not just the superficial symptomatic. I knew the importance of this from the first journey I had with cancer. I also knew the importance of harmonizing our emotional and mental fields and how the Aboriginals felt that all illness came from spiritual illness, how when the spirit was squashed or undernourished, the rest of the being broke down, and how when the spirit was fed and focused on, this established and maintained a more powerful and healthy and happy person.

I sat in the clinic picking Dr. Zhan's brains regarding what signs to look for in my body to plot the course of any cancer, if by off chance it woke up again and began to spread. He told me how lumps would form in the lymph nodes in my groin or under my arms or behind my ears and pointed out other signs to be aware of.

I remembered someone saying how when you combine herbs like aloe vera with others, the herbs can direct the chemo to target the appropriate places and not pulse so randomly through the body, and how dosing the body up with massive amounts of vitamin C helps the immune system handle the effects of the chemo. And I thought of Brigitte, who, after a long period in coma, had so recently suddenly awoken and sat up in her bed, talking and laughing as if nothing had happened. I thought of how her doctors wanted her family to transfer her to a hospice for the terminally ill, how they refused to give her any chemo saying her cancer was too far advanced and so instead they kept her on a drip of glucose and morphine to dull the pain.

In the end, we decided to do the blood test just to check my general health indicators, tests which later came back looking perfect. I left Dr. Zhan with the realization that he could be of far greater benefit to his clients if he embraced more of his heritage and added an understanding of Chinese herbs to his treatments, thus combining traditional and ancient remedies to broaden the healing spectrum. He was in wholehearted agreement when I shared this with him, and I gave my thanks for his open mind.

It was slightly ironic to me that the thing that currently made my heart sing the loudest was the presence of my part-Aboriginal granddaughter, a wise, loving, slightly mischievous soul who was still thankfully awake and fully aware, having not yet—and hopefully will not ever—succumbed to the amnesic game we call being a child. Instead she appears to retain the enlightened view that she is a divine being journeying back to Earth for her own soul's learning and pleasure. Being with an awakened one is always fun! Our bloodline bond and genetic link opened me, via the inner-plane matrices, to the indigenous healing cultures, cultures far more advanced than my own. I had always admired the connection, the understanding of oneness maintained by the indigenous peoples, plus their honor of nature and the higher laws of cosmic consequence and knowledge of the power of cause and effect and attractor patterns.

After my appointment with Dr. Zhan, I went to the pathologist to give blood for the tests, then headed straight to a session with John, the holographic kinetics facilitator. When we had finished, John informed me about the free lecture the Aboriginal founder of holographic kinetics, Steve Richard, was giving at the clinic that night. The synchronicity was amazing, as I had already decided to call Steve for an interview to discuss his findings in more detail—and now the universe was delivering him to my door.

Steve specializes in youth suicide and prison work, and his passion for human rights and the injustice of the continued genocide of the Australian Aboriginal people was enlightening. But I had not come to his free lecture for a political view—I had come to learn more of the dreamtime healing, for I sensed that only the dreamtime healing could bring back a state of emotional harmony and bridge the rifts between the old and new Australian worlds. Based on ancient truths and universal laws, I knew that these laws needed to be known and applied by all. As multicultural as we may be here, we have also neglected to respect and honor the culture that has kept the spirit of our land so pure. To the human rights watchdogs, Australia's treatment of its Aborigines has been disgraceful.

Listening to Steve explain how kinetic energy is the change of movement of matter growing out of motion and hearing him talk about the harmony of free-flowing energy, about universal equilibrium and how it involves unfolding space-time to reset limiting patterns, I thought again about the power of education and began again to feel my passion expand further for providing more options for people in our world.

In the development of the holographic kinetics dreamtime healing system, Steve Richards has spent much time dealing with the release of disembodied spirits, particularly in his work with Aboriginal youth. One of the things that he stresses is to always only work with the divinity within and to not call for any external help from the interdimensional plane. Although many in the metaphysical field may be skilled in working with interdimensional-plane beings, he says, many lack the skill to discern just who is real and what entities are presenting themselves in the guise of, say, Archangel Michael, although it may be a lesser entity who comes in response to their call. Some entities come to feed off a field of fear and any trapped emotions that act as negative-attractor patterns. Obviously, this would not apply to those who have eliminated their physical, emotional and mental toxicity, yet nonetheless I realized, as I spent time researching more of holographic kinetics, that perhaps it was time to refine things a little further.

Although I have always been a proponent of DOW power, I began to sense that as our world continues to move through its current pattern of change, it is so important for all of us to align only with our DOW. Immortal, incorruptible and interconnected as the essence of All That Is, the holiest of holy, our DOW will weave us quite naturally with whatever we need. Hence we do not need to seek interdimensional help or alliances, for there is no separation and we are all one, individual cells in the body of the divine, and we can choose to express as much or as little of our divinity as we like. Our DOW is our incorruptible bridge between all worlds—all knowing, all powerful, all loving and all wise; our master computer controller, perfect programmer and virus controller when invited to do Its job. It is pure and perfect in Its essence and pure and perfect in Its expression through us.

When I returned to Ingrid for a third LISTEN system diagnosis, I hoped that the analysis and readings would be back in the healthy forty to fifty range, where they nearly all were in my first test so many months before. As we went through each pressure point to gain the electrical response and reading, the good news was that everything was no longer too tender to touch. The readings from the second test for my liver and spleen had been nearly critical, but with this third reading, everything was back up into the twenties and thirties, so I was no longer in the system shutdown zone. Still, it was obvious that the body had had a great shock and was still in need of tender care.

Although the Simian virus had gone back to sleep and was no longer active, the formaldehyde poisoning was still present, and so we bombarded my system with harmonizing and potent vibrational medicines to take with me on the road. After we confirmed my continued need for ganotherapy and stabilized oxygen, although now in smaller doses, I left Ingrid feeling relieved, yet also just a tiny bit disappointed. It seemed that although the cancerous cells had stopped their spread and were sleeping, their march through my system had left its toll.

Much better informed than when I had left the doctor's office, I knew that my coming work time would put me into such an intensified field of grace that I hopefully would access whatever else I needed. Still bringing myself into a new health pattern, I knew that once I found it again, I also needed to stabilize into it and hold it.

That day I came to realize that as the Earth changes unfold and the polarities continue their path of rebalance, perhaps we could all do with some assistance at this time. For so long my guidance had been to teach people the art of DOW power radiation so that we can move beyond our human limitations and remember and experience ourselves as divine beings once more. Although this is still the goal, my exposure to MWO and GenMed has made me realize that some of the new light technology that is coming through can be of great assistance as we all make the transition to a time when DOW radiation can rebalance all the negative electromagnetic field radiation that currently pollutes our world.

I also realized again that so often we think, "What am I doing wrong that I have manifested this?" rather than, "What am I doing right that I have manifested this?" If I hadn't manifested my squamous cell carcinoma on my mouth, I would never have undergone this journey, or written this book, or been led to the light machines, or had the opportunities to experience the higher properties of the reishi gano mushrooms, or learned about holographic kinetics as the system based on ancient Aboriginal healing arts, or met all the fascinating people I have met along this very confrontational journey.

It has been a journey that has required great focus and faith: focus on being committed to life, faith in the healing path we choose; focus on fulfilling it and harmonizing ourselves back into health, faith in the UFI in delivering any help we need; focus on applying the tools that this help may provide, faith that we can regain our health. All of this is part of the healing process. So is having faith that our body has the innate intelligence to self-heal, plus faith that if our time here is complete, we can exit consciously, completely aware and without the need to succumb to disease if this is what we choose. All of this can come by retraining ourselves to hold a different perspective in life.

The journey of harmonious health is also the journey of enlightenment, as the light that we are in essence flows most brightly within us the more we are in harmony within. The more it flows, the healthier and happier we become. Having the faith in its ability to heal us is a challenge that we all face from time to time, for everyone needs to be healed of something— whether it is one of the seven deadly diseases or feelings of loneliness or separation or the mental illness of superiority or greed or the spiritual illness of "one way, my way" and self-righteous behavior.

A healthy body does not always house a healthy spirit and mind, nor do a healthy spirit and mind always dwell in a healthy body. In his book *Destiny of Souls*, Michael Newton talks about souls who select weak genetic lines so that they can dwell in an unhealthy body with all the challenges that this can bring, just so that the souls can perform their service work this life with greater empathy and compassion.

There are so many reasons for the experience of dis-ease, whether it is physical, emotional, mental or spiritual, and yet we can gain clarity as to why the disease has been made manifest in our life and, having gained this insight, we can also discover a recipe for our healing. All we need to do is ask and then focus—with faith—on applying what we receive.

I still don't know how to create passion for life; it seems as if we either have it or we don't, and for some it's not until it looks as if they may lose their life that they discover how passionate they are about being here.

Dealing with family and friends is also an amazing part of our enlightening journey here. Whether it is the journey of harmonizing ourselves into a state of physical, emotional, mental and spiritual health, or the journey of just sharing and surviving, seeing and feeling our loved ones surround us and step forth when the path becomes rocky is enriching.

A friend was telling me of her cousin, a thirty-year-old man who had manifested Hodgkin's lymphoma, and the problems he had with his mother. Distraught at the prospect of losing her only son and loved companion to cancer, all she could do was cry. Anchored in the depths of a sorrow too great for her to bear, his mother wore his challenge like a heavy anchor around her neck, allowing it to weigh her down and drag her into her own path of illness through her worry and despair. Too vulnerable dealing with his own challenge, the young man had no energy left to handle this level of sorrow from his mother. Seeing that he was ready to no longer see her and to cut their ties in order to save himself, his mother did a major readjustment via a 180-degree shift in her attitude. Deciding to be cheery, positive and supportive, she joined him on the adjustment path, and they refined their physical, emotional, mental and spiritual diets until they both regained their health.

It was a heart-warming story that I was seeing being lived out with my family all around. Aware and supportive, everyone rallied with positive care, sensitively delivering what they felt was needed. "So many have suffered so needlessly due to family interference," a healer I knew had recently said of those patients submitting to their cancer, allowing it to deliver them to death's door.

"Family interference, their lack of trust in their loved one's choice of alternative methods, their insistence on the more traditional path of chemotherapy and surgery, all of it can create such problems in a person's healing field. It's enough having to deal with one's own stuff without having to take on other people's fears. You know, someone can be coming along nicely, when suddenly the family starts freaking out because it may be taking a little longer than they expected, and so they start the pressure for the patient to go back to traditional methods. We know that people often appear to get worse before they get better as they let go of all their toxicity, but ill-informed family? It really doesn't help . . ."

"It's just lack of holistic education," I declared, so aware of my own unnecessary surgery and how easily early knowledge of the black Cansema salve would have circumvented so much—but also denied me the revelation of such an interesting journey.

As I looked back on all the events and the endless string of sacred synchronistic occurrences I had experienced, I realized how perfect and how blessed it all had been and how much I had learnt and gained. Thankfully I was able to tell my family to just send love and light and to not add their worries to my field, and thankfully they understood quickly that it didn't help me if I had to also deal with their issues around what I had created.

It's been hard to see my family suffer as they have been dealing with my very real potential demise. Being confronted with losing someone we love is never easy, yet the last thing a person needs is to deal with negative projections and people's grief around one's possible death. Staying focused, having faith and trusting in the triumph of overcoming our challenge is crucial in our healing path, and it helps when families do this too. Deciding to stay, knowing it's not our checkout time; being prepared to discover the right path of our healing, to address its causative and symptomatic issues; being discerning and clear in our actions; having faith and focus in the outcome we desire—all of this is a requirement of the path of harmonious healing.

As I typed up all the research I had found and put my own experiences on paper, I rang my friend in Paris and asked her what was happening with Brigitte. Still languishing in and out of her comatose state, I couldn't believe that her journey was to be one of surrender and morphine meandering. I described what I had discovered, and my friend was amazed, declaring, "There's so little of this in France now, all of it has been squashed by traditional medicine and government controls. Please email me what you have so I can get it to Brigitte and her family and at least give them more choice."

"But they've been using MWOs in hospitals in France and Italy and Germany for years, haven't they? What about bioresonance machines?"

"There's nothing like this that I know of anymore . . . perhaps in Germany. I'll do some research, just send me what you have."

And so I did.

On one level, it is none of my business that Brigitte's journey has taken her to where she is now, but perhaps there is still time for her to choose to stay and stem the tide of the cancer marching through her body, and maybe my research will help her—maybe not. Most of the time, she is too weak to have a say, and so her family does with love what they feel is best. Yet without education as to what is available to us, we have so little choice.

There is so much data around for using alternative therapies for the treatment of things such as cancer; there are so many stories of triumph and so many stories of loss. Like so many, I can see the need to embrace the holistic view of healing, yet I also feel that it is time to combine the traditional and alternative paths.

Not all get the information they need when they need it, and so holistic education is the first key. I would love to think that all cancer clinics and doctors who come across skin cancers like mine have access to both ganotherapy and the black salve; I would love to think that as soon as a suspicious growth appears, all we have to do is cover it with the black salve and let it do its work, and then take a course of the reishi gano to draw out anything that might be left. Still, the path of harmonious healing is not that simple, for as we all know, treating just the physical symptoms will provide only a temporary reprieve.

I see my world through new eyes now and know that I still walk a fine line. The immortal's way beckons as a choice preferable to the road that I was facing, and I trust that my DOW will keep me on this path. Whether to stay or go still doesn't really matter on one level, as to me, there is no separation between life and death, for the divinity we are still goes on and on.

Every time I access my emails, little loving messages flow in from the psychics in the world who've been intuitively tuning in—messages of appreciation and love and invitations for me to stay. The universal field and the inner net seem to be working overtime, doing whatever is needed to settle me back into life. And so it is and so the game goes on.

I catch my flight to Japan, where long-standing work commitments are waiting to be fulfilled. Feeling a little stronger yet unprepared to work again so soon, all I can do is trust that I would triumph in it all now that I have made my choice to walk the immortal's way.

As the days go by, I notice another strange formation on my top lip, to the right of the surgery scar. I am watching it closely, hoping and praying that it is not a squamous cell carcinoma regrowing. It has that familiar craterlike dip in the middle of a round lesion. One day I finally realize that I could use the north-sway tool to check and then hopefully stop worrying, as what we focus on, we can bring into being, and the last thing I want is to open the door to another growth.

I stand facing the north and first ask for a clear connection to my DOW. My body sways forward to confirm this, and I then ask my DOW to indicate clearly through my body if here is a squamous cell carcinoma regrowing. I breathe deeply and remain relaxed so that the chi can move me, and thankfully, I begin to sway backward. Simple! The answer is a clear "No!" so I trust and let all the worry go. My mouth is still undergoing its healing process with the scar tissue still tender to the touch. I choose not to focus on it anymore and instead just tell my body how much I love it and what a great healing job it is doing and how perfectly it is regenerating itself.

After Japan I spent two weeks in Thailand in a darkroom retreat with an amazing group of people. Every day we sat in silence and deep meditation to merge in oneness with our DOW, and every day new insights and revelations flowed as the final pieces of my puzzle all clicked in. During this time, I learnt so much more about the immortal's way as I repatterned myself back into the state of health I was in before the cancer had made itself seen. I was finally able to let go of all my pills and potions and moved back into the pure prana beam.

Steps Taken

Here is a summary of some of the steps I have taken so far:

1. I asked the universal field of intelligence (UFI) and my Divine One Within (DOW) to bring me into the presence of wisdom and deliver me to a healer of integrity who could help me regain a state of harmonious health exactly as I needed it.

2. I used the dependable discernment testing tools (described in detail in Part 2) to check what I needed regarding therapies and medicines for my body. In this I looked at both alternative and traditional medicine.

3. I applied regular checks for treatment refinement and adjustment using the dependable discernment tools. It's important to remember that healing can take place quickly, so we need to tune in regularly to our body to check its changing needs.

4. I kept my focus and had faith that my selected course would deliver the outcome of harmonious health. We need to look at the positives of everything and not focus on the negatives.

5. I applied the other tools and meditations I describe in Part 2, particularly those for accessing my perfect healing program.

Postscript

March 2005

O n March 22, 2005, having regained consciousness long enough to release herself from hospital and settle comfortably back in her apartment in Lyon, Brigitte Testut passed peacefully from this world. Although the news did not shock me, I still felt saddened by it all. It was expected and yet unexpected, as I had hoped that somehow she would choose to stay. It seemed so strange that we began our journey with cancer so close together, although I was still unaware of what I was creating when she shared her own prognosis. It was her choice to go and my choice to confront it, clear it and hold a new pattern of health and hence to stay. We had similar challenges that provided different outcomes.

At the time of the revelation of Brigitte's news, I knew that it was not necessarily the end of her Earth journey, and we both knew that she still had choice. Even though most people's exit time is predetermined and they will create an accident or disease so that they can leave at the appropriate time, this is not always the case.

What makes us choose? What gives us the passion we need to maintain life?

The answer to this last question finally came to me in the darkroom retreat, when I realized that the level of my passion is completely determined by how well I am listening to the voice of my DOW. When I listen and apply Its guidance, life sings; when I ignore It, my zest for life dies down. It is as if my DOW was saying, "Well, you have forever, that's true; and yes, although you have completed the main work you came to do this life, there are other personal encodements that you agreed to fulfill. If you don't want to do them, then fine, you can leave the body, rest awhile, reflect on it all and come back in another space and time, for this gift of rest time is also a gift of the eternal nature of your being." And this is the freedom of choice that we all have as we learn to walk the immortal's way.

Facing our mortality is such an important part of the play, for in order to embrace all the freedom that our DOW has to give us, we need to let go of all the inhibiting factors and trust enough to merge so deeply with It that It can exhibit all Its power.

For years I had tested, using trusted sources, to determine exactly what I had agreed to fulfill this lifetime. And when we have made agreements to fulfill certain things, then all the universal forces will rearrange everything in life to support us as the divinity we are so we can do so. But we are also beings of free will, and we can choose to plateau on any step along the way or to hold on to our patterns of limitation, until we get the call to let it all go and then move on again.

I am cancer free now, relaxed, at peace, happy with all I have gained. My new mantra is that I always choose the highest option, knowing that to compromise in the future could lead me back to paths I have now rejected. I trust that as I joyously fulfill that which I have come to do, perhaps it will inspire others to do the same, for to walk the immortal's way is to walk hand in hand, heartbeat entwined with heartbeat, embraced by the divine One who loves us enough to gift us with life.

Yes, It is immortal in Its nature.

Yes, It requires never to age or die.

Yes, It absorbs cosmic particles enough to provide food and nourishment on all levels, for any human existence It chooses to have.

Yes, It loves us deeply and fills our heart with great song and passion and joy—passion and joy for the miracle that life is.

Yes, It exists multidimensionally through many fields and planes of time.

Yes, It is wise and loving and incorruptible and pure in the essence that It is; and

Yes, It unifies and harmonizes us all.

Through It is the path for harmonious healing, and as we heal on all levels of our being, only then do we discover the path of the immortal's way.

PART 2

THE MAGICAL MEDICINE
OF MIND MASTERY
AND MEDITATION

Harmonious Healing Tools

Effective healing is about self-mastery, a subject about which I have written twenty-two metaphysical manuals—from *In Resonance*, with its understanding that our body is a system of energy that we can operate in harmony or disharmony, to the additional lifestyle tuning tools I offer in *Four Body Fitness*, to the more extreme research manuals of the Divine Nutrition program.

The common thread weaving through all of these manuals is divine power, how the One who breathes us and loves us enough to give us life has the ability to wisely provide all that we need on any level, and how we can access all that our Divine One Within (DOW) has to offer. Although so many healing tools are offered in all of these manuals, in this section I will attempt to synthesize the ones that are relevant to the harmonious healing path as far as freedom from dis-ease creation goes. What I do not discuss here is no doubt covered in my previous work, which you may also wish to read.

To me, self-mastery is about creating and maintaining perfect health on a physical, emotional, mental and spiritual level, in a way that respects and harmonizes with all. In my own healing journey, I discovered the need to repattern my mortality schisms and release any death urges. These discoveries form a deeper part of the immortal's way and will be covered in depth in my next manual.

However, there are enough insights and tools in this current book to bring anyone either into a state of health or into a state of understanding regarding what he or she needs to do to achieve perfect health. The dependable discernment tools are particularly beneficial for obtaining clear guidance in all areas of our life, and having clear inner guidance allows us to be in greater harmony with all life.

Statistics of Diseases Today: Facts to Stimulate Action

As I clean up files on my computer, I find a long-forgotten report titled "Your Health Is in Danger" by Robert Allen. He talks about the seventy-seven million baby boomers who were born between 1946 and 1964, and how many of them are now beginning to experience any one of the seven deadly diseases, which to me is a way of checking out of this body and shutting down the system so that their soul could freely move on. The facts and information he provides are fascinating. He shares how heart disease is the number-one killer of people in our western world and how it is a relatively new disease, with the first cases of heart disease being reported in 1912. He also shares how over a hundred years ago, only 3 percent of people died of cancer, whereas today almost 30 percent of people die from this disease. He looks at Alzheimer's, which is the third on the list and wasn't even diagnosed till 1907; 40 percent of people over eighty-five now suffer from it. And diabetes has increased 600 percent in just one generation.

I realize, as I read these figures, that these changes are perhaps due to the fact that we have improved diagnostic tools and that we now record data better, but from other research that I have done I know that it is more than that. It is the change in our diet; it is the change in the chemical ingestion in our world, the pollutants; it is the change in our stress levels; and it is the allowance of many other issues that has sped up the spread of these diseases.

Allen points out that when a million people die of heart disease each year or half a million people die of cancer, there is so little attention given to this, even though it's the equivalent of a jumbo jet full of people crashing every hour of every single day of every single month for an entire year, year after year—an event that, if it actually occurred, would cause such physical outcry across our world and insistence on the changing of plane safety levels. And yet although it is happening that so many people die from preventable diseases, there is no outcry; it is as if humanity has surrendered to these realities, as if they were the norm.

Further on in Robert Allen's report, I read that the seven deadly diseases are the cause in more than 80 percent of deaths on our planet. Heart disease, cancer, stroke, diabetes, arthritis, osteoporosis and Alzheimer's allow so many people to leave this planet every day, to free their souls for rest time in other planes. Allen also states that every thirty-two seconds in North America, somebody will die from heart disease, and he points out how improper diet causes plaque to slowly clog up the arteries, stopping the flow of vital oxygen and nutrients to the heart muscles until the arteries are so blocked that the heart goes into spasm and attack—and for most people, this comes as a total surprise, for they had no idea that their arteries were congested. These death exit ways and dying mechanisms serve their purpose on many levels; however, the suffering that people undergo as they submit to these diseases can be avoided, for there are other ways of dying as I have discussed earlier in this book.

Such statistics need to be shared, both the good and the bad, for statistics can also help us track the changes as we share more of the benefits of holistic education.

Allen also talks about fantastic research on people who live to be over a hundred, who are not old or suffering from these types of diseases, who function very well and who rate their health as excellent. Their secret seems to be that they exercise regularly, have a balanced nutritional diet, often take mineral and vitamin supplements, are positive thinkers and laugh and love a lot. A hundred years ago, the average person lived to be forty-seven; today it's seventy-six, and the risk of dying before age forty is very small, so the news is not all bad.

Allen's report includes a statement from Dr. Michael Colgan, the world-famous expert on nutrition, who tells us not to fear cardiovascular disease since it is the easiest of all man-made diseases to prevent and even to reverse. All we need to do is follow the right nutrition and add a little exercise to blow away the cobwebs.

Robert Allen says of cancer that at least over a million North Americans will be diagnosed with cancer every year, and 50 percent of those will die within five years—which is the equivalent of fifteen hundred people a day, or one every minute of every day. One person will die from cancer every three or four seconds somewhere else in the world. His research shows that the incidence of cancer has increased 44 percent since the 1950s; breast cancer is up 60 percent, and prostrate cancer is up 100 percent. Soon cancer will bypass heart disease as the number-one cause of death in America. Yet there has been some improvement on this; the rate of death from cancer has peaked and is dropping a little, thanks to educational information on the need for good nutrition.

Robert Allen reports that according to the National Cancer Institute, 18 percent of women who are diagnosed with breast cancer will survive it for at least five years, and that in 1950 only one in twenty women was diagnosed with breast cancer, whereas today the number is one in eight. He also shares how tests show that these experiences can still decrease the life span by an average of nineteen years for the women who are cured.

Robert goes on to talk about strokes, how strokes kill more women than breast cancer and more men than prostrate cancer, and how in the causing of the stroke, the arteries of the brain harden and plug up, eventually shutting off the flow of blood to vital parts of the brain, causing, in essence, a brain attack. According to him, researchers at the Research Institute in Cincinnati have found out that 730,000 strokes occur on average in the U.S. each year. Of these victims, at least 150,000 will die, and the majority of the survivors will be left with some sort of major or minor disability, including paralysis, speech loss, impaired vision and memory.

Although a lot of research is heavily based on statistics from North America, we can see the same trend spreading through Asia into Australia as our foods become less nutritional, deprived due to poorer farming methods and too much chemical input and genetic modification.

The statistics go on . . . 30 percent of American men sixty years and older develop prostrate cancer, and 50 percent of men over the age of seventy-five will develop this disease. The ten-year survival rate among those dealing with prostrate cancer is over 86 percent, because this cancer grows slowly and can be treated.

Robert Allen points out that 20 percent of cancer is hereditary, and 80 percent is under our control. He goes on to quote Dr. Virginia Livingstone Wheeler, who has cured many people in her clinic in San Diego and who points out that we all have cancer in our bodies, but our immune system is keeping it in check. When the immune system breaks down, cancer is allowed grow. If we maintain a strong and healthy immune system, our chances of ever getting cancer are virtually nil.

As I read this, I realize the importance of adding the information on oxygen therapy, something that I have recently begun to increase my use of, as it helped me with the first cancer I manifested over a decade ago, and I make a note to share more of this information in Part 3.

Dr. Phillip Lee Miller from the Los Gatos Longevity Institute once wrote about the human body being an amazing array of competing forces that constantly strive to maintain internal stability and balance. One way this is done is by eliminating and combating invading pathogens and sterilizing and detoxifying the body through oxidation. The body also needs antioxidants, which prevent damage to the DNA or the cellular membrane from oxygen-free radicals. Our body knows how to orchestrate all of these processes simultaneously. Thus an oxygen-rich body combined with water and the proper nutrients for cellular regeneration means optimal health.

Dr. Patrick Quillin, a cancer expert in North America, says that nearly all people develop undetectable cancer about six times in a seventy-year life span, and scientists agree on this number. However, only one of three people actually develops detectable cancer. This indicates again that the body is equipped to deal with cancer. However, in order to do so, the body needs proper nutrition, which could prevent 50 to 90 percent of all cancer.

Robert Allen's research paper goes on, providing more statistics that on one level I am reluctant to share here, for I wish to focus more on the good news. Yet perhaps it helps to deliver statistical research before we offer a higher level of awareness as to how disease creation can be prevented. But before we can prevent something, we need to look at what causes it in the first place. Poor diets; sedentary lifestyles; mental, emotional and spiritual as well as physical pollution—all of it takes its toll, as we can see by the above statistics.

Meditation and Mind Mastery

Before I address the power of mind and meditation as magical medicine for our healing path, it is important to look at the power of emotions.

The Power of Emotions

Research by many alternative therapists plus some medical practitioners, including Dr. Deepak Chopra, has shown that emotional dis-ease is a significant factor in the creation of disease. Our inability to cope with stress, often due to feelings of uncertainty or lack of control, is also very damaging to the physical body and can lead to a nervous breakdown or to the creation of a deadly disease. The level of emotional distress that we can experience when we are diagnosed with a potentially fatal disease is even more acute.

Even though it may appear that our emotional reactions are automatic, the nerve pathways that carry the information to the brain take approximately three seconds to relay this information before the emotional responses—and our mind's experience of them—are triggered. In these three seconds, the rest of the brain has already received the information via faster nerve pathways, so even though we are unaware of this process, according to some research sources, we are built to think before we feel. We are not "victims" of our emotions.

When we "spontaneously" have an emotional reaction because our buttons are being pushed, we need to learn to deal with these emotions effectively so as not to create energy blockages and, eventually, disease. If we already have dis-ease, then we need to release built-up emotional blockage and learn how to not create any more. If, as Einstein says, cancer grows from a bed of resentment, then the emotional clearing for healing is imperative, as is learning how to effectively deal with future emotions.

Remember, events are emotionless; we assign an emotion to them according to our perception. Strong emotions that are unresolved are stored in the body and create blockages, as they impede the flow of energy through the body's energy systems.

If we wish to increase both the quality and quantity of life and if we desire to experience more joy, happiness, health and harmony in our life, we must firstly decide to accept nothing less. By deciding to focus on and accept positive feelings in our lives, we learn to bring our attitude into line with positive thinking and always look to see the silver lining in every cloud. Both positive and negative views exist, yet free will allows us to choose which view to hold, and what we focus on grows.

Remaining positive as we deal with a life-threatening illness can be an incredible challenge, and yet it is easier when we understand that all experiences are here to teach and inspire us. By understanding how we assign an emotional response to an event via our perception of it, we gain more control over the quality of our experiences. Even if a situation initially appears negative, we can choose to see it and accept it instead as positive. We can, and will, learn from it, so it can be embraced for its teaching power.

Storing negative emotions in the physical body serves no purpose. If we were to dam a free-flowing river by building a wall, the plant life beyond the dam wall would atrophy and die due to lack of water. So it is with our bodies. Emotions must flow freely for the body to be healthy. They must be accepted and not denied. They need to be dealt with in a positive manner, through honoring, acceptance and release without overindulgence. The computer hardware of the body stores negative emotions in databases called our organs—for example, the liver stores anger, the lungs store sadness—simply because we have not learnt how to effectively deal with these emotions.

In his book *Ageless Body, Timeless Mind*, Dr. Deepak Chopra states that emotional pain in the present is experienced as hurt; in the past, it is remembered as anger; and in the future, it is perceived as anxiety. Unexpressed anger redirected against you and held within is called guilt, and the depletion of energy that occurs when anger is directed inward is called depression. If, as he says in *Quantum Healing*, cells are just memories clothed in matter, then it is extremely important that we begin to look at and access cellular memory with a view to releasing energy blockages as we cleanse our cells of negativity and toxicity so we can harmoniously heal on whatever level required.

We can learn to deal with our emotions on a two-fold level: Firstly, we can release negative emotions from past experiences that are stored in the cells and organs of the body. Secondly, we can learn to deal more effectively with negative emotions as they confront us daily and do it in an effective manner. By meditating regularly, we can take this one step further—we can learn detachment; we can act and not react; we can constantly experience life from that deep place within and see things in perspective.

Releasing Negative Emotions Held in Cellular Memory

This can be achieved by using creative visualization techniques such as the simple one described later in this chapter.

A large selection of healing modalities is also available to aid the physical body to effect this release quickly and effectively, for example, kinesiology, homeopathy and body harmony. Aid in realigning and cleansing the cellular structure and energy fields of the body can be obtained through a number of alternative therapies, which can achieve in hours what may otherwise take years of meditation.

We can also ask that our emotional body be cleansed and released of all negative beliefs and patterns of limitation while we sleep at night. Simply tune in to your Divine One Within (DOW) and ask for this to be done. Do not doubt. You can ask for awareness of this being done via your dreams, or you can specifically request that it be done without conscious memory.

I feel that all emotional release work can be a gentle and free-flowing experience and not a traumatic one unless one requires it to be. I do not support the saying "No pain, no gain," and I feel that all can be achieved gently and lovingly if that is our intention and desire.

Learn to Deal with Negative Emotions and Hurt Effectively

Dissipate negative emotions through breathing to regain a calm mind, body and emotions. Establish a deep, fine, rhythmical pattern and continue until you feel settled.

Express your feelings in a nonattacking, nonthreatening manner to the person who triggered the hurt, and then deal with the issues that allow your buttons to be pushed. Remember, the external situation is only a mirror; if you held no issue within, you would not react. A good indicator for the success of the release work conducted is when you cease to react strongly to a situation that in the past was guaranteed to make you react.

Take responsibility for how you think and feel. Feelings always follow thought and perception. If you don't like how you are feeling, change what you are thinking.

Approve of yourself and don't seek approval from others. Set your standards of what is acceptable to you. We all have different standards of what we wish to experience and accept in life.

Top up your own energy by accessing your limitless inner reservoir in meditation. By merging with the Divine One Within, we learn to love, honor and accept others and become our own well of happiness. Don't depend on others to make you feel good.

Remember, the most important person is you. If you are happy, you can positively deal with others and all life situations much more effectively.

Be in touch with your physical and emotional responses—do not deny how you feel. Burying something under the carpet or holding emotional dis-ease within—"swallowing your tongue"—for the sake of peace or to not create waves will lead to disease, peptic ulcers, cancer, heart problems and so on. And remember:

- Resolve why you feel hurt, and let it go.
- Learn to live in each moment, but do it with a passion for and an appreciation of life.
- Be willing to change; after all, the only constant thing in the universe is change.
- Don't poison your body with harmful food, thoughts or emotions.
- Release judgment. Choose to have only positive thoughts and assessments about others and about yourself.
- Replace fear motivation with love motivation. One of the most powerful tools in healing the emotional body, and consequently the physical body, is forgiveness—forgiving both ourselves and others.

Meditation as a Preventive Tool

The major benefit of meditation is in dealing with the emotions and the detachment we can achieve so that we no longer feel that we are "at the mercy of others." It allows us to be responsible for our own happiness in a dependable, guaranteed manner and to readily identify problem ownership.

Chris Griscom, in *Time Is an Illusion*, states that apart from past-life regression work, meditation and changing the frequency of our energy fields to higher octaves are the most powerful ways to release the old, negative patterning held in the emotional body and cellular memory. Holographic kinetics achieves the same thing.

Mastering the emotional and mental bodies does require discipline. After years of thinking that we are powerless to our thoughts and subsequent feelings simply because society teaches us to adopt this attitude, we now can be aware and learn to discipline our thinking. An Indian guru once said that you cannot expect a wild horse that has roamed the plains since birth (like our undisciplined minds) to come into a corral simply because we whistle.

Television has created expectations of instant results, which makes spending time in inner silence and disciplining and stilling the mind quite difficult for many. TV soap operas reinforce victim mentality, game shows reinforce greed, newscasts reinforce fear and negativity. All are powerful emotions that are reinforced subliminally in our day-to-day lives. However, television is also a powerful communication device, and we can control, via selective viewing, this device in a manner that can be used to our advantage. We have the power to choose our perception, our thoughts, our reality and our emotional experience.

Most importantly, meditation places us in a state of stillness where we can learn to listen to and experience our DOW.

Set the Standards

I call the following technique and exercise "positive memory association." It is designed to achieve two things: firstly, to set a minimum standard of what is acceptable to you regarding your emotional experience, and secondly, to tune your day when you get up "on the wrong side of the bed" or are overwhelmed by negativity. The technique is simple, but the effect is powerful.

Positive Memory Association
1. Sit in contemplation; breathe deeply, finely and connected until you feel a sense of inner peace. This will allow you to access memory more quickly.
2. Go back in time, search through your memory database. Find a time when you experienced your life to be just great, happy and fulfilling.
3. Recapture the details, the time, the place, who you were with, what made it so special. In particular, pay attention to how you felt.
4. When you have accessed the feeling of this event, decide to accept no less. The exact form the memory takes is not relevant. What is important is how you can use this memory to trigger feelings of joy and harmony, especially when you are feeling emotionally upset by your healing crisis.

The majority of people I have done this exercise with report that the most common feelings remembered were ones of joy, contentedness and being carefree. They also report that these are the same experiences they miss most in their current lifestyle and their adult world of "responsibility."

The fact is that we have had these experiences in the past and, although we may not be able to re-create the same circumstances, we can set the standard for ourselves of what we wish to accept on an emotional level. Simply by beginning each day accessing a positive memory from our personal database of memories, we can set the tone for the day. We can decide to accept no less and then evoke the feeling by reliving the memory. This will allow the day to begin on a positive note and is most helpful for calming us and changing our emotional state as we journey through our path of self-healing.

If the universe responds to our expectations and if we always expect the best for ourselves while vigilantly counteracting negative thoughts by being persistently positive, we will find our life changing quite magically—guaranteed!

Dreaming and Guidance

The dream state can be used most effectively for receiving guidance, emotional and mental body clearing and/or healing and training. If ever I am unsure over an issue or a decision, I meditate before going to sleep and ask the higher mind of my DOW presence to give me a clear answer via the dream state, plus total clarity in recall and easy understanding of the symbolism of the dream. This technique never fails! I always wake up immediately after receiving the dream with its answer or instruction and can interpret it as well as any symbolism it may contain.

However, it is very important that we spend time in meditation and contemplation prior to sleep so that the subconscious mind can bring to the conscious mind any unresolved issues from the day's events to avoid that those issues preoccupy our dream state. Dream interpretation is an excellent way of gaining self-knowledge, especially about crisis-causative factors, and there are many wonderful books on the subject for those interested.

We can go beyond the subconscious mind and its need to communicate issues to the conscious mind for attention and resolution via dreaming, when we pay attention to ourselves via meditation and contemplation at the end of each day. This leaves our dreamtime free to explore other realms of reality, especially other healing systems that are held in other dimensions within the universal field. Personally, I find that my nighttime "activities" are often divided. The earlier part of the evening is spent in training, whereas the latter part is spent working through issues of a more personal nature via dream instruction. One state is where one actually leaves the physical body to work in the etheric realms; the other is the interaction between the subconscious, conscious and superconscious minds.

Here is an affirmation to program ourselves to remember dreams:

I ask my DOW to allow me full memory and easy conscious recall of dreams, instructions, preparation and teachings that I receive during the sleep of my physical body. Reveal to me via my dreams the perfect healing program that I need.

We can also ask our DOW to take us to the perfect plane for healing as we sleep.

Meditation for Emotional Fine-Tuning: Cleansing and Realigning the Emotional Body

This meditation is designed to release emotional baggage that is held in cellular memory from unresolved past issues and to allow us to effectively deal with negative emotions on a day-to-day basis.

Get comfortable in a place where you won't be disturbed.
Tune yourself with breath and lightwork.

When relaxed, visualize yourself to be standing on a mountain. In front of you, see steps leading downward.

As you step down, begin to count. Between each step take one full inhale and one connected exhale.

Let yourself relax deeper and deeper as you count. With each step down, you feel lighter and freer, knowing that you are about to enter a special, safe place.

Breathe in and out . . . 9, breathe in and out . . . 8, breathe in and out . . . 7, . . . 6, . . . 5, . . . 4, . . . 3, . . . 2, . . . 1, . . . 0 . . .

As you reach the ground, you feel deeply relaxed. Take a few deep, connected breaths; look around you, open up all your inner senses.

You see—visualize or imagine—that you are in a most beautiful sanctuary, a place that is yours alone; a place where you feel completely safe, at peace, nurtured and loved. This is your internal cubbyhouse, like the one children have to enact their games and fantasies.

Let your mind wander. See the trees, the flower beds. See yourself picking a flower. Hold it to your nose and smell its fragrance (allow your sense of smell to be activated).

Listen to the birds singing and the wind rustling in the trees.

Feel the sun on your skin and the wind in your hair.

Pause for a moment. Allow higher mind to create this inner sanctuary. Remember, this is your place. You can create it to be whatever you wish— there are no limitations to your vision here.

Take a few deep, fine, connected breaths. Allow yourself to bathe in the beauty of this place. If you could have a place of physical perfection, what would it be? A beach, a rainforest, a valley or a mountain top?

See before you now a pathway lined with flowers. Intrigued, you begin to follow it. The ground feels soft beneath your feet, and as you continue to breathe in the cool, fresh air, you feel lighter and lighter, energized and freer.

You notice that you are wearing long, flowing robes. Your feet are bare and you feel as though you are gliding through a forest.

You come to a clearing, a beautiful leafy glade, and in its center is a large, clear, sparkling rock pool that is fed by a beautiful, cascading waterfall at its far end.

The sunlight dances on the surface of the crystal-clear water. The air feels regenerating, alive, energized with oxygen and prana.

Scoop water from the pool and bring it to your lips to taste it and refresh your thirst.

The plant life is lush and tropical and abundant and lines the perimeter of the pool.

You notice a large, flat rock jutting out over the water, and you sit yourself gently down upon it. Breathing here is easy—the oxygen and prana flow naturally into you, filling your lungs with their healing power, and as you exhale, you give yourself permission to release all the cares and worries of your world.

You sit in a glorious beam of healing light energy that streams out from the clear blue sky above you. It surrounds you and seems to penetrate all the pores of your skin.

You feel as though you want to surrender to its healing power, to allow it to transform and reenergize and realign you to its purity.

As you breathe in its golden-white light energy, you feel it fill your lungs and then flow into your cells and organs. It feels as though all the pores on your skin are also absorbing this light into themselves—as you exhale, you do so through your mouth, sighing gently as you begin to release the emotional baggage that has been stored in your cells and organs for eons of time.

Breathe in the light.
Exhale and affirm: "I now release all _____." Allow your being to release what it feels; the first thought that comes into your head is what you should be releasing, whether it is anger, fear, jealousy, sorrow and so on.

Allow your vocal release to be louder, sighing or groaning.
Feel all negative vibrations flow out of your being and be dissolved by the light around you.
Breathe in the light and affirm: "I am healthy. I am vibrant."
Exhale deeply and affirm: "I now release all _____."

Continue this until you feel you have released all of the energy of that negative emotion from your being, then ask yourself what else you need to release.

Alternatively, simply release all harmful vibrations with this affirmation: *I now release all dross, all toxicity, all pollutants, all stress and all negative emotions stored in my cellular memory and everything that no longer positively serves me at this point in my life!*

(You can use this technique to release any anger, frustration or stress that you may have accumulated during that day or week.)

As you release it from your cells, visualize an intense beam of light coming in through the top of your head and cleansing all the energy pathways, all the cells and organs, dissolving all the garbage and filling your being with healing light energy. It is like a gigantic inner spring cleaning!

Continue to affirm as you inhale the light energy from the beam that surrounds you: "I am light; I am love; I am free; I am a glorious, radiant being!" Affirm whatever feels right to you.

Alternatively, visualize that you are holding a knapsack or container on your lap. Visualize your hands filling with what it is you've released and dumping it all into the knapsack in a strong, forceful motion. When the knapsack is full, seal it shut and then see yourself offering it up to the light—see it dissolve in love and light. Feel as though you have been deeply cleansed.

As you breathe in the light and prana, feel yourself becoming stronger, healthier, free from all disease, free from all discomfort. Feel yourself becom-

ing transformed and willing to accept only love and joy and laughter in your life from this moment on.

Cast your memory back to the best time in your life (positive memory association) *and decide to accept only the best for yourself emotionally from this point on.*

Affirm: In joy, in safety, in harmony I step into the unknown, I willingly embrace all that is for my highest good.

When you have completed this or feel you have done enough, visualize the top of your head opening like a lid on a jar of honey and healing, loving, liquid light pouring in and filling your entire being with its beautiful energy.

Then see it close up and continue to breathe deeply. Feel calm, fresh and energized.

Be grateful for the use of this tool. Ask your higher self to allow you to deal positively with all future emotions and situations and to recognize that all occurs for us to learn or be inspired by.

Now visualize yourself slipping into the beautiful rock pool. Feel its waters energize you, soothe you and restore you as you swim gracefully and joyously.

Swim to the waterfall. Stand under it and allow it to cascade gently over you. It recharges and energizes you. Then allow yourself to be dried by a whispering breeze and the rays of the Sun as they gently caress your skin.

When centered and relaxed, feel your arms, your legs and the cushions or chair on which you are seated.

Bring back the feelings of peace and tranquility from the time in your sacred place by the rock pool. Know that you can go there any time you desire. Savor your feelings. Take five deep breaths. Bring your attention back to the room and open your eyes.

Dependable Discernment Tools

I n the chapter on dependable discernment, I discussed at length the need to avoid information overload and to be able to develop dependable methods for us to discern the perfect healing course of action. This was something that I found a need for early in my journey, and it inspired me to share a three-level system that I had discovered previously, when I wrote *The Law of Love*. As I have said earlier, I have since found the need to add more tools for the level-two system test, tools that are a little more reliable than kinesiology and can be used to access the perfect step-by-step healing program. Such tools can also help establish a stronger Divine One Within (DOW)-mind-body connection and hence help bring clarity when we are confused or unsure about a situation.

A Confirmation System in Three Parts
(Based On an Excerpt from The Law of Love)

System 1:
Guidance from our DOW

Generally, guidance from our DOW, our inner voice, must always be our first method of testing, since it is the only reliable source of confirmation that is completely incorruptible. Doing this requires us to establish a clear line of communication between ourselves and our divine nature—whether we call this our DOW, Monad, Atman or whatever. This level of commu-nication comes via our sixth and seventh senses of intuition and knowing and needs to be, in my opinion, our first barometer of guidance in every-thing that we do in life, particularly when accessing and manifesting our perfect health plan.

Our DOW is the only thing that all humans have in common. It is pure; It gives us life; It breathes us, loves us and guides us to evolve into our perfection. Learning to listen to our DOW and trust Its guidance is a basic part of self-mastery, self-knowledge and self-healing.

System 2:
Guidance Confirmation from Muscle Responses

The second level of testing is to use a system like the art of kinesiology to gain information confirmation by using muscle responses in the body. Kinesiology, as many who are trained in this field know, has its limitations, because it depends on how it is used and how strongly people's muscles test. It also depends on the calibration purity of the one being tested as well as the calibration of the one doing the testing and of the questions being asked. Reading David Hawkins' book on this subject, *Power vs. Force*, will provide a deeper understanding. I also recommend that when we use kinesiology, we ask the DOW to confirm information, using the muscle-testing system through the body rather than asking the body's con-sciousness itself.

Remember, there is a huge difference between the voice of our DOW and the voice of the body consciousness, which sees everything through a very limited perspective. Asking our DOW to express Itself through the body movements in all system-two testing methods is essential.

There are additional systems apart from kinesiology that we can also use here, and I will elaborate on this later in this manual.

System 3:
Guidance Confirmation from the Universal Field of Intelligence

The third level of testing that provides a wonderful support system for us is to ask to receive clear confirmation from the universal field of intelligence (UFI), which is all around us. This goes back to the story of people who, looking for answers, walk into a book shop, find that a book falls off the top shelf and hits them on the head, then spirals around and falls at their feet, open, the right way up, and when they pick this book up, there is the answer to the very question they had been thinking about. This is one way in which the universal field of intelligence responds to our telepathic thought patterns when we have a strong desire for further knowledge, particularly when the knowledge that we are seeking is supporting our own evolutionary path in a posi-tive way and is also beneficial for the world.

Using the alchemical system of three—where we ask that the data we need is received from the universe three times, from three different sources—we can then trust that this is the course of action for us to take, particularly if it is confirmed by an intuitive sense of knowing.

Muscle-Response Testing Tools

Systems 1 and 3 need no further elaboration. System 2, however, can give incorrect readings when people are feeling overly emotional and are unable to tune in to their DOW and hear Its voice. For example, when my body said yes when asked if more surgery was required, on a higher level, this was an incorrect reading. The body has to have confidence that we can receive clear DOW guidance and calmly apply the right course of action. Had my body had confidence in me that day, I would have received a different answer. So if system 2 can sometimes be unreliable due to our emotional states, how do we get the right answers? Are there more dependable tools that we can use as a second-level system test other than kinesiology?

The answer to this question is yes, and so we provide additional discernment tools now. The breath/tummy testing tool is my favorite, and it ranks high in its dependability. Then we have the sway tests and the heavy/light arm test and the eye test. Many of these come from Einstein, whom I interviewed about this matter near the end of my healing journey, and they all make the path of discerning the perfect course of action much easier. All also serve to free us from the problem of information overload or from giving our power away to external sources as we seek answers to our healing dilemmas.

Please note that as I have shared before, the more our body feels loved by its master, us, the more willing it is to release any information that we need. Hence I recommend that daily you bathe your body in love and appreciation using the following three tools: the body-love tool, smiling at each of your organs and the love-breath tool. Information on these tools is provided in the section on life enhancement tools starting on page 143.

Please be aware that if you are under emotional stress and are not thinking clearly, then your body may have no confidence in your ability to help heal it via alternative methods, so if it feels under threat, your body may opt for traditional methods of surgery instead. This may not be the best approach, so you need to use the testing tools when you are calm and centered. Therefore, it's best to use the body-love tool and the love-breath tool to settle your system and center yourself first.

The North-Sway Tool

The north-sway testing tool was given to me by a young Aboriginal woman in Cairns, northern Australia. I call it the north-sway tool (NST), as the woman did not provide its name or its source.

- Buy or borrow a compass and find the direction north.
- Face this direction to align yourself with the north magnetic pull.
- Breathe deeply and relax. Center yourself so that you are in a place of stillness and ask your DOW to express Itself clearly, through your body, through this tool.
- When you are calm and breathing in a relaxed manner, test the tool by stating something simple, for example: "I am in a female body." If this is true, you will find yourself being pulled or swaying slightly forward. If it is false, you will find yourself swaying backward.

This can be a trick question for some, as some people can inhabit both a male and a female body concurrently as the research in Michael Newton's book Destiny of Souls shows. Hence if you state, "I am in a female body" and you get no reaction, you are perhaps doing the split soul game. So you might want to make another statement, like "My name is _____," and insert your name. Like with kinesiology, the art here lies in asking the correct question. (The first question is enough for most people to feel how this works.)

Now you are ready to move on to ascertain other things. For example, I received this tool at the end of my chosen course of healing, after I had already discerned the right path of cure for my challenge through using kinesiology when I was in a state of calm and control. So I was seeking confirmation for the following statement: "There are no more active cancer cells in my mouth and lip area." Remember, like with kinesiology, we need to make assumptive statements rather than ask questions. Here is another example: "My body will now benefit by taking stabilized oxygen." Wait and feel the sway response as you chant this statement over and over, then pause to feel the sway.

I also used this tool to confirm and adjust both my daily required oxygen intake and my body's need for additional minerals and nutrients as well as to ascertain what type of treatment it required to address the deeper causative issues.

The problem I saw with the north-sway tool is that we are dependent on using a compass to ascertain north. When I mentioned this much later to Einstein, he told me that the sway tool, in his opinion, is superior to kinesiology, as it allows our DOW to express through us through chi movement. He also pointed out that we don't need to face north. Rather, we can just ask our DOW to express Itself through us as we relax deeply by swaying us forward and backward for a yes and sideways for a no, which is similar to a pendulum response; we could also ask our DOW to magnetize us forward for a yes response and push us backward for a clear no response. I loved his input and tested his suggestion successfully, for it frees us further from another limitation.

Einstein then offered me the tests below to add to our testing toolbox.

The Arms Test Tool

Stand up, relax deeply, center yourself through your breath, raise both your arms straight out to the side, holding them at ninety-degree angles to your body. Ask your DOW to express Itself through you by making your arms feel heavy for a no answer and lighter for a yes answer. Make an assumptive statement of the question you want to get answered, for example: "My body now needs additional vitamin and mineral support." Say this over and over, and slowly you will feel your body's response. If it's not true, then your arms will feel heavier and heavier as if weighted down by gravity. If the statement is true, they will feel light and energized.

The Eye Test Tool

Again get relaxed and centered and ask your DOW to express Itself through you, through your eye movement. Begin to roll your eyes around and around in a circular motion—the direction is irrelevant; it doesn't matter whether you roll them clockwise or counterclockwise—as you make your statement. If it's a statement of truth, your eye flow and movement will become freer and easier. If it is a statement of falsity, the movement will slow down and become "sticky" in its response, as if the flow was being hindered.

The Breath Test Tool or Tummy Test Tool

This is my preferred level of system testing, as it follows the smooth, deep flow of the One who breathes us, our DOW. The basic principle is that when we are in alignment with our truth on an issue, our breathing gets deeper and deeper, dropping naturally down into our tummy area. On the other hand, when we are in a state of incongruence or falsity on an issue, our breathing naturally becomes shallow, rising higher up into the chest or throat.

Get relaxed and centered and again ask for your DOW to clearly express Itself. Think of a statement you want verified. Chant it over and over as you have your right hand resting gently on your abdomen and your left hand on your chest so you can detect more easily the change in your breathing rhythm.

There is also the tummy-tension tool: Feel the area around your belly button—press in with your fingers—and you will find that the tissue in this area is relaxed when you are in truth and tense when you are not.

Sample Statements for the Testing Tools

Here are some statements you can use to verify your healing program:
1. "In my healing process, my body will now benefit from a change in my diet." If you get a yes reaction, then check further, for example: "My body now prefers a _____." Fill in vegetarian diet, vegan diet, raw-food diet, juice diet and so on. Ask to confirm each, one at a time, and listen to yes and no.

2. "In my healing process, my body will now benefit from my taking additional nutritional and mineral supplements." Again confirm each, one at a time.
3. "In my healing process, my body will now benefit from increased meditation time."
4. "In my healing process, my body will now benefit from _____ drops per day of stabilized oxygen therapy."
5. "In my healing process, my body will now benefit from _____ therapy." Insert the name of the therapy you are considering.

The above are just some examples. Read through the rest of this section and also Part 3, and then use this method to determine your perfect action path.

Meditation Magic

Meditation can be utilized for many things—from creating a state of inner peace and destressing the body to using focused mind mastery and healing violet laser light to transmute cancerous or diseased organs and cells; to exploring other, more refined and even healing dimensions of existence; to developing detachment so that we act rather than react in life; to creating a loving mind/body connection; to setting up connections with loved ones who have died and now exist in another plane; to accessing higher and purer, pranic forms of nourishment that feed us on physical, emotional, mental and spiritual levels. Many of these issues are discussed in my other manuals, and in this book, we will focus on using meditation and mind mastery for harmonious healing purposes only.

Challenge or Checkout?

The purpose of this first meditation is to determine the correct course of healing and nurturing for you, once you have ascertained whether you have manifested a potentially fatal disease simply as a learning tool and challenge, or because it is your time to leave this plane.

Relax yourself. Create a space of silence and stillness, tune yourself to the rhythm of your breath using the body-love and love-breath tools (described in "Life Enhancement Tools" on page 143) or any meditation technique that you like, that you know will center you and allow you to hear the voice of your DOW.

Once you are still and centered, with your imagination, fill your body up with pure violet-light energy. This will change the frequency of your cells and allow for an easier release of your divine inner knowing regarding such matters.

Next you are going to ask some basic questions that require a simple yes or no answer. Pause after each question and wait for an intuitive answer to come. Trust the first response that comes.

Breathe deeply. Take three deep, fine, connected breaths or however many you need to feel centered. Once you feel connected and still, ask the first question:
1. *"Is it in my blueprint to learn how to become and then be free from the need to create disease?"*

If you get either a yes or a no to this question, then clarify it further by asking the next question.
2. *"Is it in my blueprint, in my preagreements, to learn how to cure the challenge of this disease, _____?"* Insert the name of the health challenge you are facing.

If you get a no to this question, then go on to the next question, but also be aware that it may not be in your blueprint to self-heal and that you may have to learn to live with this disease unless it is potentially fatal. We only ask the third question if the disease we have is potentially fatal. You may also need to clarify the second question with a simple statement and a question like the following:

"I can now cure myself of _____." Again, insert the name of the disease you are dealing with.
3. *"Is it in my blueprint, in my preagreements, to exit the Earth plane in this coming time via the creation of this disease?"* or *"Is it my time to die from _____?"*

Note: If you get a clear yes answer for the first and/or the second question, then you need to use the dependable discernment tools and apply what I now share here and in Part 3 of this book to find the perfect action path for you. Also be aware of the words that you use. Keep them simple, as too many words can give a different answer because your inner being interprets them all. For example, sometimes we manifest a disease as a challenge to gift us a new virtue, like empathy, and yet the details of this manifestation were not part of our divine blueprint—we only agreed to learn about empathy, and the details how we achieved this were to be a free-will game.

If you get a clear yes for the third question, then confirm this by using the dependable discernment methods and act accordingly: Take care of your family/business affairs and focus on improving the quality of your time here. As we have discussed in the chapter on dignity and dying, if you do receive and confirm a yes for this, then your harmonious healing path alters dramatically.

Firstly you need to come to terms with the fact that no healing path you choose will give you an outcome other than enhancing the quality of your time here. As I have mentioned previously, in his book *I*, David Hawkins says that the time of our death is known to us as clearly as the time of our birth.

If I were to receive—or had received—a yes to the third question in this meditation, then I personally would not spend my time engaging in debilitating treatment methods such as chemotherapy and other traditional treatments that can create great suffering. Instead I would focus on improving the quality of the time I had here, spending it with family and friends, enjoying each moment of each day and doing what I could of the things covered in this section of the manual to improve the quality of my life. I would also become a regular practitioner of the bilocation meditation so that I'd get used to consciously being out of my body and thus could leave it permanently when I'd be ready.

Some people have healed spontaneously purely by focusing on enjoying what time they had left. Spontaneous remissions are not that rare, and you may get a yes-it's-time-to-check-out response just so that you can learn to relax, love and let go, which in itself may also heal you as you increase your stressless-fun quotient in life. Our inner guidance does not always give us answers for the reasons we think, and although an answer may appear to be wrong, in retrospect it is always right at the time, when we look at it in the context of our learning.

Revitalizing and Energizing the System

The following meditation for self-healing and reenergizing the body comes from my book *The Law of Love*, and the violet-light data and meditation come from the book *The Food of Gods*. I offer it here as a way of boosting and revitalizing our systems, and it is suitable for all of us to do, regardless of what the answer is that we receive in the first meditation described above.

Revitalizing and Healing the
Biosystem with Nourishing Violet Light

When the DOW is invited to flood our system with violet light, it acts like a computer virus cleanup program that can automatically heal and nourish us, particularly when used with the programming code of "Perfect Health Now." Once the inner doors of our atoms are open, we can then flood the cells of our body with the pure violet light that streams constantly through our inner energy centers, or chakras. I call this system flooding. Flooding can also operate via a system of biofeedback looping once the original energy dynamics are established.

To begin, imagine pure, violet light flowing in through your crown and flooding and expanding each chakra with its power.

Then imagine each energy center growing and expanding with this nourishing light until each chakra touches the next one to form one spinning column of light.

Now imagine this spinning column radiating out millions of rays of violet light into your cells, then into your atoms, healing and rebalancing each cell.

Next imagine these violet-light beams of energy radiating through your atoms and opening the inner doors. Imagine that the rays increase to their maximum expansion, attract the violet light from the inner planes and then contract back. (Maximum expansion is determined by the velocity, power and potency of the beam being transmitted.)

Now imagine these violet light-filled rays flooding back further into the atoms, then into the cells, then into the organs, bloodlines, meridians and so on, until your entire biosystem is flooded with this violet light.

Finally imagine that this expansion–attraction–contraction process occurs naturally and automatically, just like breathing, keeping your cells tuned to the inner-plane fields of violet light.

The Eleven-Strand Healing System of Violet Light

When you flood your system with violet light, you hold the intention that the violet can heal and regenerate your body. But there is also another method that you can use—a violet-light matrix mechanism, which is a system that can be used for recalibration, healing and also for nourishment. Drink a glass of water before you start to stabilize the system and allow it to distribute the higher frequencies you are about to receive.

To start, sit comfortably in meditation, spine upright; this is not a meditation to do lying down.

Now visualize pure violet light, the pink, the blue and the gold streaming in through the crown chakra, coming from the heart and mind of the Source of creation. Imagine that as soon as it hits the crown chakra, a laser beam of violet light flows into the energy matrix of the lightbody.

Now imagine another strand or beam of violet light going into the meridian system, which is the bridge between the lightbody and the physical system.

Next imagine another strand of light coming in through the whole chakra system, going through the major and minor chakras in the body.

Imagine yet another line of light going straight through the crown and into the skeleton, like a river of laser light flowing through the skull and down the spinal column, through the vertebrae, through the shoulder blades, down the arms, through the major bones, down into the hands, right down into the finger tips. Imagine the light going right down into the pelvic area and down through the major bones of the legs, the femur, the knee joints, the tibia and the fibula, right down to the toes. Imagine the whole skeleton lighting up like a Christmas tree, a violet light-filled tree.

Now, as these strands begin to move through the body as rivers of violet light, imagine that this violet light is regenerating you and is capable of transmuting any stuck energy, any blocked energy; imagine that it is healing any disease and any decay, whether this is in the bone structure or the muscular structure, or whatever it encounters along the way. Imagine that it is a pure, healing, laser ray of energy that is flowing through you and bringing you back into a state of perfect health.

Next imagine that a laser beam of violet light is going through the muscles surrounding the skeleton and doing exactly what we have shared above—healing and transmuting as it flows through all the major muscles of the body.

Then imagine that another strand or line of light moves through all the bloodlines of the body—through all the major veins, arteries, capillaries—branching right through you like a river of tingling, golden, violet, healing light.

Imagine that it flows through all the blood streams, charging and nourishing the white corpuscles and the red corpuscles, exactly as they need it, feeding the blood so that the blood holds pure nourishment as it works its way through the body exactly as required.

Imagine that as the violet light hits any arteries or veins that may be in need of healing, that are beginning to collapse, that are bleeding from problems with valves or things like this, it immediately heals and reconstructs these problem areas.

Imagine rich, nourishing blood coursing through the heart and all the violet light moving in such a way that it is healing any damaged or clogged arteries or capillaries or any other problems within the ventricular system of the heart.

Next imagine another laser beam of light flowing in through the crown chakra or branching off from the crown chakra; imagine this going through the lymphatic system. Similarly as above, imagine it carrying through all the fluid of the body, through the glandular system, through the endocrine system, through the fluid in the spine and around the brain the perfect frequency for all of it to be revitalized, recalibrated back into a state of perfect health.

Next imagine another line of light going through the whole nervous system of the body, following the whole system of nerves from deep within the body to every organ and right out into the skin.

Also imagine another line of light going through the body into the organs, first through the brain, like a river coursing through the left and right hemispheres of the brain, feeding the brain, nourishing the brain, activating all centers of the brain that need to be activated for you to experience your paranormal powers.

Imagine the violet light coursing through the synapses around the cerebral cortex, through the cerebrum, through the cerebellum, through the hypothalamus, through the thalamus, through the pituitary and pineal glands.

As you think it, imagine this happening immediately as I say these words or as you hear these words on your tape. See your whole brain being recalibrated and activated. Hold this idea that this is real, that this light has the power to do all that you intend.

Imagine this healing light going through all aspects of the brain and then flowing down into the lungs, coursing through the lungs, filling the lungs with violet light, transmuting all sadness or sorrow or anything else within the lungs that is no longer serving you.

When you imagine that the lungs are totally overflowing with this healing light, then imagine the violet light moving through the heart and healing the heart, reenergizing the heart, cleansing the heart; then moving down into the spleen, dissolving all worry and anxiety; and then, after it has moved through the whole spleen, send it into the kidneys. Imagine it dissolving all fear and any other old energy patterns that you no longer need in the kidneys. From there, imagine that this beam of violet healing light goes down into the liver and dissolves all patterns of anger and resentment or jealousy or anything else that has been stored there.

Just imagine following this beam of violet light and, if you can, scan your body and look to encounter any dark patches of energy that you intuitively feel no longer serve you. Then imagine this laser beam of violet light zapping these dark clouds of energy and dissolving and transmuting them, making every organ as the light enters it be totally, crystal clear and dancing with the golden, violet light of health, vitality and youth, regeneration, rejuvenation and transmutation. Trust that this is what this beam does.

Now send this light beam through to the stomach, to cleanse its way through the stomach, and then see it flowing, like a river, through all your intestinal organs and then out into the sexual organs.

See another beam of light moving from the crown chakra and spreading its way like a river around the skin, moving through the subtle levels of the skin as it encases the whole body, the miles and miles of skin. Imagine the skin being hydrated properly, healed of any lesions or scar tissue or moles that you may not wish to be there.

Just take the time to visualize each area that has scars or moles, imagining that the laser light is healing these as more and more of this light floods in from all the other systems, from the energy lines flowing through you to now support this instant body transmutation and the transformation of your skin.

Imagine one other beam of violet light moving from the crown chakra up above it and beginning to wrap its way horizontally, very snugly, around your whole body. Imagine this beam moving through an area only about half an inch to an inch away from your body, moving through the auric field. As it does so, imagine it having a vacuum effect while also pulsing through the auric field, healing any schisms and severing any psychic ties, any energy bonds that no longer serve you. Imagine that it is now moving its way through the energy-field emanations of the emotional body and the mental body as they extend through the auric field.

Imagine your whole body now being mummified and totally encased within these circles of violet light. Imagine again that this violet light swirls around your head, down your neck, around the shoulders, around the arms. Imagine extending your arms out and the violet light mummifying each arm, encasing every part of your arms before swirling up again to begin making its way around the torso, then around the individual legs down to the feet and down to the individual toes.

It is as if your whole being is being sealed within this beautiful matrix of pure violet light that is healing, transmuting, realigning, regenerating and youthing your body and recalibrating all of your energy fields back into a state of harmony with the energies of divine love, divine wisdom and divine power as all the lines of light now run through your whole physical biosystem.

Imagine the lines of violet light now all connecting through the soles of your feet and flowing out from the feet, energizing the root chakra and moving down into the Earth to energize the Earth with every step that you take as you move through the world.

You may wish to add to this meditation that as the violet light moves through all aspects of the physical system and as you lay these energy lines through this matrix one by one, through each system, you program the violet light for perfect healing plus the perfect delivery of vitamins, nutrition, minerals—everything that you need to feed the system, plus, for perfect elemental equilibrium, you program the violet light to hydrate each level of your body with the perfect fluids that it needs now and to do this forevermore. Imagine that this violet light, as it flows through you, is constantly connected to and drawing from the universal ocean of all cosmic particles and energy in a way that you need to feed and hydrate your internal system.

Check to see that your inner system now has all these strands or beams of light flowing into your crown chakra and that all are now permanently hooking into your lightbody; into your chakra and meridian systems; into your skeleton, muscles and bloodlines; into your endocrine and nervous systems; into your organs and skin tissue; and into your emotional- and mental-body energy fields.

Ask your DOW to make any final adjustments required to this matrix system so that you can become and remain healthy and well-nourished and so that your system can be held in the perfect state of regeneration.

Imagine these adjustments occurring. Then chant three times: "So it is! So it is! So it is!"

Drink a full glass of water and imagine the water as a conductor of energy carrying all these new programs into every cell as it flows through you.

Finish with a few minutes of deep, fine, connected breathing and chanting, "I am love. I love. All is love."

There are countless ways to energize and strengthen our physical system, and many of these are outlined in detail in *The Food of Gods*, for example, diet, exercise, meditation. Rather than repeat the whole manual and its tools for a healing lifestyle here, I recommend that if you are serious about nurturing your physical system, you absorb and apply the tools provided in that manual.

Bilocation Practice and Checkout Preparation

I have taken the information and meditation on bilocation presented below from my book *In Resonance*, modified it and expanded it for the purpose of this discussion.

Once we have trained ourselves to be comfortable coming in and out of our body at will, the next step for some is to exit and stay out.

The final part of this exercise is for terminally ill people only who would like more control over their exit process. Before I offer the exercise and tools to do this, though, let us look a little deeper into what bilocation and the ability to leave our bodies is about. I also recommend that you read *Journey of Souls* and *Destiny of Souls* by Michael Newton to familiarize yourself with the planes we can move through when we are in the bilocated, out-of-body state.

Bilocation is the ability to be in two places at once, *bi* meaning "two." Throughout the ages, there have been various stories of great masters who were reported to have been seen in different places at the same time. In modern times, devotees of Babaji and Sai Baba have also reported this phenomenon.

The ability to bilocate comes naturally when our vibrational frequencies are tuned closer to the speed of light. Many techniques are available, but I have found, from personal experience, that vibration is the key, not technique. Consequently, although we may practice various techniques—like the ones recommended in this meditation—the shift will not occur if our frequency is not aligned. I have also found that we all have our own personal key, so what works for me may not necessarily work for someone else. Practice and desire make perfect. Desire will attract to us the appropriate way, which will be revealed when we are ready, that is, tuned.

Having had regular contact with various beings of light, both telepathically and in the dream state, I began to feel as though the visual relationship was one-sided. They seemed to tune in to me at will, and I wished to be able to visit and communicate when I desired. Often I could feel their presence and sometimes detect shimmering waves of light energy as thought transmissions began. Consequently, I began to consciously develop those skills. Others before me had suggested spinning the chakras alternately to build up a certain momentum, then—by will, command and desire—projecting out. So for some months I practiced. I would call a friend, say I was tuning in, go through the routine, send my consciousness to my friend at his or her place of residence, try to see with spiritual eyes what he or she was doing, wearing and so on, then call back, via telephone, to confirm. These efforts were met with varying degrees of success, but I soon became dejected as it all seemed like hard work.

At this point, I was offered the choice—a common one in the path of every initiate—to serve divine will and allow no distraction, or to continue focusing on my own unfoldment and my own "games." Both are valid choices, and both lead to the same point. I chose service. A few months later, as a gift, my by then forgotten desire for bilocation was fulfilled.

For me it seemed as though the secret lay in where I was bilocating to. After all, it was easier to get in the car and visit a friend than trying to bilocate there, but to go to the etheric retreats of the beings of light was another matter altogether! So the first step in bilocation is the intensity of the desire. The second is the motivation behind the desire. And the third step is being tuned to the right vibrational frequency.

There are dimensions within dimensions, the majority of which we cannot connect with by our normal energy band of consciousness. We cannot pick up the transmission broadcast of channel nine on television if our television is tuned to channel ten. We must consciously and physically switch channels.

Bilocation is a shift in our conscious awareness. For those beginning or interested in this training, it is well to understand that there are varying degrees of bilocation, depending on the skill and ability of the bilocator. There are those who can project a solid appearance of themselves that others see with physical eyes; they are literally in two places at once. Another possibility, often due to the intensity of concentration involved with this method of projection is, that we have other individuals look after and watch over our physical body, which may be left in a meditative or sleep state. However, the energy projected is fully animated and appears solid, although it is said to have a luminescent quality. These two methods involve bilocation within this physical plane for various purposes, and it's usually a case of an embodied master appearing before a student. The book *The Nine Faces of Christ* by Eugene Whitworth describes this process in beautiful detail.

As the fourth dimension is the last requiring a physical body, beings of the fifth dimension and above can take a body at will and often choose to appear to the initiate in the form of their last incarnation, for easy recognition. Generally, their vehicles are lightbodies. When I first began to bilocate to these other realms, all who appeared before me materialized in a form resembling a physical body clothed in robes. Now when I visit, they remain as energy, since I know their individual vibrations as they know mine. In order to tune in to these realms, we need to send only our conscious awareness.

I have not fully explored bilocation and teleportation within the physical plane, as mentioned above, and can give no guidance. I assume the methodology is similar, but greater command by mind over molecular structure would be required. Although I have practiced—and have had limited conscious tuition in—dematerialization of the molecular structure and have actually felt my feet disappear, I have not advanced enough to give a workable formula or guidance at this point.

What I am aware of is that it has to do with the implosion of energy; the technique I have practiced is to raise the vibrational frequency to the highest octaves of light. You have to shift your conscious awareness beyond the confines of the physical form and then, through the power of will and intention, gather up into that higher energy band the molecular structure of the physical form. You must allow yourself to dissolve and let go of any fear that is often common with any new experience of expansion. The technique can be likened to a fisherman in a boat (your conscious awareness in the bilocated state) who casts a net out into the water (your will and intention) and allows it to gather all the fish (your molecular structure) before drawing the net plus fish up and into the boat again. Implosion is moving inside out through frequency bands, where the boat is the highest-frequency band, the water surface is another band and the area underneath the water is a lower-frequency band.

This technique was confirmed to me by another channel, who recently received the same information. Those interested in teleportation should enroll for these classes on the inner planes and gain tuition while the physical vehicle is in meditation or sleep.

The following then can be applied as the individual cares to apply it, making note that the information has been gained from the split of conscious awareness and consequent visitation to the etheric retreats of the ascended masters.

Now, you might imagine that you will just zip off and have no awareness of your physical body and where you leave it. However, a split in conscious awareness is just what the words imply. We have what I call the watcher, a part of ourselves that stays behind to keep watch over the physical form. When we relax in that knowledge, we find that we can fade in and out of either realm at will.

Secondly, when we find ourselves at the place where we have projected, we might have to spend some time, in the beginning, to tune ourselves and hook into the frequency band there. Fading in and out is common, like when you first tune to a TV channel and need to adjust the picture to get the clearest image. Being able to hold the vision and frequency may take practice.

Thirdly, be aware that all beings will present themselves to you in a form that has maximum recognition potential or appeal to your programming. So for example, if you have always held a vision of Mother Mary in long, blue, flowing robes, then that is how she will manifest to you—if it is your desire and highest will for you to meet her.

Fourthly, if you find yourself asking whether what you are experiencing is not just a figment of your imagination, you may be told, as I was, that in these realms, all is manifested as a result of thought. So as you desire it to be, it will be. Why not take a leap of faith? Let go of doubt. Allow the energies of these places to move through you and manifest in your physical body.

Your energy fields are connected by the antakarana, or rainbow bridge. This is the bridge from the physical to the spiritual realms that you have created through your meditations. The antakarana allows for the transfer of energy from the higher to the lower planes of frequency, for readjustment and realignment.

So basically you can practice the routine described below remembering that you may need your own unique key/s; my keys were purity of intention and strength of desire. Also note that, as I like to do a number of routines in one go, I have combined other affirmations for purification and reprogramming here. I suggest you play with it all, adding and eliminating according to your inner guidance and success.

Some of the following steps I have already covered in the ascension meditation in *In Resonance*, and points five, eight and nine are not required for bilocation. What is required is to build up the light quotient and chakra momentum to project the consciousness from the confines of the physical body. I also found that unless I spun the chakras alternately—counterclockwise, then clockwise, then counterclockwise and so on—I could not build up enough velocity, spin and momentum and seemed to need to create a double-helix, woven-strand type of effect to achieve success. Again, it is necessary to practice and find the right formula for you.

In the past, I bilocated by building up the light quotient within my four-body system together with the spin and velocity of the chakras. The exit point for me has been through the crown chakra, then up through the five chakras above, joining with the energy of the DOW and, by the power of will and command, tuning in to where I wished to be, then being there. However, of late I have been programming prior to sleep to go to my DOW's perfect place of choice for whatever lightwork may be required. As I had been consciously receiving tuition each night while the physical body was asleep, I felt this learning may be intensified and absorbed easier if I went for a tune-up first.

One morning I decided to go for an alignment while I lay in bed in contemplation, so I simply willed myself to the ascension chamber my DOW chose. I was told this was the retreat in Luxor, which I had not consciously visited before. I felt some energy swirl lightly within the physical body, but then the phone rang, so I got up. (I was obviously not well prepared for this impromptu experience, nor was I aware of how easy my nighttime jaunts had allowed the daytime jaunts to become). Distracted, I decided to give up and had a shower, but I felt completely faint, as though I had undergone an enormous energy drain somehow. A quick tune-in, and I was advised that I was operating at half capacity, that the rest of my energy was still in Luxor and to go and lie down, complete what I had started or regroup my energies. I returned to bed, impressed at the ease of this bilocation, and sent my full focus to the happenings at Luxor.

I am sure that with practice, we can maintain physical activity while we send ourselves off to retreat for realignment or whatever. The process continued for some twenty minutes with some in-depth discussion with my inner-plane friends, and then I felt to regroup. Interestingly, the moment I thought it, I was back in my body, followed instantaneously by swirls of energy that were also absorbed back into my body via the front top chakras. So no technique is set and all are to be experimented with until we find our own formula that can be applied at will. Happy travels!

I recommend that you practice exploring the inner planes and becoming familiar with them before you decide to leave your body permanently. Step 1 of the following meditation is suitable for all who wish the freedom to come and go from their body at will. Step 2 is for those wishing to exit permanently.

Bilocation Tool for Practicing Leaving Your Physical Form: Step 1

Desire stillness and communication. Program that all will unfold for your highest good and for the highest good of all with whom you may share. Be clear in your intention, motivation and desire. Get comfortable, so you can be easily freed from the physical body and not return until ready. It is very important that you are at a place where you will not be disturbed.

Imagine encasing yourself in a cocoon of pure, golden white light. Activate the pituitary and pineal glands with a crystal and/or white light to receive and transmit telepathically; also ask your DOW to activate both glands.

Affirm: "I release all old programming and instruct my pituitary, pineal and all the glands in my body to be open, activated and operating to their fullest potential."

Feel these centers expand and visualize them explode in light; also visualize the thalamus and all major brain centers fill with, and be activated by, violet light to change their resonance.

Breathe in light and allow it to fill your cells and change their vibrational frequency to closer to the speed of light.

Activate all the chakras with liquid light pouring in from the crown center. See the crown chakra expand and spin, then move down to the brow, throat, heart, solar plexus, sacral and base chakras. Do the following chakra affirmation with each: "I call upon divine wisdom, divine intelligence, the infinite power of God Most High, to activate this chakra to resonate to its highest potential and flood my being with this wisdom NOW!"

Instruct your DOW to bring your base chakra into perfect alignment with the perfection of the physical body. Repeat this procedure with the emotional body and the sacral chakra, as well as with the mental body and solar plexus chakra. All chakras are to be huge balls of spinning light, spinning in opposite directions—counterclockwise, clockwise, counterclockwise and so on.

Draw the light into every cell, every organ, visualizing all being cleansed and aligned to the light right down to the feet, then feel the energy wind its way up around and through the body, spinning the chakras as they go.

Feel the whole body resonating and vibrating as if being rocked.

Feel the energy vortex rise up, up, up, intensely lighting up each chakra spinning to maximum capacity.

Bring in your intention to leave. Go up through the eighth, ninth, tenth, eleventh and twelfth chakras.

Visualize being where you wish to be as you command: "I am at the perfect place for me to be free from my body and my physical-plane existence NOW!"

Do not doubt. Your body should stop rocking and/or reverberating. Settle back and watch. Be open. Allow the energy fields of any who appear before you to solidify. All communication will be via telepathy. You may see or feel or hear, depending on your tuning.

Keep alert. Keep your senses open to receive. Be still and listen. The watcher will be aware of the physical body. You will find a part of your awareness still anchored in the physical body. Be fluid and relax and let the "vision" flow.

Know that you have programmed all to unfold for your highest good.

Bilocation Tool for Practicing Leaving Your Physical Form: Step 2

When I discussed this with my father, his first question was, "What if there is no one to meet me at the other side because I get the timing wrong?" The answer to this is that your guides and guardian angels are always aware of you and what is happening.

Before you take this step, I again recommend that you read Michael Newton's books *Journey of Souls* and *Destiny of Souls*. Michael Newton is a clinical hypnotherapist who has spent decades researching life between lives and what souls go through as they depart this realm—the resting, healing, reflection and growth periods they enter into, plus their preparation for reentry. He also discusses guides, soul groups and so much more. I must admit that after reading his research, I became more excited about life without a body than life with it, and others say that they lost their fear of dying.

For the next part of this meditation, practice the same as for the step above, but once you have become familiar with coming and going, on the day that you sense the time is perfect for you to exit and not return to the body, you need to do the following.

Firstly, again use the dependable discernment tools to check that it is the perfect time for you to complete your physical body time on Earth. Double-check using kinesiology or meditation with your DOW.

Next double-check and make sure that all your earthly affairs are in order. What sort of funeral have you arranged? What about your will and any financial obligations to your family?

Next set the intention and request that your guardian angels and your DOW will guide you perfectly and joyously through this exit process and allow you to arrive at your perfect destination. Ask that you be met by all those who love and support you on the inner planes, who can beneficially assist you at this time in a way that is for your highest good.

Ask that you be intuitively guided to do this and exit the Earth-plane dimension at the perfect time for you:

Build up your momentum using Step 1 of this meditation, and then, when you are out of your body and find yourself in the presence of your guides, feel loved, safe and supported. Tune in again to confirm that the time is right for you to do this.

Ask your DOW to permanently disengage Itself from your physical form and also ask for any other guidance you might need to be successful in joyously ceasing your Earth-plane existence now. You may notice a silver cord connecting you back to your body; if so, then see your DOW severing this cord now. I have not yet done this complete process in this life, so at this point, you need to trust that your DOW—as asked—will guide you perfectly to do this now.

Please note that many advanced souls are not met by guides or angels when they cross over. Many have been through the life/death/rebirth cycles so often that they do not need guides. After a period of rest or rejuvenation and reflection, they may meet with higher lightbeings to review their past and future life-path choices.

Note: This meditation will be successful only if it is your time to go and to do so in this manner. If you have the calibration and the skill to successfully bilocate, then you'll have the skill to know what is right for you and to trust in this process.

Reprogramming and Mind-Medicine Healing Tools

Many are now aware of the fact that thoughts emit and transmit "unseen" energy fields that operate via biofeedback loops. These fields thus rebound and are received by their original transmission source. Consequently, everything that comes to us in life, everything that stands before us, we have attracted to ourselves by the nature of the energies we have emitted.

We—our physical, emotional, mental and spiritual bodies—are energy fields in motion, all resonating and vibrating at specific frequencies and transmitting energy waves. In simplistic terms, the human body can be seen as the computer hardware, the mind as the operating system, the thoughts as software programs and our lives as the printout of the three. The physical body reacts to the emotional body, which reacts to the mental body which, when in alignment, serves Spirit and divine intelligence. So our mental programming affects not only our emotional well-being but also our health.

Our thinking processes are habitual and learned but may appear automatic and beyond our control. In his audiotape of the book *Unconditional Life*, Dr. Chopra says, "We are prisoners of our thoughts. Through memory and habit, we literally become bundles of conditioned responses and nerves, constantly being triggered by people and circumstances into predictable outcomes of biochemical response in our bodies. And so the conditioned mind leaves little room for anything new. Emotions seem beyond our control. We erect and build a prison, and the tragedy is that we cannot even see the walls of this prison. The lack of meaning we currently endure can only become worse if we remain within this prison."

We are taught our thinking processes by those we have associated with in our formative years, where we often learn to generalize, think only in terms of black and white, draw conclusions without evidence, assume the worst in a situation or blow things out of proportion, take everything personally, focus always on our failures or our problems.

When we understand that thoughts are energy (that can also trigger emotions) and that universal laws govern this energy and we have the power to create our personal reality, we can be forever free from limited thinking and the belief that life "just happens to us." Then we become apprentices in mind mastery. We realize that we need to be disciplined and vigilant with each and every thought. We also need to question the basis of our beliefs, habitual thinking patterns and reactions. If our lives are abundant on all levels, then we have mastered the mind and its ability to create. If we still feel limitation and lack, then we need to scrutinize our thought forms carefully. A positive thought followed by a negative thought will neutralize the energy field or vice versa. So if we catch a negative thought, we must follow it with positive ones and watch our reality change.

In the short-term, mind mastery and being responsible for every thought, word and action require far more energy and application than victim mentality, where we blame the world and others for our sorrows and circumstances. In the long run, once we have graduated—through discipline and discernment—from apprenticeship to mastery, the benefits are abundant and the quality of our life improves dramatically. Dr. Deepak Chopra reminds us that "there is no objective world to the observer" and that "perception is a learned phenomena."

Perception is governed by environmental influences, genetic encoding and previous life experiences, all of which are held in cellular memory. These memories can be accessed through meditation, hypnosis and/or past-life regression and can, and do, influence our current life experiences. As all creation is birthed in love on light rays of divine wisdom and thought and as we are made in the image of the divine One, with all of Its creative power, then we need to be aware of the power of our thoughts and how through the use of affirmations and mantras, we can create great healing and life changes.

Healing Affirmations and Mantras

Center yourself through deep breathing and/or use the love-breath and body-love tools (see pages 144 and 146, respectively).

When deeply relaxed, imagine sending a beam of pink love light to any part of your body that needs healing as you smile to this part of your body.

Then send a beam of green healing light to it, imagining that the green heal-ing light is feeding and transforming the cells.

Do the same again, but with violet light.

While beaming light into the damaged cells or organs, chant over and over: "With love I heal now, with love I heal now."

You may also use the chant: "Body, heal and regenerate yourself now!"

Life Enhancement Tools

As I have written extensively about the healing lifestyle in my book *Four Body Fitness—Biofields and Bliss*, I will not go into great detail with this here. Suffice it to say that the eight-point lifestyle presented below is a wonderful tool to be used for preventive medicine and to improve the quality of our life as we tread the harmonious healing path. I include additional breathing and programming tools that are also designed to bring our body into a state of greater harmony by allowing us to access and feel more of our healing, divine essence. I have taken the following information from my book *The Food of Gods* and have adapted it for the harmonious healing journey.

Breathing is used to calm, oxygenate and flood the body with the healing energy of prana. Our breath is one of the most powerful tools we have for feeding and fine-tuning our biosystem. Free and at our constant control, we can utilize various breath techniques to achieve many things.

These techniques include but are not limited to: calming and destressing the biosystem, leaving the body to travel through the inner planes via bilocation techniques and astral travel, fine-tuning our energy fields to be in a more healthy and harmonious state and many more. Although there are many techniques of breath work, I recommend the following two.

Love-Breath

This technique is designed to tune us to the divine love channel from which the healing energy of the food of gods flows. I call it the love-breath meditation.

Do the first three steps for at least five to ten minutes each morning and evening, or until you really feel as if all you are is love and all you do comes from this love. Know and trust that the more you flood your system with love, the more you increase the quality of your life. Do this meditation at least every morning and see how you feel after a month or so.

Imagine yourself connected on the inner planes with a beam of pure love that flows from the heart of the Divine Mother into your heart chakra.

Inhale of this love deeply and chant as you reclaim, "I am love." Keep chanting this mantra over and over with sincerity.

Exhale this love slowly out into your body and chant, "I love!" over and over with sincerity as you imagine this love filling every cell and then flowing out from your auric field into your outer world.

Add the mantra: "I am love, I love, all is love." Chant it over and over in rhythm to your inhale and exhale. Also tell your body over and over, until it tingles, "I love you, I love you, I love you, I love you."

This exercise opens up your cells and atoms to receiving pure Divine Mother love as it strengthens your divine heart and your ability to attract, hold and radiate love in this world. And it changes your brain-wave patterns from beta-alpha to the more healing theta-delta patterns.

It is also a great technique to use if ever you feel uncomfortable around someone or judgmental toward another person and you wish to feel more compassionate. It is also a good technique to remind us of who and what we really are when our masks, personas and shields are stripped bare.

This is definitely a try-it-and-experience-the-difference tool that takes some focus and discipline. As I have shared in other manuals, a basic breathing technique like this one that uses the "I am love, I love" mantra is also a wonderful way to train what the Indian yogis call our "monkey" mind to remain still and focused. Many people are unable to focus their mind on just their breath for more than a minute or two without finding themselves thinking of work or shopping or other things, yet mind mastery is absolutely necessary to find and access the food of gods channel. Untrained in the art of stillness, the Western mind in particular requires this type of training as a prerequisite for attaining inner and outer peace. Maintaining a stress-free biosystem is vital for our healing journey.

The Ancient Vedic Holy Breath.

Over five thousand years old, this technique achieves a number of things. Firstly, what actually breathes us is our Divine One Within (DOW), who is here to have a human experience and who utilizes our physical, emotional and mental bodies to do so. Without Its energy, we could not and would not exist, and when we match Its breathing rhythm, we begin to glimpse Its power. Using this tool is also like saying to your DOW, "Are you there? I really want to feel you." Releasing more of its innate healing energy is very beneficial on many levels.

Take a few moments and sit in stillness, then:
Breathe through your nose with deep, fine and connected breaths, not paus-ing as you inhale then exhale, so that you are literally breathing circularly. Once you have an even rhythm, move your awareness to the energy behind your breath and just watch and feel your breathing rhythm.

Remember, you are focusing now on the inner force that breathes you, and you will know when you have found Its rhythm, as you will begin to feel Its waves of love pulsating through you. After a while, you will no longer be focused on deep, fine connected breathing and instead will feel as if you are being breathed.

With training you can find the bliss of your DOW's love beat within maybe four or five breaths. Imagine being able to switch yourself into the bliss zone this quickly.

For those already trained in the art of meditation, I recommend that you do both of the above techniques sitting in the middle of some chaotic scene like peak-hour traffic. Again, this is focus training. It's easy to be a yogi and meditate in the stillness of nature; however, many live in busy cities where experiencing a constant state of inner peace can be a challenge at times. Maintaining mastery in all situations in life is also basic training for the mod-ern-day yogi and for anyone who wishes to achieve and maintain health. (Although the female yogi is known as a yogini in India, throughout this text I choose not to discriminate, as to me a yogi is neither male nor female.)

Inner-Smile Taoist Master Practice

Here is an additional tool: smiling to our organs to establish a loving mind/body connection and to promote faster healing. The inner-smile Taoist master practice prepares our organs and biosystem to get and stay connected to the theta-delta field by tuning each organ to the healing and nourishing frequency of unconditional love. It also opens the inner doors to an experience of a more conscious and positive mind-body communication, which is necessary for our harmonious healing journey.

Sit quietly and imagine that you are inside your body, as if your mind has taken you inside somehow. You see your lungs before you. Imagine beaming a great, big smile at your lungs, and at the same time think how thankful you are for the job that your lungs have been doing for you your whole life—filtering the air you breathe, extracting the chi or pranic particles from the atmosphere around you. Say over and over to your lungs as you smile at them, "I love you, I love you, I love you" and/or "Thank you, thank you, thank you."

Do the same with your brain, then your heart, then your kidneys, then your liver and your sexual organs, until you have smiled at every organ in your body. Do this daily, and soon your organs will begin to feel appreciated and loved and will cooperate quickly with your new programming codes.

Body-Love

The body-love tool is a way of, again, expanding our atoms' and cells' ability to accept and receive more healing energy and nourishment, which in its purest form is love.

Every morning and evening take five minutes to tell your body that you love it by sincerely chanting over and over: "Body, I love you; body, I love you; body, I love you." When said sincerely, from a point of really appreciating every part of your body, from your head to your toes, after a while, your body will tingle in response as if to say, "Do you? Do you really?" and your response, of course, will be, "Yes I do!"

Although this is a simple tool, it is one of the most powerful we have for gaining the physical biosystem's cooperation for the cocreation of health and happiness. In metaphysics love is the foundation for all change and expansion.

Love-Lifestyle

Lifestyle medicine means a lifestyle for harmonious health, and the love-lifestyle tool provides a perfect program for physical, emotional, mental and spiritual nourishment and healing. This includes the use of water, diet and exercise to create a biosystem that, again, is capable of being well-tuned as well as accepting and coping with energy of the theta-delta field. This energy needs to be downloaded safely without burning out the electrocircuitry of the biosystem. Diet refinement is also to be applied as a cleanse and detoxification program while applying the 3-to-2, then 2-to-1 system (see below, under "Additional Tools for Health and Longevity"), then the meat to vegetarian to vegan to raw food to fruit detoxification system, which I will elaborate on below, and the programming code system.

Luscious Lifestyles Program

One of the first steps for successful healing is the adoption of the luscious lifestyles program of Recipe 2000. Briefly, the program entails a daily lifestyle of the following points:

1. Meditation
2. Prayer
3. Mind mastery
4. Vegetarian diet
5. Exercise
6. Service
7. Spending time in nature
8. Using devotional songs and mantras

I've discussed these points in great detail in *Four Body Fitness: Biofields and Bliss*, Book 1. Here I would like to add the following: The meditations given throughout this book actually suffice to effectively tune our emotional, mental and spiritual fields and to open the correct channels for theta-delta field feeding. Meditation allows us the stillness to experience DOW power.

Pray. Not only does prayer heal, but this daily communication with the cosmic computer called God keeps the pranic flow strong within us, for this is the universal law of resonance where like attracts like. Focus on divinity allows all that is divine to be fed by our attention.

Mind mastery and programming is the most complex part of this lifestyle. In dimensional biofield science, light rays act as computer hardware that is then operated and directed by specific software programs that are comprised of thought, will and intention. A basic fact in dimensional biofield science is that all thoughts, words and actions that are beneficial for all will be supported by the purest and most powerful fields.

A vegetarian diet tunes us to the fields of kindness and compassion, which are a natural part of the theta-delta field. A vegetarian diet also improves health and decreases our draining of the world's resources, as it takes twenty times the resources to put animal products on the table compared to vegetables and grains. Until we have mastered our biosystem, it is also much better for our health as has already been proven.

Exercise keeps our physical fields strong and hence allows us to attract, hold and radiate more of the theta-delta field frequencies. In that way, exercise helps us become a clearer and stronger transmitter of these frequencies and more able to imprint quite powerfully in the world.

Service keeps us tuned to the kindness and compassion channel and attracts more love and support to our personal field.

Spending silent time in nature is one of the most amazing foods for the soul, as it really allows us to gain peace, quiet and solitude and lets us feed off the pranic particles that are generated by nature and the trees, sunshine and the earth. This is part of Surya yoga.

The use of sacred music, chants and devotional song also keeps us tuned to the theta-delta fields, as it both destresses our physical, emotional and mental bodies and allows us to feel and recognize the divine in Its purest form.

This eight-point lifestyle plan—the luscious lifestyles program, or L.L.P.—promotes fitness on all levels and keeps our personal field tuned to the divine love, divine wisdom channel, and in time, it anchors our brain-wave patterns in the theta-delta field. This in turn affects our personal keynote and frequency and attracts more grace into our life, allowing us to make a more joyous and easy transition into personal and global paradise, which is the true gift of being nourished by the food of gods.

The daily practice of the above eight points makes us healthy, happy and harmonized within and without, and as we change, so do our societies. By refining ourselves energetically, we also release our highest potential and experience who we really are—the Self who breathes us and gives us life.

Now that we know how to activate this divine power that lies within, our DOW, by frequency matching with it via our lifestyle, then the next question may be, "What's in it for me?" Apart from the divine rapture, divine revelation, harmonious health, overwhelming joy and fulfillment, the practice of L.L.P., if done by the masses, will eliminate all war and violence and hence bring world peace, as inner peace brings outer peace. It will eliminate disease by acting as a system of preventive medicine, hence it will save governments and taxpayers billions of dollars on traditional and alternative health care systems, as L.L.P. delivers to each person improved health and vitality on all levels. The main benefit of the practice of L.L.P. is that people's needs and desires are satisfied on the deepest levels, so that they naturally become more altruistic and caring toward all, thus promoting global harmony.

L.L.P. also increases communication with the divine self as the perfect inner teacher, who will then guide all people to always be in the perfect place at the perfect time doing the perfect things for themselves and their planet. It activates the four-fifths of the brain we usually don't use, the part that houses our higher-mind and higher-nature consciousness.

The sincere practice of L.L.P. will fulfill all our deepest needs and move us into a state of such satisfaction that we are free from all desires and free to know and demonstrate our highest, most divine natures. We also become more detached, discerning, impeccable and filled with love and free of dis-ease on any level.

The 3-to-2 and 2-to-1 System

To continue your dietary adjustment for your healing journey, I also recommend the 3-to-2, then 2-to-1 system, which can be applied immediately. This system simply means that if you currently eat three meals a day, cut it back to two; if you currently eat two meals a day, then cut back to one. The reason for this is that research has proven that if we halve our calorie intake, we can increase our lifespan by 30 percent. It also means that we immediately reduce our consumption of the world's resources by 30 percent just by having two meals each day instead of three.

Our body will feel better, as it will have less digestion time, and if we choose a healthy diet, we will begin to detox slowly, lose weight if required and take stress off our organs, provided we also provide the body with proper nutritional supplements.

Concurrently with this, I recommend the meat-to-vegetarian-to-vegan-to-raw-food-to-maybe-just-fruit detox system. This means immediately stopping your consumption of red meat. Then, when you are comfortable with this, stop your consumption of all other animal or marine flesh. If you are dealing with one of the seven deadly diseases, the sooner you lighten up your diet and detoxify your system, the sooner your body can utilize the energy it uses to consume these products and divert it to healing.

Next, after you have adjusted to the no-meat-or-chicken-or-fish diet—in other words, if it has a face, don't eat it—then cease your consumption of all other animal-derived products such as cheese, eggs, butter, honey and so on and become a vegan. Once you are comfortable with this, go to eating raw foods only.

The slower you take these steps, the easier will be the emotional adjustment and the general detoxification of your system. However, for quicker results with healing, the sooner you lighten up your diet, the better. Your initial discomfort with detoxification—nausea, sore muscles and headaches—will pass and will be helped enormously by the addition of regular colonics.

Adopting a vegetarian diet is usually a natural choice for someone tuned to the kindness and compassion frequency, particularly when that person has been well educated on alternative choices and has made the conscious decision to no longer support the slaughter of life. It is also important in speeding up the detoxification process to promote healing.

Please note that experimenting with a raw-food and even a fruit-only diet can be wonderfully beneficial for your biosystem, as the cleaner and lighter the physical form, the better you will feel on all levels. I would also recommend the use of vitamin and mineral supplements plus ganotherapy to cleanse and strengthen the system. (There is more detailed information on the detoxification and healing power of ganotherapy in Part 3.)

Perfect Personal Programs

Below I describe a step-by-step process that you can begin immediately to support your body with its perfect healing process. To improve the quality of your life, I recommend that you follow the steps listed below.

1. Immediately lighten up your diet to minimize strain on your digestive system. Know that due to modern-day farming methods, few people receive the correct nutritional dosage through food these days.

2. Supplement your diet with high-quality vitamins and minerals.

3. Begin stabilized-oxygen therapy to boost your immune system.

4. Begin detoxification using colonic irrigation.

5. Begin a detoxification and regeneration program using ganotherapy.

6. Do the meditations and use the breath tools outlined earlier in this section.

7. Ask your Divine One Within (DOW) and the universal field of intelligence to bring you any other meditation tools that may be beneficial to you in your harmonious healing journey.

8. Establish a strong mind-body connection. Learn to listen to both the voice of your body—through cleansing it and feeding it live, light food—and the voice of your higher mind, your DOW, through regular silent meditation time.

9. If you are well enough, learn yoga, qigong or tai chi; exercise your body regularly to strengthen your chi flow, which aids healing, and to

increase your physical flexibility. Even if you are greatly weakened by an illness, you can still learn and practice one of the gentle energy-moving arts, such as tai chi.

10. Be aware of what you say—remember that your cells have ears and think that you literally are their master, and so they will eventually manifest whatever you believe to be true. If your doctor says that you have only three months to live and you accept this as a truth, then you will only have three months to live—self-talk can be self-fulfilling. Be aware of the power of words.

11. Have an open mind and research both alternative and traditional therapy options before choosing your path. A guide to help you with this is in Part 3, plus details on some beneficial new technologies.

12. Do the appropriate emotional body cleansing that you need to support your physical system to eliminate the causative factors that created your dis-ease.

13. Apply the eight-point lifestyle program to immediately improve the quality of your life.

14. Apply the personal program described in the following chapter, "Accessing and Creating Our Perfect Healing Program."

15. Use the dependable discernment tools to discover your correct daily doses for points 2 and 3 above. You will find more detailed information on points 3, 4 and 5 in Part 3.

Accessing and Creating Our Perfect Healing Program

The following program is for you to use if you have a debilitating illness and need to gain clarity as to the correct healing path that your system needs. Remember—whatever we have created, we can un-create, and our body knows exactly how to do this.

Step 1: Gathering Data and Diagnosis

Sit in meditation and ask your Divine One Within (DOW) for clarity as to why this situation has been created in your life, that is, ask what the dominant learning is for you.

If it is a potentially fatal illness, ask your DOW for a clear indicator—yes or no—if it is your time to leave this plane via the death process. If you get a clear yes, then there is no point having debilitating treatments such as chemotherapy, as it is your time to go, so attend to all your practical and family affairs. Please note that it is advisable to still apply alternative therapies as mentioned in this manual, since they will improve the quality if not quantity of your life.

If you get a clear no, then ask your DOW for a clear healing structure for you to follow. Ask for yes-or-no answers to questions like: "Would it be beneficial to lighten up my diet?"

Next use the dependable discernment tools and/or a trusted, well-informed kinesiologist to confirm what you received in meditation and/or to discover what sort of support your body needs to bring itself back into a state of harmonious health on a physical, emotional, mental and spiritual level. This may include increased doses of nutrients, minerals, oxygen, meditation, yoga, programming and prayer, to list just a few helping mechanisms. It may also include the use of alternative or traditional technologies, from the multiwave oscillator (MWO) to the bioresonance machine to Reiki and more.

Be sure to investigate and then set a program to deal with the causative factors of any disease you may have; do not just treat the symptoms. Remember that surgically removing a cancer without dealing with the underlying conditions that caused it in the first place will only buy you more time—it will not break the cycle of creating more in the future.

Be aware of the limitations of kinesiology and that the north-sway tool (NST) and all body-testing answers depend on the clarity and intention of the questions. Always make assumptive statements rather than ask questions. Here are two examples: "Taking more than twenty drops of stabilized oxygen is good for my body now." "Right now my body will benefit from additional nutritional supplements."

Use dependable discernment tools to discover which modalities in the traditional and alternative therapies fields will be most useful for and beneficial to you.

Ask the universal field of supreme love and intelligence to bring you the perfect support systems you need, including the perfect traditional and alternative therapists who can support and assist you. Do your own research on the physical level. Do research on the Internet to understand more of the disease you have been diagnosed with. Research all healing modalities. Research background and successes of alternative and traditional therapists, then use the dependable discernment tools to test which therapy or therapist is perfect for you.

Do not give your power away to a therapy or therapist. Know that you have created the imbalance, and consequently, you have the tools and innate intelligence to heal yourself. Healing comes from a combination of internal and external modalities, including physical, emotional, mental and spiritual fine-tuning. Utilize what the therapy and therapist can provide in the best way you can while trusting that you hold the power within you to bring yourself back into a state of harmonious health.

Use the dependable discernment tools to communicate with the limitless intelligence within your body to discover on which plane—physical, emotional, mental and etheric—the source of this dis-ease was first created, and then set a treatment program to address each one. Cancer usually begins in the emotional plane, which of course is linked into the mental plane via our self-talk and perceptions. As the imbalance grows in these two planes, it then manifests in the physical.

I also recommend that you look back to the time when this pattern of imbalance was first created and recapitulate and release it as per the holographic kinetics system or via neuro-linguistic programming (NLP) time-line tools.

For your own peace of mind, I also recommend that you do traditional medical blood tests to discover the state of your blood's health. Test for minerals, vitamins, proteins, hormonal changes, cholesterol levels and so on. Also use hemaview analysis to discover additional data that normal blood tests will not pick up.

Have a full medical checkup with a doctor who is also open to combining traditional and alternative methodology for holistic health.

Have a full medical checkup with the LISTEN or the bioresonance system as alternative diagnostic and rebalancing tools. You may also wish to receive an iridology diagnosis to gather additional data or to confirm what you already know.

Have a checkup using Chinese medicine procedures such as pulsing. Use whatever herbs you need to boost your system.

Step 2: Treatment

Use the dependable discernment tools to set the perfect healing plan. This may be a program like the one that I underwent, which combines various treatments. Keep an open mind—by using the dependable discernment tools, you will not waste time or money chasing nonbeneficial therapies. Remember, your body knows what you need.

Once you have a clear program from your body, check it and then adjust it regularly, for as you heal, your body's needs will change. Use the dependable discernment tools to determine how many pills of each nutrient or how many drops of stabilized oxygen you need each week or each day. I recommend that you use the dependable discernment tools weekly to refine your program, or even use them every few days if you are under an intense program using light technology and/or the multiwave oscillator.

If you do not already do so, then learn to meditate to destress yourself during this trial and also to keep yourself stress free in the future. Apply the steps mentioned previously to support your body into healing through diet and lifestyle refinements. Use additional vibrational medicines such as homeopathy, Bach flowers and what is offered via the bioresonance and LISTEN systems for rebalancing. Start to oxygenate your system to boost your immune system so that it can repair the body.

If your body has stated its need for something like chemotherapy, investigate adding alternative treatments such as the use of herbs to direct the chemo to target only the diseased cells, and take massive doses of vitamin C and oxygen to keep the immune system strong. Do not assume that your doctor is informed as to all the perfect treatments that are available for you. Take responsibility for your own health and be open to combining systems.

Be prepared to lighten up your diet and change or increase your exercise program.

Look at the use of plasmonic lightower nanotechnology, which changes positive ions into negative ions, which are more beneficial for your external field. These technologies are said to negate harmful effects from TVs, mobile phones and other energy pollutants in our world. Investigate these to see which are suitable for you.

Read Part 3 and do your own research.

PART 3

HARMONIOUS HEALING HELP:
AN ALTERNATIVE VIEW

DIAGNOSTIC, CLEANSING AND
HEALING TOOLS AND
NEW TECHNOLOGIES

An Alternative View:
Diagnostic, Cleansing and Healing Tools and New Technologies

This chapter provides more information on the modalities and technologies mentioned throughout this book, in alphabetical order. Detailed articles on many of these follow in the next chapter.

Akasha: The metaphysician's universal library. Part of the universal field of intelligence where all data and all answers to all questions are stored, along with all that has transpired throughout all dimensions.

Bioresonance system: Diagnostic and rebalancing tool. Bioresonance accepts that the cells are controlled by electromagnetic fields, and hence it is possible to introduce healthy frequencies to rebalance the whole body and provide an environment where the body cures itself. See more in the article in the next chapter.

Black salve: Also known as Cansema, an herbal mixture historically known as escharotics, which is based on the original formula that was discovered and refined by John Hoxsey in 1840. (His book *You Don't Have to Die* provides a history of his formulas). Cansema has the ability to discriminate between healthy and abnormal tissue, which can be used as both a diagnostic tool and a skin cancer remedy. Herbal mixture of bloodroot and other ingredients helps to draw out and combat cancer cells in the body. Applied topically. Available through various naturopathic sources or through David Highman, Bsc ND; Inn Harmony Centre, davace60@hotmail.com, www.holisticproducts.com.au, phone +61 7 4038 2064, fax +61 7 4038 2095 or through Alpha Omega

Laboratories, Mail Bag 67, Drake, NSW 2469 Australia, phone + 61 2 6737 6767.

Calibration: In this manual the term is used to refer to David Hawkin's system of testing mass consciousness. Using Dr. John Diamond's system of kinesiology, Hawkin's developed "a calibrated scale of consciousness, in which the log of whole numbers from 1 to 1,000 determines the degree of power of all possible levels of human awareness." In this model, 200 represents emotions of positive stimulus where muscle response remains strong, and below 200 is where muscle response weakens as emotions such as anger, fear, guilt or shame begin to influence the body.

The number 200 represents the energy of truth and integrity, 310 is the calibration for hope and optimism, 400 is the energy of reason and wisdom, 500 is the energy of love, 540 of joy, 600 is perfect peace and bliss, and the numbers 700 to 1000 represent even higher levels of enlightenment. Another word for calibration is frequency or resonance.

Dependable discernment tools: Tools to help us discern the perfect healing path, or to gain or confirm clearer insights.

Detox with colonic irrigation and juice fasting: As meat and other toxic matter can sit undigested in our intestines for up to twenty years, slowly putrefying, I recommend periods of fasting after a period of colonic irrigation as a step to regaining health and vitality. Combined with fasting with alkaline-inducing fruit and vegetable juices such as carrot, apple and beetroot juice, colonics give the body's digestive system a chance to rest and be refreshed. For further details on this, do your own in-depth research and also read Dr. Walker's book *Raw Foods*. Some research has found that many diseases, such as cancer, thrive in the highly acidic environment created by junk food diets and too much coffee and sugar.

Electromagnetic field radiation (EMR): Electromagnetic field radiation coming from electric appliances and transmitters. A large number of appliances emit extremely low electromagnetic frequencies, often in the same frequency area as the fields that control the biological processes in our bodies. This radiation can disturb our hormonal and biochemical processes and create disease. See detailed article under "Plasmonics" in the next chapter.

Ganotherapy: Therapy using the king of herbs, the red *Ganoderma lucidum*, or reishi gano. Taken in capsule form, the king of herbs scans, detoxifies and regenerates the body, bringing to the surface any imbalances such as cancers. Also used by the Japanese royal family for immortality. See more in the article in the next section.

GenMed: Light technology using sound waves and light rays designed to recalibrate our DNA back to our original DNA harmonic signature and blueprint; removes any generic and emotional disease signatures from our DNA. New technology is so far restricted to Australia. Violet-light rays pulse through 180-quartz crystals at a frequency of the individual's original DNA pattern. GenMed is a rebalancing and healing tool. For more details contact David Highman, Bsc ND, Inn Harmony Centre, davace60@hotmail.com, www.holisticproducts.com.au, phone +61 7 4038 2064, fax +61 7 4038 2095.

Hemaview analysis: System for testing the health of the body by analyzing and viewing the blood. See short article in the next chapter.

Holographic kinetics: A healing system developed by Steve Richards. Based on Aboriginal dreamtime healing principles of universal law and combining neuro-linguistic programming and kinesiological testing methods to release harmful trapped emotions from crystals in the body and break negative attractor patterns.

Kinesiology: Diagnostic tool. Founded by Dr. George Goodheart and given wider application by Dr. John Diamond, behavioral kinesiology is the well-established science of muscle testing the body where a positive stimulus provokes a strong muscle response, whereas a negative stimulus provokes a weak response. Please note that in order to establish a disease-free existence where there is no physical, emotional, mental and spiritual disease, a human biosystem needs a personal calibration of 635 as per David Hawkins' calibration system described in his book *Power vs. Force*. There is a wealth of data on this on the Internet and therefore no need to elaborate further. Finding a skilled practitioner is crucial, so ask your Divine One Within (DOW) and the universal field of intelligence (UFI) to bring you the perfect person, or use the dependable discernment tools.

Laser technology: There are two formats for laser work: the actual technology of laser therapy and the mind power and creative visualization using laser light to regenerate and heal.

Lightower: Based on plasmonics, which is said to be the next big thing in nanotechnology (New Scientist on "Bright New World," 26/4/03). When the lightower, which acts as an antenna, is aligned with the magnetic north-south, it changes positive ions into more healing negative ions that support us and protect us from harmful EMR.

LISTEN system: Diagnostic and rebalancing tool that uses meridian point readings to check and rebalance the body's harmonics. See detailed article in the next chapter.

Multiwave oscillator (MWO): Rebalancing tool based on Tesla/Lakhovsky technology using radio waves to produce ozone in the body and to recharge and restore the natural voltage around every cell to seventy-seven millivolts. The charge around cancerous cells is often as low as fifteen millivolts. See detailed article in the next chapter.

North-sway tool: Diagnostic, confirmation and guidance tool.

Oxygen: With proven research that states that disease cannot exist in a highly oxygenated environment, the ingestion of stabilized oxygen has been known to support the immune system so that it can do its natural job, which is to fight disease in the body. See detailed article in the next chapter.

Plasmonic nanotechnology: See article in the next chapter and information on lightower above.

Pranic nourishment: The ability to be able to draw nourishment in the form of vitamins and minerals from the universal force, or chi field, to the degree that we no longer need to take nourishment from physical food. A way of being physically, emotionally, mentally and spiritually nourished by tapping into the force behind creation. Read *The Food of Gods* for more information.

Radionics: A distant healing and diagnostic system similar to LISTEN and bioresonance systems. See detailed article in the next chapter.

Universal field of intelligence (UFI): The supremely intelligent and loving energy field from which all life springs and is fed by. Known by many other names, the UFI can be accessed via meditation, and when asked, the UFI will provide all the tools and information we need for our journey into harmonious health, whether this be on a personal or global level.

Universal laws: Laws of the higher light science that govern the mechanics of creation. Covered in detail in my book *In Resonance*.

An Alternative View Continued:
Information on Research and Diagnostic, Cleansing, Healing and Rebalancing Tools

Although I am reluctant to nominate any particular group or institution that I have not dealt with personally, and although I recognize that there are now a myriad of wonderful alternative research centers and practitioners, I offer a few connections for you to research, and maybe utilize, below. However, I recommend that you use the David Hawkins model discussed in his book *Power vs. Force* to determine the calibration of anyone you are thinking of dealing with. If they—or their organization—do not calibrate at two hundred or above, which is the level of truth and integrity, then do not get involved with that person or organization. Remember, many of these therapies need to be used in conjunction with other methods and according to the personal healing program that your own being will provide, as discussed earlier.

Bioresonance: A Diagnostic and Rebalancing Tool

I was first exposed to the bioresonance system a number of years ago in Germany and then later in India. Back in Australia, I found its equivalent in the LISTEN system. A pranic nourisher for the past decade, I would use the LISTEN system, plus a yearly hemaview analysis, as a diagnostic tool to confirm that I was maintaining a good state of health. I also used it as a rebalancing tool when needed. The information below is taken from two different websites to provide a more complete view. The first is http://www.bioresonance.co.uk/page3.html.

Many different forms of bioresonance therapy exist today as a result of the pioneering research by the scientist Hans Jenny and others who carried on his groundbreaking work such as Dr. Peter Manners.

These therapies consist mainly of various methods of application of certain frequencies or magnetic fields to the body. The underlying theory behind this is that all matter has a resonant frequency and every cell in the body resonates at a particular frequency.

This takes the form of an electromagnetic field and groups of cells in an organ or system have multiple frequency patterns that are unique. Hence, the whole body has a complex frequency makeup that can change or become distorted when affected by illness. If you accept that the cells are controlled by electromagnetic fields, then it is possible to introduce healthy frequencies to re-balance the whole body and provide an environment where the body cures itself.

This treatment therefore appears to have connections with the principles of acupuncture and homeopathy, which rely on energy flow and imprinting of frequencies on aqueous solutions. The application of frequencies to the body or water is usually by vibration, electromagnetic fields, or by light.

The following information on bioresonance therapy is taken from the website http://www.naturaltherapycenter.com/bioresonance_therapy/

The treatment of pathological oscillations is to return them back to the body in a modified form—in this case, as a mirror image. This action is based on the principle, well known in physics, that oscillations are influenced by their exact mirror image. Returning the oscillation to the patient in this modified form can diminish, or even eliminate, the pathological oscillations of the allergen or toxin, allowing the body's own healthy oscillations to become dominant. If the practitioner decides that medicine would also be useful in treatment, the oscillation of that specific medicine could also be returned to the patient.

These returning oscillations help to balance the patient electromagnetically, and are again fed into the BICOM device [bioresonance therapy device] for further analysis. The process is repeated constantly in fractions of a second. The pathological signals in the body are consequently reduced and finally extinguished, and the physiological endogenous regulatory forces can regulate the biological process unhindered.

The patient's body signals are conducted from the right hand into the input of the device using a BICOM electrode. In the BICOM device, the disharmonious frequencies are filtered out and inverted. These inverted therapeutic oscillations are now given back to the patient via the left hand using another electrode.

Ganotherapy, or Reishi Gano:
A Cleansing, Rebalancing and Rebuilding Tool

The following text is based on information from http://www.hbp.usm. my/wanb/ganotherapy/sihatlingzhi.htm and http://www.hbp.usm.my/ wanb/ganotherapy/ganobook/English/3rg.htm.

Ganotherapy is a method of attaining good health using *Ganoderma lucidum*, the fungus also known as lingzhi, reishi, kulat and cendawan. The therapy is based on the premise that illness is caused by two sources: toxins in our body and disharmony in body functions. Ganoderma lucidum does not cure the disease; rather, it helps balance our body system and improve immunity against diseases. The appropriate dosage is not related to the disease but to the individual. Any physical reaction we experience during ganotherapy is caused by our body system and not by the intake of Ganoderma.

Reishi gano is a mushroom essence (*Ganoderma lucidum*). It is effective for cleansing out toxins, regulating body functions, helping the body maintain good health and preserving youthfulness. The essence contains more than two hundred active elements, which can be divided into three categories:

- 30 percent water-soluble elements
- 65 percent organic soluble elements
- 5 percent volatile elements

Water-soluble elements include polysaccharides (the "cleanser") and organic germanium (the "balancer"). The polysaccharides strengthen the natural healing ability of the body, reduce blood sugar levels and assist pancreas function. They also help to clean toxic deposits from the body, strengthen the cell membranes and increase the oxygen-carrying capacity of red blood cells. Organic germanium is partially soluble. It helps increase the oxygen content in the body, regulate the balance of electrical charges in the body and remove abnormal electrical charges found around abscessed cells.

Organic soluble elements are adenosine (the "regulator") and triterpenoids (the "builder"). Adenosine can help lower the cholesterol level in the blood and the amount of free fat, lower the level of blood lipid and stabilize the red cell membrane, lower the level of platelet agglutination and enhance thrombolysis, improve the function of the cortex of the adrenal glands to maintain endocrine balance, regulate the metabolism for a youthful energetic feeling and balance the pH level of the blood. Triterpenoids, which are bitter in taste, can enhance the digestive system, prevent allergy caused by antigens (because they inhibit the histamine-releasing mast cells), reduce cholesterol and neutral fat in the body and activate the nucleus of body cells.

The volatile element is the ganoderic essence (the "regenerator"), which assists in the treatment of skin diseases. It can be used for beautification of the skin and for external application on skin diseases, mouth ulcers and external wounds. It also stops bleeding and rejuvenates the body tissue.

How Reishi Gano Works

Reishi gano works in five phases: scanning, cleansing, regulating, building and regenerating.

Scanning takes one to thirty days. Diseases are caused by an imbalance of body functions, and reishi gano can help regulate these functions. The effect reishi gano has on the body identifies the ailing area.

Cleansing/detoxification takes one to thirty weeks. Uric acid, excess cholesterol, fat deposits, calcium deposits, bad tissues and chemical accumulation are some of the toxins present in our bodies. These toxins are removed from our body by sweating and the circulation system (the kidneys and liver). They are then discharged from the body through urination and stool, boils, rashes, phlegm and mucous discharge.

Regulating takes one to twelve months. Reishi gano's balancing effect works to regulate body functions.

Building takes six to twenty-four months and refers to the process of building and healing the body parts that have sustained injuries or damage. The immune system is strengthened, physical strength and mental calmness are built, and the body is made more resistant to disease. Reishi gano also supplies essential elements to the body, such as minerals and triterpenoid for the recovery of bodily functions.

Regenerating takes one to three years. This is the ultimate aim of consuming reishi gano. It is the process whereby the body is functioning at its optimum level, which actually has a rejuvenating effect wherein youthful appearance, strength and peace of mind are restored.

It is said that there are four things we can use to obtain good health:

• Like cures like. Cold things cure cold conditions or hot things cure hot conditions. For example, we can take ginger to cut down a high body temperature. This is homeopathy.

• Opposite cures opposite. To overcome feeling cold, we consume something hot—for example, ginger. This is traditional medicine.

• Poison cures poison. To kill a virus (poison), we use antibiotics (poison). This is modern medicine.

• Function cures function. We help the immune system to function so it can get rid of whatever it is that has caused the dysfunction. This is ganotherapy.

John of God: A Rebalancing and Healer Tool

I always pay attention when information comes to me three times from three different sources, particularly when I am writing a book, and so it was with news about John of God, a Brazilian healer who says, "It is not me who cures. God is the healer; I am simply the vessel." I have taken the following information from his website, www.johnofgod-healing.com. Again, please use your own discernment.

John of God, (João de Deus) is without a doubt one of the most powerful channeling mediums and healers alive today. João has been at the Casa de Dom Inacio for over thirty years. There are some thirty-three entities he incorporates at the Casa, so named after one of the entities, St. Ignatius de Loyola, founder of the Jesuits. His work is free of charge.

In 1991 João traveled to Peru and worked on over twenty thousand people, including the president, who suffered with atrophy of the hands, and his son, who had a mental disorder. In gratitude he was awarded a Peruvian medal of honor. He was also given a march of honor by the entire provincial Peruvian army. This was usually reserved only for heads of government. He has also treated Shirley Maclaine and the author and spiritual teacher Ram Dass. On his days off, he travels to other parts of Brazil and may treat tens of thousands of people at a time.

João Teixeira da Faria was born on June 24, 1942, in a small village in central Brazil. His father was a tailor, and despite his efforts working as a tailor, João and his family were often faced with hunger and poverty. As a child, he displayed clairvoyant abilities. Because of his rebelliousness, João's formal education was cut short after only two years. Perhaps this was a blessing in disguise, as it allowed him to develop in such a way as to better serve the future that was ahead. It was not until João was a teenager that his life was transformed forever.

At sixteen he traveled to Campo Grande to begin a job as a tailor. For unknown reasons, the job was terminated on his first day. With the reality of hunger and poverty staring João in the face, he was filled with despair. He went swimming in a nearby creek to refresh himself and wash away his anxieties. Then suddenly he heard a voice call his name. He was amazed to see a beautiful, fair-haired woman next to a tree. He sat near her, and they spoke for a long time. Later that night João realized she was Saint Rita of Cassia. With many questions still unanswered, he returned to the same spot the next morning, hoping to speak to her. A beam of light sparkled in the place where she had stood and her voice then emerged from the light. She instructed him to go to a Spiritualist center in town; the people there were expecting him. Not understanding the meaning of this, he nonetheless did what he was told.

When he arrived at the church, members were indeed expecting him. Then João lost consciousness. When he woke up a few hours later, he apologized for passing out and explained that it was due to hunger. To João's surprise, a senior member told him he had not merely passed out but that he had incorporated the spirit of King Solomon. He went on to say that in those three hours that John couldn't remember,

João had healed many people and performed amazing surgeries. João naturally thought this was a mistake. But after he was served a meal and more discussion took place, João began to reflect on the possibility that it could be true. So began the spiritual career of João de Deus— John of God, as he is affectionately known—whose healings have benefited hundreds of thousands of people throughout the world.

Please note that there are many talented people who allow the healing power of the divine One to flow through them. Use your discernment to determine the right ones for you to work with.

Hemaview Analysis: A Diagnostic Tool

The following information is taken from the website http://www.ess-health.com.au/tests/live_blood_analysis.phtml.

Live blood analysis involves a fascinating examination of your blood to analyze your health. A single drop of blood is taken from the tip of your finger and is viewed through a microscope, which will provide resolution of these features without drying or staining the blood. This technique enables the evaluation of blood features in their living state, hence the term "live blood" analysis.

Observations are made on variations in the size, shape, ratios and fine structure of red cells, white cells, platelets and other structures in your blood. Observations can infer:

• Nutritional deficiencies
• Organ-system dysfunctions
• Gut permeability and digestive health
• Antioxidant levels and free-radical load
• Certain biochemical imbalances
• Immune surveillance and activity.

Why Use Live Blood Screening?

Live blood analysis detects functional imbalances otherwise known as "precursors" to disease (inflammation, sluggish immune surveillance, poor red cell structure, and more) very early on, in some instances well before that of standard blood pathology. A recommendation can then be implemented to rectify the change in the initial stage, prevention being far easier than cure.

Lightower Technology: A Rebalancing and External Energy Support Tool

In his booklet on nanotech products, inventor Neil Orchard writes: "Every form of life has a unique electrical imprint and its own mathematical signature, wavelength or frequency. Creating beneficial harmonic energy frequencies requires tremendous mathematical research and analysis plus an understanding of the subtle energies and factors that influence all biological systems."

Apparently, when the lightower, which acts as an antenna, is aligned with magnetic north-south, it changes positive ions into the more healing negative ions that support us. The negative ions harmonize the surrounding energy field by rebalancing any disturbances from the electromagnetic field radiation (EMR) of appliances that surround us and bombard us daily. Using plasmonics, the lightowers restore the delicate balance of light in both the external and internal environments of our bodies.

Over twenty years of research has linked EMR to a range of health problems, from headaches to leukemia and cancer. Contact inventor Neil Orchard at NANOTECH Products by phone +61 438 288 882, or 0438 288 882 within Australia. For overseas suppliers, search the Internet and use your discernment. In Europe, Germany is most advanced with this.

LISTEN System: A Diagnostic and Rebalancing Tool

Computerized Electrodermal Screening (CEDS)

The following information, both on CEDS and the LISTEN Orion system is taken from http://www.energyhealthcentre.com/ceds.html.

What is CEDS?

CEDS is a computerized health screening technique that collects data related to energy imbalances within a person's body. It measures skin resistance at the acupuncture points on the body that correlate to major organs, glands and systems of the body. The information gathered allows a trained CEDS practitioner to determine the cause of an energy imbalance and identify what product or technique will help produce a balance. CEDS is part of the emerging field of bioenergy medicine, or bioelectromagnetics, which includes devices that measure energy changes in the body (such as a thermometer) or use energy to measure structure or function in the body (such as x-rays).

LISTEN Orion

The history behind this state-of-the-art technology dates back to Germany in the 1950s. Dr. Reinhold Voll, a medical doctor, acupuncturist and homeopath, theorized that, since the acupuncture system was based on energy flow, it was an electromagnetic force that could be measured with simple electrical measuring devices. He developed a special system of measuring electrical skin resistance, which became known as "Electrodermal Screening."

In the late 1960s, James Hoyt Clark, a computer scientist from Utah, was approached to develop a computer program able to process these electrodermal screening/readings into a viable computer system. With over twenty years of research and clinical studies now backing it and in its twelfth stage of development, this system is currently known as the LISTEN Orion.

In October of 2000, a U.S. patent was granted to James Hoyt Clark. The actual patent document states: "This invention relates to methods and apparatuses for providing treatment or promoting health through the application of electromagnetic radiation or electric current to the body and in particular to methods and apparatuses for providing therapeutic treatment and promoting health of the body or for treating food, chemical, vitamin, mineral, metal and biological sensitivities."

How Does It Work ?

It has been known and accepted by the Chinese for thousands of years that there are many points on the body that connect with all the organs, glands and systems, and the pathways from these points are called meridians. These points, commonly referred to as acupuncture points, are considered to be access windows to the meridian pathways, and in turn, a way of tapping into the energy system of the body.

Simply put, the actual testing procedure involves holding a ground electrode (earth) in one hand while the operator contacts an acupuncture point on the patient's opposite hand or foot with a probe that looks like a small pen.

The procedure is noninvasive. The skin is only touched with a small amount of pressure. The patient becomes part of a closed electrical circuit. The electrons flow from the ground electrode of the system, through the cable and the patient and back through the probe, which is in contact with the skin. In effect, the system operates as an ohm meter for the body by recording the responses to stimuli. This data is stored and processed within the computer, and a printout in graph form is generated, giving a visual energetic snapshot.

The LISTEN Orion has within its memory electrical frequencies relating to over 45,000 items found in our environment. By sending these signals through the body, the LISTEN Orion is capable of measuring the body's response to many items in a matter of minutes. A trained LISTEN practitioner can then determine the data, to make relevant therapeutic suggestions designed to rebalance the body. It may involve any number of combinations of modalities.

What Does This All Really Mean?

It means that this technology represents an extremely valuable missing link, not currently found in today's mainstream medical practice. It lets your body do the talking! It enables a practitioner to interrogate the body and observe changes, often before they can be detected by currently available medical technology, by interfacing with the subtle energy fields of the body.

Multiwave Oscillator (MWO): A Rebalancing, Support and Reenergizing Tool

The following information on the Lakhovsky multiwave oscillator is taken from the website http://www.toolsforhealing.com/products/MWO/MWOHomePage.html.

Georges Lakhovsky developed and presented the idea that each cell in the human body works as a microcellular oscillator with energy fields resonating with a "twisted filament" (like a tiny oscillator) in the nuclei of living cells. The cell acts like a transmitter and receiver of radio-electric waves that produce an energizing effect. With help from Nikola Tesla, he built the first Multiple Wave Oscillator (MWO) in the mid-1920s. He applied for a U.S. patent (#1,962,565) and received it in 1934.

Lakhovsky, unfortunately, died in 1942 at the age of seventy-two. His patent expired in 1951 and is now readily available in the public domain. The MWO and other similar devices continued to be used in clinics throughout Europe after his death, but the technology seems to have been almost forgotten in America. After achieving a 98 percent success rate over an eleven-year period, it's more than a bit curious as to why his work was suddenly withdrawn from use and patients told treatments were no longer available. MWOs have been documented to be of value in treating cancer, arthritis and other illnesses.

Lakhovsky's goal when designing the Multiple Wave Oscillator was to produce and transmit a full spectrum of harmonic frequencies within the body, allowing each cell to resonate with the appropriate frequency. Cells that were sick would be entrained by the correct harmonics, bringing them into a normal state so they could heal themselves through natural processes. With the proper resonant frequencies, normal mechanisms of detoxification could work to bring about greater health and well being.

Lakhovsky recognized the nucleus of each cell in the body as an oscillator in resonance with (controlled by) the cosmic rays that Nikola Tesla often spoke about. The continuous bombardment of cosmic radiation from space is very different from the conventional radio frequencies commonly used today. The basic thought is that the cell structures in the body are blocked, impeding the flow of cosmic radiation, allowing poor eating habits, toxic items or stress to cause improper functioning. The MWO acts as an entrainment device that allows cosmic radiation to flow without interruption through the cells, allowing and stimulating proper function and health. Lakhovsky recognized the fact that the universe is basically energetic in nature—everything is energy, vibrating at its own particular frequency. If you produce enough harmonics at a high enough level, they will affect the cells in the body. And there will never be a shortage of cosmic energy flow from the universe, so our only real problem is reversing blockages and removing the high levels of toxicity that tend to exist in most of us, causing poor health.

The following information on Lakhovsky's multiwave oscillator is taken from the website http://www.altered-states.net/barry/newsletter161/.

In the 1925 Georges Lakhovsky in France developed a coil for the protection of trees; copper wire was stuck into the ground, turns were made around the tree, and the loose end was pointed toward the sky as an aerial. In 1928 he formed a variation of this that was geared to improve the health of humans, which he called the multi-wave oscillator, based on his then new theory that cells are microscopic oscillating circuits.

This was successfully used in French, Italian and Swedish clinics, and when Lakhovsky escaped to the U.S. in 1941, it proved successful in a major New York hospital. Among problems successfully treated were cancerous growths from radium burns, goiters, arthritis, chronic bronchitis, congenital hip dislocation and many others.

What Lakhovsky discovered was simply mind boggling. He postulated that all living cells (plants, people, bacteria, parasites) possess attributes that are normally associated with electronic circuits. These cellular attributes include resistance, capacitance and inductance. These three electrical properties, when properly configured, will cause the recurrent generation or oscillation of high-frequency sine waves when sustained by a small, steady supply of outside energy of the right frequency. This effect is known as resonance. It's easiest to compare it with a child swinging on a playground swing. As long as the parent pushes the swing a little at the right moment (the correct frequency), the child will continue to swing high and continuously. In electronics, circuits that generate these recurrent sine waves can be called electromagnetic resonators, but more commonly they are referred to as oscillators. All living organisms have specific resonate frequencies and micro currents associated with them including bacteria, viruses, parasites and fungi.

Fact 1: If one has two tuning forks of the same frequency, vibrating one will cause the other to vibrate. Similarly, an opera singer can shatter a crystal glass by sounding its resonate frequency.

Fact 2: Viruses are living organisms.

Theory 1: Broadcasting specific frequencies through the body can overload and destroy living pathogenic organisms when their specific frequency resonance is included.

Theory 2: Broadcasting a broad range of frequencies (microcurrents) throughout the body adversely affects the replication process of many different pathogens.

The MWO is a multiple wave oscillator. It saturates the cells of the body with energy. In turn the chemical processes of each cell are brought into balance, allowing proper repair and operation. When you use the machine regularly, it maintains the electrical health of the body at a cellular level. All chemical processes in the body require energy to take place and the MWO feeds that need.

This is accomplished by setting up a high energy field in and around the body through resonance. The MWO doesn't pass current through the body. All that is used is the oscillating field. The process is similar to shaking a box of marbles: After a while, they organize themselves neatly into the order that their shape dictates. This is true of the body's molecular structure too. When this is achieved, the cells work at maximum ability without stressing themselves.

One scientist explains it this way: A normal cell has an electrical potential of 70 millivolts (mV), an aged cell has 50 mV and a cancerous or ill cell has 15 mV. When a cell is in electrical difficulty, the mV and the sodium-potassium balance are out. The high potential brings the cells to an equal level, basically resetting them. This allows healing to occur at a higher pace without stressing the cell. And the additional energy restores cell integrity by reorienting its molecular structure to allow for easier potential movement. Basically, it bolsters the field of each cell individually so that all cells can support each other more easily.

Moving the damaged areas while on the machine helps to increase the recovery speed of mechanical injures. Many people meditate while on the machine, using the machine as the focal point. Others just sit and watch TV or put on a movie. Don't sit rigid like a statue; shrug the shoulders and move your head around. Think pleasant thoughts; negative thought patterns consume more energy than you think.

The MWO is a harmonizing energy source that is capable of generating electrical and magnetic fields with a broad spectrum of frequencies. Cells, tissues and organs become under the influence of these fields harmonized and activated in their correct state. By applying these harmonizing fields to living cells, tissues and organs, all imbalances, blockades and internal quarrels disappear and the mutual cooperation in the body is enhanced. This in turn leads to the disappearance of sickness, afflictions and ailments.

In all probability, the original design of the MWO came from Nikola Tesla. George Lakhovsky has in turn elaborated on this design and has done many experiments on plants, animals and people with stunning results. In his book *The Secret of Life, Electricity, Radiation and Your Body* (ISBN 0939482-08-8), he stated that cells from living organisms behave like small radio transmitters and receivers. When cells are irradiated with a correct polarized electromagnetic field (which has a broad range of frequencies), each cell will pick up on a frequency and assimilate the energy out of that field. This has a tremendous stimulating and harmonizing action on the cells and thus interacts with surrounding tissues and organs.

Every atom in the universe has a frequency. Whether it's a grain of sand, a piece of steel, a plant, an animal or an organ in your body, each cell resonates, or vibrates, at a specific frequency or oscillation. Your body consists of a variety of atoms, which contain photons, electrons and an overall bioelectric energy that runs through it. The way you take care of your body physically, emotionally and mentally determines how many negative frequencies or toxins are being built up in it. There are four general ways imbalances in the body are created: toxic substances we eat, pollution we breathe, exposure to a negative energetic environment and how we process information in our thinking and feeling.

Plasmonic Nanotechnology and Lightowers: A Rebalancing and External Environment Support Tool

Please see also the information on lightower data above. The following article on electromagnetic field radiation, its effect on our health and how lightower technology combats this and is an effective solution is taken from http://www.odemagazine.com/article.php?aID=4046. Tijn Touber wrote the article.

Why Good Health Begins with Magnetism

When Russian cosmonauts first spent long periods of time onboard the Mir space station, they got sick. Their symptoms indicated this was more than a simple lack of exercise, too much zero gravity or an overdose of canned food. Their illnesses appeared to be caused by a lack of contact with the magnetic field surrounding the earth. After the Russian space station was equipped with a special "magnetism generator," the cosmonauts' symptoms disappeared.

After the experiences of the Russian cosmonauts, some scientists must have thought to themselves: "If the natural magnetic field surrounding the earth is so important to health, what does it mean that this field is increasingly being disturbed by the explosive growth of electric machinery? After all, every electric current produces an electromagnetic field and those fields increasingly compete with the earth's natural magnetic field."

Cells are ordered by magnetism. The smallest building blocks of life—atoms and molecules—are micromagnets with a plus and minus pole, comparable to the earth's poles. Because everything is made up of atoms and molecules, every structure is determined by magnetism. Communications in the body take place via miniscule electric currents and the electromagnetic frequencies they generate. If electromagnetism orders the very process of life, then a disturbance to this magnetism will result in an increase in chaos and degeneration. And that is exactly what's being observed: a strong increase in degenerative diseases and chaotic explosions of violence among humans and in nature.

This growth in disorder around us may be explained by the increasing disruption of the natural magnetism that supports health and harmony. The explosive increase in unnatural electromagnetic fields is making increasing numbers of earth dwellers space-sick. Just like the cosmonauts, people are losing contact with the natural frequencies that support life on earth. A large number of appliances emit extremely low electromagnetic frequencies often in the same frequency area as the fields that control the biological processes in our bodies. This radiation can disturb hormonal and biochemical processes.

Back in the 1970s the American physician Robert O. Becker, now professor emeritus of orthopaedic surgery at the State University of New York, warned that our health would be affected by artificially generated electromagnetic frequencies. Becker, who was twice nominated for the Nobel Prize for health, is convinced that the increase in these frequencies is directly linked to the rise in rates of cancer, birth defects, depression, learning disabilities, chronic fatigue and Alzheimer's.

His argument: "All matter living and non-living is an electromagnetic phenomenon. The material world, at least as far as physics has penetrated, is an atomic structure held together by electromagnetic forces." His concern: "The human species has changed its electromagnetic background more than any other aspect of the environment."

How damaging is it, Becker wondered, "that the density of radio waves around us is now 100 million or 200 million times the natural level reaching us from the sun"? The question is, how exactly are these waves affecting us? Experiments with animals have showed that disturbing the electromagnetic fields can have serious consequences. Bees, fish and termites veer off course and are no longer able to perform certain functions. When you destroy half a termites' nest and then disrupt the workers' electromagnetic communication, they no longer know what to do. The strength of the electromagnetic field with which termites communicate came to light several years ago in the Peruvian capital of Lima. The fire brigade was sent to clean up a termites' nest because the waves were so strong they completely scrambled radio reception in a neighbouring area. The positive effect of magnetism has been demonstrated in the case of animals as well. Flies that ate magnetized sugar in experiments lived twice as long, and exposing mice to a strong magnetic field twice a day also increased their longevity.

The importance of the magnetic field for orientation was demonstrated by Hans Fromme and Friedrich Merkel of the Zoological Institute in Frankfurt, Germany. In an experiment, they kept European robins in a cage. Away from sunlight and stars, the birds continued to stare longingly to the southwest—precisely the direction they would normally migrate. But when the magnetic fields around the birds were disrupted, they lost their orientation. Magnetic crystals have been found in a number of animals, including salmon, that enable them to tune in to the earth's magnetic fields. Recently Robert Becker, among others, found these crystals in humans. Becker believes that people unconsciously tune in and navigate thanks to the magnetic field around them. When these fields are disturbed, people become disoriented—literally ungrounded. The reverse also appears to be true: magnetism can be specifically used for healing. There are indicators dating back thousands of years that ancient Chinese, Japanese and Egyptian people used magnets for healing. Descriptions of magnetic therapy have also been found in the works of Aristotle, Plato and Homer. They wrote of using the therapy to help paralysis, rheumatic disorders and swollen joints, among other things. Cleopatra evidently wore a magnetic amulet on her forehead to maintain her youth.

These ancient cultures not only worked with actual magnets, usually made from magnetite, but there are also descriptions of people who could "magnetize" their hands. This type of magnetism was also successfully applied in the 18th century by Austrian physician Franz Anton Mesmer, among others. The success of his treatment method was so striking that the medical and political authorities of his time felt seriously threatened and wanted to have Mesmer beheaded. Mesmer was eventually vindicated, and this type of "magnetization" is still practiced by healers today.

What Mesmer was not able to prove scientifically back then, has been proven now. Robert Becker has demonstrated that the brain waves of healers who magnetize their hands are in sync with the frequency of the earth's natural magnetic field. This same frequency has also been measured among meditating monks. Researchers at the Menninger Clinic in Kansas, U.S., found that healers will often produce up to a million volts of charge during healing work. In other words, meditating is not just some cosmic practice; it can actually ground you to the earth. Many healers, too, do nothing more than reconnect their patients to the earth using their magnetic powers.

Robert Becker calls this form of healing "energy medicine." In his book *The Body Electric: Electromagnetism and the Foundation of Life,* he writes: "The idea of an energy medicine that postulates a common basis for all of these disciplines has arisen lately because of new discoveries in biology that cast serious doubt on strictly mechanistic concepts of life and seems to reintroduce the old idea of body energy. These discoveries are not vitalistic in the sense that they prove or even hint at some mysterious, unknowable life force. Rather, they reveal the presence of electrical and magnetic forces at the most basic levels within living organisms."

Oxygen: An Immune System Support Tool for Rebalancing

The following information comes from the booklet *The Oxygen Answer for Health and Healing* by Tonita d'Raye.

"All chronic pain, suffering and diseases are caused from a lack of oxygen at the cell level."

—Arthur C. Guyton, M.D., *The Textbook on Medical Physiology.*

"Virtually all heart attacks come down to a failure to deliver oxygen to the hardworking heart muscle."

—Phillip Stavish, M.D., "Oxygen Deficiency Linked to Increase in Disease."

"Lack of oxygen clearly plays a major role in causing cells to become cancerous."

—Dr. Harry Goldblatt, *Journal of Experimental Medicine.*

"Hypoxia, or lack of oxygen in the tissues, is the fundamental cause for all degenerative disease."

—Steven A. Levine, Ph.D., and Paris M. Kidd, Ph.D, "Antioxidant Adaptation."

"It is the lack of oxygen in proper amounts in the system that prevents oxidation and oxygenation, which energizes the cell to biological regeneration. These processes are the foundation of life and death."

—Stephen R. Krauss, "O_2xygen: Nature's Most Important Dietary Supplement."

Doctor Phillip Lee Miller from the Los Gatos Longevity Institute once wrote, "The human body is an amazing array of competing forces always striving to maintain homeostasis (internal stability and balance). One process, through oxidation, is eliminating and combating invading pathogens, and sterilizing and detoxifying our body. Another process requires a rich array of antioxidants to prevent DNA or cellular-membrane damage from oxygen free radicals. The body knows how to orchestrate all of these processes simultaneously. Therein lays the answer to promote homeostasis. An oxygen-rich body combined with water and the proper nutrients (fuel) for cellular regeneration equal optimal health."

Dr. Miller has been practicing medicine for twenty-six years. He has a degree in Biochemistry from the University of California Berkeley campus and has training in Neurology. He is board certified in Emergency Medicine and a charter member of the American Academy of Anti-Aging Medicine (www.AntiAging.com).

Give Me Oxygen! Oxygen (O_2) = Life

Oxygen is essential for combustion (oxidation), and acts as a disinfectant, deodorizer, sanitizer, and preserver. Oxygen makes up almost 50 percent of the earth's crust by weight, 42 percent of all vegetation, 85 percent of seawater, 46 percent of igneous rocks and 47 percent of dry soil. This colorless, tasteless and odorless element so essential to life comprises 65 percent of our body. We develop permanent brain damage if robbed of oxygen for a mere eight minutes and blood is, in essence, a river by which oxygenated red corpuscles are transported to every cell in the body.

All functions of our body are regulated by oxygen. It must be replaced on a moment-to-moment basis because 90 percent of our life energy depends on it. Oxygen energizes cells so they can regenerate. Our body uses oxygen to metabolize food and to eliminate toxins and waste through oxidation. Our brain needs oxygen each second to process information. The ability to think, feel, move, eat, sleep and even talk all depend on generated energy from oxygen.

Oxygen is the only element capable of combining with almost every other element to form the essential components necessary to build and maintain our body. For instance, nitrogen + carbon + hydrogen + oxygen = protein. Carbon + hydrogen + oxygen = carbohydrates. Hydrogen + oxygen = water. The combination of oxygen in the air, water, proteins, and carbohydrates creates life energy. None of this energy could be produced without oxygen. Since 1783 the therapeutic use of oxygen has been well researched, and its benefits have been documented by thousands of experts in various scientific and medical fields.

Symptoms of Oxygen Deficiency

Initial symptoms of oxygen deficiency may include overall body weakness, fatigue, circulation problems, poor digestion, muscle aches and pains, dizziness, depression, memory loss, irrational behaviour, irritability, acid stomach and bronchial problems. Oxygen deprivation can also lead to life-threatening diseases such as cancer. Cancer and most other infections or disease cannot live in an oxygen-rich environment. Dr. Otto Warburg, two-time Nobel Laureate for cancer research, stated: "Cancer has only one prime cause. It is the replacement of normal oxygen respiration of the body's cells by an anaerobic (i.e., oxygen deficient) cell respiration."

Just as modern-day farming methods have depleted the vital nutrients in our food, we have almost 50 percent less oxygen available to us today. Before the advent of the industrial revolution, the oxygen content of our air was 32 percent. In the early 1900s, this was reduced to 24 percent. In the year 2000, the oxygen content of our air dropped to an average of 19 to 21 percent by volume in relatively unpolluted environments. In large cities the content may be as low as 15 percent and in industrial areas, 10 percent. This is dangerously low. Scientists believe that if the oxygen content of air were to drop to 7 percent, it could not support human life.

The average person's diet today only increases the problem. Many of our diets consist of processed foods that are high in saturated fats and sugars and low in fiber, enzymes, water and oxygen. A diet high in processed foods and "junk foods" requires tremendous amounts of oxygen in order to be metabolized. A deficiency in the oxidation process of our body leads to an accumulation of toxins that would ordinarily be burned (oxidized) in normal metabolic functioning. Our body has to use precious oxygen needed for other essential metabolic functions in order to process oxygen-deficient food.

Dr. Samuel West, a noted scientist in the field of lymphology, proved that food present in cells that are oxygen-deficient will turn into toxic waste products and fat. When cells are oxygen deficient, they start producing improper chemicals that soon cause them and their neighboring cells to become unhealthy. If this continues for a prolonged period of time, the immune system is compromised and pathological disease conditions are given a chance to manifest.

Our body is constantly being stressed to use its oxygen reserves to neutralize excess acidity and get rid of toxic accumulations. Leading biochemists and medical physiologists say that aging and many diseases (including cancer) result from the accumulation of acid waste products in body cells and tissues. In an acid condition, red blood cells can function at only 5 percent to 10 percent of their oxygen-carrying capacity. The result is unhealthy cell metabolism, which can lead to serious problems, including the suppression of the thymus gland.

The thymus is vital to the immune system due to its production of T-cells that protect us from toxic invaders such as bacteria, viruses and cancer. The thymus starts to shrink at about age twenty. By age sixty, it is only about 5 percent of its original size. The thymus will enlarge in an alkaline environment and shrink in an acidic environment.

Free Radicals: Friends and Foes

Free radicals are oxygen molecules that have lost an electron. These molecules are highly reactive, unstable and capable of destroying an enzyme protein molecule or a complete cell through oxidation by stealing electrons from other nearby molecules. Sunlight, radiation, drugs, tobacco, smoke, pesticides, chemicals, solvents, fried foods and alcohol are just a few examples of free-radical generating substances.

When our body is overburdened with out-of-control free radicals, the result is oxidative stress, which may seriously compromise the immune system and give rise to life-threatening disease and decay. All forms of stress, whether from chemical toxins, or from physical or emotional sources, deplete our body of precious oxygen. Regardless of the health-promoting potential any nutrient may have, very little metabolic value can be experienced from it if our body is oxygen deficient.

Our Body's Oxygen-Delivery System

We take in oxygen through our lungs, skin and digestive system. The dissolved oxygen content in the blood of a healthy person is approximately four times that of air. Haemoglobin molecules in each blood cell become over 95 percent saturated with available oxygen. Haemoglobin in red blood cells is the liquid carrier of dissolved oxygen to our body's trillions of cells. Oxygen is consumed in the complex oxidative process of converting proteins, carbohydrates and fats into the energy and heat needed for healthy cellular metabolism and for the body to rid itself of toxins and other cellular waste. This vital process is key to healthy metabolic function, including assimilation, digestion, brain function, nervous-system response, circulation and elimination.

An oxygen-starved body is susceptible to premature aging, chronic illness and life-threatening disease. Fortunately, when oxygen levels are increased, our blood picks up the extra oxygen, our cells become energized and our health can be restored. Researchers reported that many patients who were in advanced stages of illness or disease fully recovered with increased oxygen saturation. This was especially true if supplement oxygen therapy was implemented before hypoxia (long-term oxygen deprivation) irreversibly damaged body systems.

Here is an Australian contact that I have used with success: Noah Yamore at Stabilized Health Products. Phone +61 2 66 843004, fax +61 2 66 843114, email noah@linknet.com.au or website www.naclo.com.

Radionics: A Diagnostic and Rebalancing Tool

Radionics is similar to the bioresonance and LISTEN systems. The following information is taken from the website:

http://www.borderlands.com/newstuff/research/superior_radionics.htm

Radionics is a method of diagnosis and treatment at a distance that utilizes specially designed instruments so that the practitioner can determine the underlying causes of diseases within a living system, be it human, animal, plant or the soil itself. Although Radionics is mainly used to diagnose and treat human ailments, is has also been used extensively in agriculture to increase yields, control pests and enhance the health of livestock.

Radionics as a healing art originated from the research of the distinguished American physician Dr. Albert Abrams. He was born in San Francisco in 1863 and became one of the most highly qualified specialists of his day. A graduate of the University of California, he wrote several medical textbooks and eventually earned a national reputation as a specialist in diseases of the nervous system.

In the course of his research, Abrams made the startling discovery that diseases could be measured in terms of energy, and he devised an instrument with calibrated dials that enabled him to identify and measure disease reactions and intensities. From this work, called the Electronic Reaction of Abrams (ERA), came Radionics as we know it today. Leading British physician Sir James Barr considered Abrams' discoveries to be among the most significant of the day. Not surprisingly, certain elements of the medical and scientific community attacked Abrams' work and sought to discredit him. In 1924, the year of Abrams' death, a committee of the Royal Society of Medicine under the Chairmanship of Sir Thomas (later Lord) Horder investigated his claims. To the astonishment of medicine and science, the committee, after exhaustive tests, had to admit that Abrams' claim was legitimate.

During the 1930s in the United States, Chiropractor Dr. Ruth Drown added further dimensions to Radionics through the discovery that diagnosis and treatment could be carried out from a distance. In the 1940s the main focus of Radionic research switched to England and the De La Warr Laboratories in Oxford. Instruments and techniques were refined and extensive work was done in the field of Radionic photography, originally initiated by Dr. Drown in California. The 1960s saw completely new concepts emerge for Malcolm Raes' research into Radionics instrumentation and homeopathic potency simulation, and the introduction by chiropractor Dr. David Tansley of a whole new basis for Radionic diagnosis and treatment based on the subtle anatomy (energy fields) of man, which subsequently revolutionized the theory and practice of Radionics throughout the world.

Some Fundamental Principles of Radionics

Basic to Radionic theory and practice is the concept that man and all life forms share a common ground in that they are immersed in the electromagnetic field of the earth, and further, that each life form has its own electromagnetic field that, if sufficiently distorted, will ultimately result in disease of the organism. Accepting that all is energy, Radionics sees organs, diseases and remedies as having their own particular frequency or vibration. These factors can be expressed in numerical values which are known as rates, or in the form of geometric patterns. These provide the means by which the practitioner identifies and treats disease at a distance. Radionics is also cognizant of the fact that there are a number of finely organized fields of energy that lie beyond those identified by science and that these fields can be utilized for diagnostic and therapeutic purposes. Thus it may be said that Radionics is a healing art where physics and para-physics, science and religion meet and merge.

The Radionics practitioner, in making a distant diagnosis, utilizes his intuitive faculty, which science now believes arises for right-brain hemisphere functions. The intuitive mind has access to information that lies beyond the reach of rational and logical abilities, which appear to be meditated through the left-brain hemisphere. By tuning in both his mind and Radionic instrument to the distance patient, the practitioner, by applying his faculties of extrasensory perception (something we all have to a greater or lesser degree), is able, through observing the reactions of the detection apparatus under his control, to determine what the underlying causes of disease are. By identifying causes which may be hidden for clinical and more orthodox procedures, the Radionic practitioner is able, then, to determine with accuracy the correct treatment to eliminate this underlying element. A Radionic diagnosis is not a medical diagnosis; as previously stressed, it is a means of identifying and assessing the underlying causes that give rise to pathological states and their systems. These may or may not coincide with current medical opinion, but this is to be expected when the practitioner's approach is along para-physical lines.

Radioic Treatment

When the Radionic diagnosis is finished and the practitioner has a complete health profile of the patient, including the functional integrity of all organ systems, psychological states and imbalances that are present in the energy structures that form the energy fields that underlie the body, treatment can then be properly determined. All pathological states and their causes have their own frequency of energy patterns; these can be treated at a distance through the Radionic instrument by employing rates or geometric patterns. The bloodspot or snippet of hair from the patient (known as the patient's witness) acts as a link between the practitioner, his Radionic instrument and the patient. Essentially, treatment is the projection of healing energy patterns; to these may be added the wave form of homeopathic remedies, colors, flower essences and herbal extracts, if they are indicated as part of treatment.

It may be difficult to accept that such treatment can be effective at a distance. However, the weight of clinical evidence shows that it is very effective in a significant number of cases—action at a distance, as this phenomenon is called, is not new to science. Today a great deal of research is being carried out by scientific institutions in this field, and they are finding out that humans, plants and animals respond to projected thought patterns and that this phenomenon occurs no matter how great the distance between the subjects under investigation. Their findings now bear out the rationale of Radionics. One of the great advantages of Radionics is that it is often possible to discover potentially serious conditions at an early stage and, by appropriate treatment, prevent them for developing to a point where they become clinically identifiable.

Moreover, as Radionic treatment takes place at a nonphysical level, it cannot harm any living tissue or produce any unnatural side effects. Radionics is concerned with healing of the whole man, with the health pattern or entelechy of the individual. The health pattern is a singular, unitary force within the structures of man that ensures adequate and optimum functioning of the systems of his body. The purpose of Radionic therapy is to help the individual to reestablish his optimum pattern of health.

The Scope of Radionics

The scope of Radionics in theory is unlimited; in practice it is limited by the sensitivity, knowledge and expertise of the practitioner [as are kinesiology and other diagnostic and healing tools such as bio-resonance and the LISTEN systems]. At one level, it can be used to determine the structural and functional integrity of the body and identify the causes of disease hidden within. At another level, the determination of the states of the energy centers (chakras) provides a picture of energy flows in the body and enables the practitioner to gain a deeper insight into the reasons behind certain physical and psychological imbalances. To this may be added an analysis of the qualities of energy within specific psychic structures. A synthesis of this data will reveal physical and psychological strengths, weaknesses, limitations and capacities and thus provide patients with insights into the personal and spiritual aspects of their nature, which can prove most useful during periods of crisis and stress. The beauty of Radionic treatment is that it is noninvasive. It can be used to complement other forms of therapy, and its efficacy is such that it forms a complete system of heaing on its own right.

Another Research Connection to Pursue

For information on future science, future medicine and future technologies, go to http://www.borderlands.com/main1.htm, Borderland Sciences' website.

Please note that there are many institutes now focusing on these issues, and there are many more valuable alternative therapies and diagnostic tools, such as Chinese medicine, acupuncture, iridology, Bach flower essences, essential oils and more. As with any of the technologies and healing or diagnostic methods above, ask your Divine One Within to connect you with the right one for you. Use discernment and confirm your findings using the tools we have provided. Most of all, trust that your journey will deliver the perfect outcome for you.

I recognize that there are many valuable therapies that I have not included here. My main objective has been to provide you with some viable alternative options plus a system of dependable discernment to determine the perfect healing program for you. By sharing a little of my own journey, I hope that you have gained further insights into the harmonious healing game, which can cover physical, emotional, mental and spiritual issues. Remember, you have all the answers within and you have the keys to reveal them.

Traditional Medicine:
New Advances in Traditional Cancer Detection Methods and Chemotherapy

In the October 2004 issue of *Australian Women's Weekly*, in an exposé on breast cancer, the following information was shared:

Vaccines: Early trials of vaccines that stimulate the immune system to recognize melanoma cancer cells as a threat. Researchers are currently looking at how repeated doses of cancer vaccines can be used to treat women with breast cancer, or those who are at risk of the disease, to keep their immune systems working properly.

Alternative therapy equivalent already available: stabilized oxygen therapy. See previous article in Part 3.

One-Dose Radiation: Instead of thirty-five visits to complete a full course of radiotherapy, women with breast cancer might soon be able to undergo radiation in just one dose, delivered directly into the tissue after surgery.

Alternative therapy tool currently being developed by the GenMed inventors: A violet light radiation system, similar to the one that repatterns our DNA, except this one is a system where the patient stands in for fifteen minutes as any diseased matter is drawn out from the body and dissipated back into the ether. Due for release within the next year or so. You can connect with naturopath David Highman for more data on this.

Revolutionary Node Biopsy: To determine if the breast cancer has spread, instead of removing the usual fifteen lymph nodes under the armpit near the affected breast, a new technique called the sentinel lymph node biopsy injects a dye into the nodes to determine which node the breast drains to first, and if it shows no signs of cancer cells, then removal is deemed unnecessary. Set to be available within the next five years.

Breast Cell Tests: Scientists are also working to improve diagnosis by removing cells directly from breast ducts, where the majority of cancers occur.

Saliva Tests: Cancer cells secrete chemicals different from those produced by healthy cells. Once the cells are identified within our saliva secretion, a simple saliva test will be able to indicate cancer or pre-cancerous changes in the body.

Chemotherapy

The following information on chemotherapy is taken from http://www.breastcancer.org/tre_sys_chemo_idx.html.

Chemotherapy is a systemic therapy; this means it affects the whole body by going through the bloodstream. The purpose of chemotherapy and other systemic treatments is to get rid of any cancer cells that may have spread from where the cancer started to another part of the body.

Chemotherapy is effective against cancer cells because the drugs love to interfere with rapidly dividing cells. The side effects of chemotherapy come about because cancer cells aren't the only rapidly dividing cells in your body. The cells in your blood, mouth, intestinal tract, nose, nails, vagina and hair are also undergoing constant, rapid division. This means that the chemotherapy is going to affect them, too.

Still, chemotherapy is much easier to tolerate today than even a few years ago, and for many women it's an important "insurance policy" against cancer recurrence.

How Chemotherapy Works

The following information is taken from http://www.breastcancer.org/tre_sys_chemo_whatis.html.

Chemotherapy is the use of drugs to treat cancer. Before surgery, chemotherapy may be used both to reduce the size of the breast tumor and to destroy cancer cells wherever they may be. After surgery, chemotherapy works throughout your system to kill cancer cells that may have spread throughout your body. Here's how this systemic treatment works.

Your body's normal cells grow and divide in a controlled manner. Cancer cells, however, grow and divide in total chaos—without any control or logical order. Chemotherapy works by stopping the growth or multiplication of cancer cells, thereby killing them. You may worry that chemotherapy will kill normal cells, too, and there is that possibility. However, remember that these drugs work best on cells that divide rapidly—namely, cancer cells. This makes chemotherapy particularly effective against cancer.

As I mentioned previously in this manual, there are some herbs such as aloe vera that can help the chemotherapy to target only the diseased cells rather than affecting the whole body. High doses of vitamin C plus oxygen therapy will help boost the immune system, which is often detrimentally affected by chemotherapy.

Stem Cell Research

The text below is taken from http://stemcells.nih.gov/info/faqs.asp#success.

What are human embryonic stem cells?

Stem cells are cells that have the remarkable potential to develop into many different cell types in the body. Serving as a sort of repair system for the body, they can theoretically divide without limit to replenish other cells for as long as the person or animal is still alive. When a stem cell divides, each "daughter" cell has the potential to either remain a stem cell or become another type of cell with a more specialized function, such as a muscle cell, a red blood cell or a brain cell.

A more detailed primer on stem cells can be found at: http://stemcells.nih.gov/info/basics.

What classes of stem cells are there?

There are three classes of stem cells: totipotent, multipotent and pluripotent:

• A fertilized egg is considered totipotent, meaning that its potential is total; it gives rise to all the different types of cells in the body.

• Stem cells that can give rise to a small number of different cell types are generally called multipotent.

• Pluripotent stem cells can give rise to any type of cell in the body, except those needed to develop a fetus.

Where do stem cells come from?

Pluripotent stem cells are isolated from human embryos that are a few days old. Cells from these embryos can be used to create pluripotent stem cell "lines"—cell cultures that can be grown indefinitely in the laboratory. Pluripotent stem cell lines have also been developed from fetal tissue obtained from fetal tissue (older than eight weeks of development).

Why do scientists want to use stem cell lines?

Once a stem cell line is established from a cell in the body, it is essentially immortal, no matter how it was derived. That is, the researcher using the line will not have to go through the rigorous procedure necessary to isolate stem cells again. Once established, a cell line can be grown in the laboratory indefinitely and cells may be frozen for storage or distribution to other researchers.

Stem cell lines grown in the lab provide scientists with the opportunity to "engineer" them for use in transplantation or treatment of diseases. For example, before scientists can use any type of tissue, organ or cell for transplantation, they must overcome attempts by a patient's immune system to reject the transplant. In the future, scientists may be able to modify human stem cell lines in the laboratory by using gene therapy or other techniques to overcome this immune system rejection. Scientists might also be able to replace damaged genes or add new genes to stem cells in order to give them characteristics that can ultimately treat diseases.

Adult stem cells such as blood-forming stem cells in bone marrow (called hematopoietic stem cells, or HSCs) are currently the only type of stem cell commonly used to treat human diseases. Doctors have been transferring HSCs in bone marrow transplants for over forty years. More advanced techniques of collecting, or "harvesting", HSCs are now used in order to treat leukemia, lymphoma and several inherited blood disorders.

The clinical potential of adult stem cells has also been demonstrated in the treatment of other human diseases that include diabetes and advanced kidney cancer. However, these newer uses have involved studies with a very limited number of patients.

Human embryonic stem cells are thought to have much greater developmental potential than adult stem cells. This means that embryonic stem cells may be pluripotent—that is, able to give rise to cells found in all tissues of the embryo except for germ cells, rather than being merely multipotent—restricted to specific subpopulations of cell types, as adult stem cells are thought to be.

Pluripotent stem cells, while having great therapeutic potential, face formidable technical challenges. First, scientists must learn how to control their development into all the different types of cells in the body. Second, the cells now available for research are likely to be rejected by a patient's immune system. Another serious consideration is that the idea of using stem cells from human embryos or human fetal tissue troubles many people on ethical grounds. The research and ethical debates continue.

As I chose to forego traditional treatments like chemotherapy, there is not much I can add here on a personal level, except to say that you need to do all the research you can so that intellectually you are well informed as to your harmonious healing choices. Having done your research, you then need to confirm with your inner being, both with your body consciousness and your Divine One Within, what the perfect course of action is for you. For some it may be a combination of alternative and traditional methods, and more positive progress is being made daily within both fields, particularly with stem cell research. Only you can make this choice, and you need to be well informed to make it.

All that I have added in this manual is for your education only. I cannot offer the exact path for you to follow, as only you have the answers. Nonetheless, I have given you some beneficial tools to find your answers. Enjoy your journey, for it has the power to bring you many gifts. Namasté.

Epilogue:
Solve All Your Problems in
Ten Easy Steps

Pay attention to your state of mind. Take note of your own assumptions, reactions, contradictions, anxieties, prejudices and projections.

- Speak up. Say what you are thinking, feeling and wanting.
- Remember that you don't know the whole truth about anything. Even when you feel absolutely certain about what you are saying, add "in my opinion" or "from my perspective" to your sentence.
- Reach out. Seek out people who have different, even opposing, perspectives from yours. Stretch beyond your comfort zone.
- Reflect on you own role in the situation. Examine how what you do or don't do contributes to things staying the way they are.
- Relax and be fully present. Open up your mind and heart. Position yourself as willing to be touched and transformed.
- Hear what is being said by the group as a whole. Listen not just to what you and others say, but to what is emerging from the collective experience of everyone.
- Stop talking. Quietly consider the questions and let answers come to you.
- Listen with empathy. Look at the situation through the eyes of the other.
- Try out these suggestions and see what happens. Notice what shifts in your relationships with others, with yourself and with the world.

—*Solving Tough Problems* by Adam Kahane

Bibliography

Chopra, Deepak. *Ageless Body, Timeless Mind: The Quantum Alternative to Growing Old.* New York: Harmony Books, 1993.

——————. *Quantum Healing: Exploring the Frontiers of Mind/Body Medicine.* New York: Bantam Books, 1989.

——————. *Unconditional Life: Discovering the Power to Fulfill Your Dreams.* New York: Bantam Books, 1991.

Griscom, Chris and Wulfing von Rohr. *Time Is an Illusion.* New York: Simon and Schuster, 1988.

Hawkins, David R. *Power vs. Force: The Hidden Determinants of Human Behavior.* Carlsbad, CA: Hay House, 2002.

——————. *The Eye of the I: From Which Nothing Is Hidden.* Sedona, AZ: Veritas Publishing, 2001.

——————. I: *Reality and Subjectivity.* Sedona, AZ: Veritas Publishing, 2003.

Hoxsey, John. *You Don't Have to Die.* New York: Millstone Books, 1956.

Kahane, Adam. *Solving Tough Problems: An Open Way of Talking, Listening, and Creating New Realities.* San Francisco: Berrett-Koehler Publishers, 2004.

Newton, Michael. *Destiny of Souls: New Case Studies of Life Between Lives.* St. Paul, MN: Llewellyn Publications, 2001.

——————. *Journey of Souls: Case Studies of Life Between Lives.* St. Paul, MN: Llewellyn Publications, 2003.

Walker, Norman. *The Natural Way to Vibrant Health.* San Diego: Nature's First Law, n.d.

Whitworth, Eugene. *The Nine Faces of Christ: Quest of the True Initiate.* Camarillo, CA: DeVorss and Company, 1980.

The following books are available as e-books at http://www.selfempowermentacademy.com.au/htm/cia-education.asp#ebooks

Jasmuheen. *The Law of Love and Its Fabulous Frequency of Freedom.*
——————. *The Food of Gods.*
——————. *Four Body Fitness: Biofields and Bliss.*
——————. *In Resonance.*

Gaia Speaks

SACRED EARTH WISDOM

Gaia through Pepper Lewis

NEW! — FROM — LIGHT TECHNOLOGY PUBLISHING!

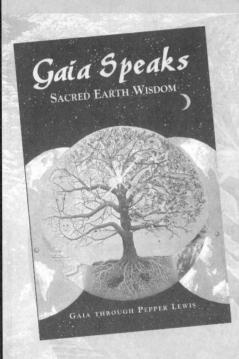

I am the nonphysical sentience of this planet—simply put, I am the planet Earth. I am the body and the soul of the planet you currently inhabit. My sentience guides and enlivens all that surrounds the planet as well as all that is upon and within her. My sentience animates the air you breathe, the energy you burn and the water you drink. My sentience—the most aware, advanced and attuned aspect of my being—is that which directs these words. Although many believe in a sentient or feeling Earth, not all are attuned to her. Channeling offers a unique advantage in this respect, because it allows the transmission of vibrations and impressions to be communicated as language.

— Gaia

- A Brief History of Religion
- Walk Your Way or Walk Away
- The Key to Dealing with an Epidemic of Global Fear
- Portals to Perfection
- Patriots, Citizens and Warriors
- Manifesting and Reincarnation
- And much more!

$19⁹⁵   SOFTCOVER 393 P.
ISBN 1-891824-48-1

available through
LIGHT TECHNOLOGY
PUBLISHING
PO Box 3540 • Flagstaff, AZ 86003

Phone: 928-526-1345 or 1-800-450-0985 • Fax 800-393-7017 or 928-714-1132
... or use our online bookstore at www.lighttechnology.com

Ambassadors of Light
Jasmuheen

Ambassadors of Light is Jasmuheen's new work and is just as controversial as her previous book as she continues to challenge the status quo and take the pranic nourishment discussion onto the global stage.

In this book Jasmuheen offers practical solutions to world health and world hunger related challenges via her Luscious Lifestyles Program, and also looks at effective ways to redirect global resources. This entails an in-depth look at global disarmament, the dissolution of prohibition, the forgiveness of Third-World debt, holistic reeducation programs and the elimination of the need for personal pharmaceutical use through the elimination of all disease.

Ambassadors of Light also looks at the undeniable long-term benefits of vegetarianism in relation to health and resource sustainability levels, and also at the lifestyles those who are now free from the need to eat food usually adopt.

Jasmuheen also compiles statistics from the Light Ambassadry's Global Research Project as well as the research of many others into this phenomena. This book is a collection of research, recipes and recommendations that, if adopted, will radically alter the path of humankind! Imagine a world without war or hunger or fear! Imagine a world that is disease-free and unified, where all life is honored! These are the dreams of the *Ambassadors of Light*.

- The M.A.P.S. Ambassadors
- Media Misconceptions
- Luscious Lifestyle
- The Return of the Qi Masters
- Challenging the Status Quo
- Bigu and Qigong Scientific Studies

- Research and Statistical Analysis
- The Global Position
- Human Evolution
- Genetic Engineering and Cloning
- Our Planet — Our Progeny
- Redirecting Resources

$16⁹⁵ SOFTCOVER 253 P.
ISBN 3-929512-70-X

available through
LIGHT TECHNOLOGY
PUBLISHING
PO Box 3540 • Flagstaff, AZ 86003

Phone: 928-526-1345 or 1-800-450-0985 • Fax 800-393-7017 or 928-714-1132
... or use our online bookstore at www.lighttechnology.com

In Resonance
Jasmuheen

This book is a manual for personal self-empowerment and self-mastery. It is filled with inspirational information of experiental research and channeled guidance from Jasmuheen and the Ascended Ones. The predominant focus of Jasmuheen's work is on bridging the worlds of science and religion, the realms of the physical and etheris, plus the cultures of the East and the West.

In Resonance offers practical tools for utilizing specific programming techniques and tuning, mind mastery for reality creation and creating a purposeful and passionate existence. It addresses issues from meditation to telepathy and Universal Laws plus the existence of the Brotherhoods of Light.

- The Art of Resonance
- The Uniqueness of Being
- White Light Energy
- The Nature of Reality
- The Power of Emotion
- Understanding the Stress and the Stressors
- Practical Techniques to De-stress
- The Chakras — The Body's Energy Centres
- Destiny and Service
- Androgyny — Our True State

- Meditation and Crystals
- Understanding and Working with Vibrational Frequencies
- Channeling
- Ascension
- Prana Nirvana
- Telepathic Communication
- Bilocation, Travel by Thought and Teleportation
- The Universal Brotherhoods
- A Bridge to the New World
- Plus much more!

$24⁹⁵   HARDCOVER 312 P.
ISBN 3-929512-36-X

available through
LIGHT TECHNOLOGY
PUBLISHING
PO Box 3540 • Flagstaff, AZ 86003

Phone: 928-526-1345 or 1-800-450-0985 ⟶ Fax 800-393-7017 or 928-714-1132
. . . or use our online bookstore at www.lighttechnology.com

NEW FROM LIGHT TECHNOLOGY...

CHANGE YOUR ENCODEMENTS, YOUR DNA, YOUR LIFE!

The first part of this book discusses what you call love. Love is the most powerful energy—you are made of this energy, so when you learn to harness it, you can do whatever you wish to do in your life.

The second part contains powerful techniques for working with your DNA encodements. Discover how this process works so that you can make great changes in your life. Encodements will help you to do what some would call miracles.

The third part contains what some call predictions, which are nothing more than my reading and interpretation of the energy at the time when the energy was read. Predictions can be changed to have a more positive result—the point of my making predictions is so that you can change them.

CATHY CHAPMAN

Cathy Chapman, PhD, is a licensed therapist who works from the mind/body perspective. She is a certified Body Talk practitioner, certified hypnotherapist and Reiki Master. She has also studied Healing Touch, pranic healing and the Melchizedek Method. She channels Amma, the divine mother of divine mothers. Cathy currently lives in Texas.

16^95 SOFTCOVER 303 P.
ISBN 1-891824-52-X

Available from your favorite bookstore or:
LIGHT TECHNOLOGY PUBLISHING
PO Box 3540 • Flagstaff, AZ 86003
928-526-1345 • 800-450-0985
FAX 928-714-1132
Use our online bookstore: www.lighttechnology.com

PRETTY FLOWER
THROUGH
MIRIANDRA ROTA

Pathways & Parables for a Changing World

This book is about practical solutions called pathways. Have you ever asked Pretty Flower a question only to have her answer begin with, "Once upon a time . . ."? At the end of her parable, did you ever find yourself saying, "Huh?" and then, "Oh!" Yes—it's easy, simple. That's what the parables are all about: a shift in consciousness, spiritual awakenings galore. But don't let me keep you a moment longer from these easy pathways, delightful parables and simple solutions for your powerful living!

—Miriandra Rota

Interwoven within your story, dear beloved ones, is the truth of who you are. Interwoven within the fabric of your being are the encodings that contain all knowing and the capability to venture forth in the fulfillment of your heart's yearning. And within your heart's yearning resides your beloved innocence, which holds the wisdom you seek while creating your story. Blessed are you.

—Pretty Flower

Chapter Titles:

- We Are All Journeyers
- The Fulfillment of Your Own Knowing
- Truth Does Burst Forth!
- Ripples in the Timeline

- Friendship and Truth
- The Light Within
- The Energy of Completion
- The Spring of All Springs

19^{95} SOFTCOVER 380 P.
ISBN 1-891824-53-8

LIGHT TECHNOLOGY PUBLISHING
PO Box 3540 • Flagstaff, AZ 86003
928-526-1345 • 800-450-0985 • FAX 928-714-1132
Or use our online bookstore: www.lighttechnology.com

THE EXPLORER RACE SERIES

ZOOSH AND HIS FRIENDS THROUGH ROBERT SHAPIRO

THE SERIES: Humans—creators-in-training—have a purpose and destiny so heartwarmingly, profoundly glorious that it is almost unbelievable from our present dimensional perspective. Humans are great lightbeings from beyond this creation, gaining experience in dense physicality. This truth about the great human genetic experiment of the Explorer Race and the mechanics of creation is being revealed for the first time by Zoosh and his friends through superchannel Robert Shapiro. These books read like adventure stories as we follow the clues from this creation that we live in out to the Council of Creators and beyond.

❶ THE EXPLORER RACE

You individuals reading this are truly a result of the genetic experiment on Earth. You are beings who uphold the principles of the Explorer Race. The information in this book is designed to show you who you are and give you an evolutionary understanding of your past that will help you now. The key to empowerment in these days is to not know everything about your past, but to know what will help you now. Your number-one function right now is your status of Creator apprentice, which you have achieved through years and lifetimes of sweat. You are constantly being given responsibilities by the Creator that would normally be things that Creator would do. The responsibility and the destiny of the Explorer Race is not only to explore, but to create. 574 P. $25.00 ISBN 0-929385-38-1

❷ ETs and the EXPLORER RACE

In this book, Robert channels Joopah, a Zeta Reticulan now in the ninth dimension who continues the story of the great experiment—the Explorer Race—from the perspective of his civilization. The Zetas would have been humanity's future selves had not humanity re-created the past and changed the future. 237 P. $14.95 ISBN 0-929385-79-9

❸ EXPLORER RACE: ORIGINS and the NEXT 50 YEARS

This volume has so much information about who we are and where we came from—the source of male and female beings, the war of the sexes, the beginning of the linear mind, feelings, the origin of souls—it is a treasure trove. In addition, there is a section that relates to our near future—how the rise of global corporations and politics affects our future, how to use benevolent magic as a force of creation and how we will go out to the stars and affect other civilizations. Astounding information. 339 P. $14.95 ISBN 0-929385-95-0

❹ EXPLORER RACE: CREATORS and FRIENDS
The MECHANICS of CREATION

Now that you have a greater understanding of who you are in the larger sense, it is necessary to remind you of where you came from, the true magnificence of your being. You must understand that you are creators-in-training, and yet you were once a portion of Creator. One could certainly say, without being magnanimous, that you are still a portion of Creator, yet you are training for the individual responsibility of being a creator, to give your Creator a coffee break. This book will allow you to understand the vaster qualities and help you remember the nature of the desires that drive any creator, the responsibilities to which a creator must answer, the reaction a creator must have to consequences and the ultimate reward of any creator. 435 P. $19.95 ISBN 1-891824-01-5

❺ EXPLORER RACE: PARTICLE PERSONALITIES

All around you in every moment you are surrounded by the most magical and mystical beings. They are too small for you to see as single individuals, but in groups you know them as the physical matter of your daily life. Particles who might be considered either atoms or portions of atoms consciously view the vast spectrum of reality yet also have a sense of personal memory like your own linear memory. These particles remember where they have been and what they have done in their infinitely long lives. Some of the particles we hear from are Gold, Mountain Lion, Liquid Light, Uranium, the Great Pyramid's Capstone, This Orb's Boundary, Ice and Ninth-Dimensional Fire. 237 P. $14.95 ISBN 0-929385-97-7

❻ EXPLORER RACE and BEYOND

With a better idea of how creation works, we go back to the Creator's advisers and receive deeper and more profound explanations of the roots of the Explorer Race. The liquid Domain and the Double Diamond portal share lessons given to the roots on their way to meet the Creator of this universe, and finally the roots speak of their origins and their incomprehensibly long journey here. 360 P. $14.95 ISBN 1-891824-06-6

THE EXPLORER RACE SERIES

ZOOSH AND HIS FRIENDS THROUGH ROBERT SHAPIRO

❼ EXPLORER RACE: The COUNCIL of CREATORS

The thirteen core members of the Council of Creators discuss their adventures in coming to awareness of themselves and their journeys on the way to the Council on this level. They discuss the advice and oversight they offer to all creators, including the Creator of this local universe. These beings are wise, witty and joyous, and their stories of Love's Creation create an expansion of our concepts as we realize that we live in an expanded, multiple-level reality. 237 P. $14.95 ISBN 1-891824-13-9

❽ EXPLORER RACE and ISIS

This is an amazing book! It has priestess training, Shamanic training, Isis's adventures with Explorer Race beings—before Earth and on Earth—and an incredibly expanded explanation of the dynamics of the Explorer Race. Isis is the prototypal loving, nurturing, guiding feminine being, the focus of feminine energy. She has the ability to expand limited thinking without making people with limited beliefs feel uncomfortable. She is a fantastic storyteller, and all of her stories are teaching stories. If you care about who you are, why you are here, where you are going and what life is all about—pick up this book. You won't lay it down until you are through, and then you will want more. 317 P. $14.95 ISBN 1-891824-11-2

❾ EXPLORER RACE and JESUS

The core personality of that being known on the Earth as Jesus, along with his students and friends, describes with clarity and love his life and teaching two thousand years ago. He states that his teaching is for all people of all races in all countries. Jesus announces here for the first time that he and two others, Buddha and Mohammed, will return to Earth from their place of being in the near future, and a fourth being, a child already born now on Earth, will become a teacher and prepare humanity for their return. So heartwarming and interesting, you won't want to put it down. 354 P. $16.95 ISBN 1-891824-14-7

❿ EXPLORER RACE: Earth History and Lost Civilization

Speaks of Many Truths and Zoosh, through Robert Shapiro, explain that planet Earth, the only water planet in this solar system, is on loan from Sirius as a home and school for humanity, the Explorer Race. Earth's recorded history goes back only a few thousand years, its archaeological history a few thousand more. Now this book opens up as if a light was on in the darkness, and we see the incredible panorama of brave souls coming from other planets to settle on different parts of Earth. We watch the origins of tribal groups and the rise and fall of civilizations, and we can begin to understand the source of the wondrous diversity of plants, animals and humans that we enjoy here on beautiful Mother Earth. 310 P. $14.95 ISBN 1-891824-20-1

⓫ EXPLORER RACE: ET VISITORS SPEAK

Even as you are searching the sky for extraterrestrials and their spaceships, ETs are here on planet Earth—they are stranded, visiting, exploring, studying the culture, healing the Earth of trauma brought on by irresponsible mining or researching the history of Christianity over the past two thousand years. Some are in human guise, and some are in spirit form. Some look like what we call animals as they come from the species' home planet and interact with their fellow beings—those beings that we have labeled cats or cows or elephants. Some are brilliant cosmic mathematicians with a sense of humor; they are presently living here as penguins. Some are fledgling diplomats training for future postings on Earth when we have ET embassies here. In this book, these fascinating beings share their thoughts, origins and purposes for being here. 350 P. $14.95 ISBN 1-891824-28-7

⓬ EXPLORER RACE: Techniques for GENERATING SAFETY

Wouldn't you like to generate safety so you could go wherever you need to go and do whatever you need to do in a benevolent, safe and loving way for yourself? Learn safety as a radiated environment that will allow you to gently take the step into the new timeline, into a benevolent future and away from a negative past. 208 P. $9.95 ISBN 1-891824-26-0

☿ LIGHT TECHNOLOGY
PUBLISHING
PO Box 3540 • Flagstaff, AZ 86003

Phone: 928-526-1345 or 1-800-450-0985 • Fax: 928-714-1132 or 1-800-393-7017
. . . or use our online bookstore at www.lighttechnology.com

SHAMANIC SECRETS
ROBERT SHAPIRO

Shamanic Secrets for Spiritual Mastery the third book of the Shamanic Secrets series due out in 2006!

SPEAKS OF MANY TRUTHS AND ZOOSH THROUGH ROBERT SHAPIRO

SHAMANIC SECRETS for MATERIAL MASTERY

Learn to communicate with the planet!

This book explores the heart and soul connection between humans and Mother Earth. Through that intimacy, miracles of healing and expanded awareness can flourish. To heal the planet and be healed as well, we can lovingly extend our energy selves out to the mountains and rivers and intimately bond with the Earth. Gestures and vision can activate our hearts to return us to a healthy, caring relationship with the land we live on.

The character and essence of some of Earth's most powerful features are explored and understood, with exercises given to connect us with those places. As we project our love and healing energy there, we help the Earth to heal from humanity's destruction of the planet and its atmosphere. Dozens of photographs, maps and drawings assist the process in twenty-five chapters, which cover the Earth's more critical locations.

$**19**^{95}$ SOFTCOVER 498 P.
ISBN 1-891824-12-0

Chapter Titles:

- Approaching Material Mastery through Your Physicality
- Three Rivers: The Rhine, the Amazon and the Rio Grande
- Three Lakes: Pyramid Lake, Lake Titicaca and Lake Baikal
- Mountains: Earth's Antennas, Related to the Human Bone Structure
  - Three Mountains: The Cydonia Pyramid, Mount Rushmore and Mount Aspen
  - Mountains in Turkey, Japan and California
  - Eurasia and Man's Skeletal Structure
  - Greenland, the Land of Mystery
  - Africa and North America
  - South and Central America and Australia

- Shamanic Interaction with Natural Life
- Africa and the Caspian and Black Seas
- Mauna Loa, Mount McKinley and Shiprock
- The Gobi Desert
- Old Faithful, the Cayman Islands, the Blue Mountains and Grandfather Mountain
- Meteor Crater, Angel Falls and Other Unique Locations on the Planet

PART II: THE FOUNDATION OF ONENESS
- The Explorer Race as a Part of Mother Earth's Body
- Spiritual Beings in a Physical World
- Earth Now Releasing Human Resistance to Physical Life
- Healing Prisoners, Teaching Students
- The Shaman's Key: Feeling and the Five Senses
- How to Walk, How To Eat
- Breathing: Something Natural We Overlook
- How to Ask and Let Go, and How to Sleep
- Singing Our Songs
- Some Final Thoughts

SHAMANIC SECRETS for PHYSICAL MASTERY

The purpose of this book is to allow you to understand the sacred nature of your own physical body and some of the magnificent gifts it offers you. When you work with your physical body in these new ways, you will discover not only its sacredness, but how it is compatible with Mother Earth, the animals, the plants, even the nearby planets, all of which you now recognize as being sacred in nature.

It is important to feel the value of yourself physically before you can have any lasting physical impact on the world. The less you think of yourself physically, the less likely your physical impact on the world will be sustained by Mother Earth. If a physical energy does not feel good about itself, it will usually be resolved; other physical or spiritual energies will dissolve it because it is unnatural. The better you feel about your physical self when you do the work in the previous book as well as in this one and the one to follow, the greater and more lasting will be the benevolent effect on your life, on the lives of those around you and ultimately on your planet and universe.

$2500 SOFTCOVER 544 P.
ISBN 1-891824-29-5

Chapter Titles:

- Cellular Clearing of Traumas and Unresolved Events
- Feeling is Our Body's First and Primary Language
- The Resolution of Fear, Trauma and Hate
- Dealing with Fear, Pain and Addiction
- Shame, Arrogance, Safety and the Inability to Trust
- The Role of Trauma in Human Life
- Letting Go of Old Attitudes and Inviting New Energy
- The Waning of Individuality
- Clearing the Physical Body
- Using the Gestures to Protect, Clear and Charge
- The Flow of Energy
- Connecting with the Earth
- Communication of the Heart

- More Supportive Gestures
- Sleeping and Dreamtime
- Responsibility and Living prayer
- Communicating with the Natural World
- Life Lessons and the Vital Life Force
- The Sacrament of Food
- Working with the Elements
- Communication with Those Who Would Follow
- Elemental Connections
- Taking Responsibility
- Creating Personal Relationships

SHAMANIC SECRETS for SPIRITUAL MASTERY

ROBERT SHAPIRO

Superchannel Robert Shapiro can communicate with any personality anywhere and anywhen. He has been a professional channel for over thirty years and channels with an exceptionally clear and profound connection.

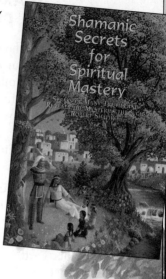

The nature of spiritual mastery is not to be completely in control, but the nature of spiritual mastery is necessarily to not have any control. The whole point of spiritual mastery is *to be in concordance, not in control.* Concordance is a little different, and it's the closest word I can find in your language to express how I feel about it. Concordance to me would mean that whatever develops as you go along, moment-to-moment in your life, you are able to act or react to it on the basis of the natural foundational love that exists between all life forms. Spiritual mastery is the underpinnings of multiple ways of being and multiple ways of understanding, appreciating and interacting in harmony with your world.

— Reveals the Mysteries

25^{00}

SOFTCOVER 475 P.
ISBN 1-891824-58-9

Highlights Include:

- ☺ My Life as a Mystical Man
- ☺ Interacting in Harmony with Your World
- ☺ Looking upon Others with Compassion and Warmth
- ☺ Rainbows Nourish the Earth
- ☺ Captured Images and the Energy in Artwork

- ☺ Physical Messaging
- ☺ The Feeling Heart
- ☺ The Human Soul on Earth
- ☺ Deep-Sleep Activity in Animals and Humans
- ☺ Death and Birth
- ☺ Special Section: Beauty of Life

EASY ORDER 24 HOURS A DAY

Order ONLINE!
www.light
technology.com

Order by Mail
Send To:
Light Technology Publishing
PO Box 3540
Flagstaff, AZ 86003

Order by Phone
800-450-0985
928-526-1345

Order by Fax
800-393-7017
928-714-1132

LIGHT
Technology
PUBLISHING

Visit our online bookstore: www.lighttechnology.com

A New Book by
Drunvalo Melchizedek

LIVING IN THE HEART

Includes a CD with Heart Meditation by
Drunvalo Melchizedek

$25 with CD
Softcover 120 P.
ISBN 1-891824-43-0

"Long ago we humans used a form of communication and sensing that did not involve the brain in any way; rather, it came from a sacred place within our heart. What good would it do to find this place again in a world where the greatest religion is science and the logic of the mind? Don't I know this world where emotions and feelings are second-class citizens? Yes, I do. But my teachers have asked me to remind you who you really are. You are more than a human being, much more. For within your heart is a place, a sacred place where the world can literally be remade through conscious cocreation. If you give me permission, I will show you what has been shown to me."

- Beginning with the Mind
- Seeing in the Darkness
- Learning from Indigenous Tribes
- The Sacred Space of the Heart
- The Unity of Heaven and Earth

- Leaving the Mind and Entering the Heart
- The Sacred Space of the Heart Meditation
- The Mer-Ka-Ba and the Sacred Space of the Heart
- Conscious Cocreation from the Heart Connected to the Mind

Drunvalo Melchizedek has been studying pure consciousness and human potential for almost forty years. His focus on the rediscovery of the human lightbody, the Mer-Ka-Ba and the way Sacred Geometry is inherent within the lightbody and all of creation is shared through workshops and books as he has brought his vision of the Flower of Life and the Mer-Ka-Ba to the world.

Now his new work, *Living in the Heart*, with the techniques that lead you into the Sacred Space of the Heart, goes even deeper into the possibilities of human potential and the creation process itself. Within these pages, Drunvalo shares his knowledge and tells you exactly how to achieve this ancient state of consciousness so that, finally, what you dream in your heart you can make real in your everyday life; a beautiful, abundant life and ascension into the higher worlds become a natural sequence of living in your heart. Join Drunvalo and be part of the large group of people who have found the joy of living in the space where you and God are one.

**EASY ORDER
24 HOURS
A DAY**

Order ONLINE!
www.light
technology.com

Order by Mail
Send To:
Light Technology Publishing
PO Box 3540
Flagstaff, AZ 86003

Order by Phone
800-450-0985
928-526-1345

Order by Fax
800-393-7017
928-714-1132

LIGHT Technology
PUBLISHING

Visit our online bookstore: www.lighttechnology.com

THE ANCIENT SECRET
OF THE FLOWER OF LIFE
VOLUME 1

O nce, all life in the universe knew the Flower of Life as the creation pattern— the geometrical design leading us into and out of physical existence. Then, from a very high state of consciousness, we fell into darkness, the secret hidden for thousands of years, encoded in the cells of all life.

Now we are rising from the darkness and a new dawn is streaming through the windows of perception. This book is one of those windows. Drunvalo Melchizedek presents in text and graphics the Flower of Life Workshop, illuminating the mysteries of how we came to be.

Sacred Geometry is the form beneath our being and points to a divine order in our reality. We can follow that order from the invisible atom to the infinite stars, finding ourselves at each step. The information here is one path, but between the lines and drawings lie the feminine gems of intuitive understanding. You might see them sparkle around some of these provocative ideas:

- Remembering Our Ancient Past
- The Secret of the Flower Unfolds
- The Darker Side of Our Present and Past
- The Geometries of the Human Body
- When Evolution Crashed, and the Christ Grid Arose
- Egypt's Role in the Evolution of Consciousness
- The Significance of Shape and Structure

$25⁰⁰ Softcover 228 P.
ISBN 1-891824-17-1

Available from your favorite bookstore or:

LIGHT TECHNOLOGY PUBLISHING
PO Box 3540 • Flagstaff, AZ 86003
928-526-1345 • 800-450-0985 • FAX 928-714-1132
Or use our online bookstore: www.lighttechnology.com

Drunvalo Melchizedek's life experience reads like an encyclopedia of breakthroughs in human endeavor. He studied physics and art at the University of California at Berkeley, but he feels that his most important education came after college. In the past 25 years, he has studied with over 70 teachers from all belief systems and religious understandings.

For some time now, he has been bringing his vision to the world through the Flower of Life program and the Mer-Ka-Ba meditation. This teaching encompasses every area of human understanding, explores the development of humankind from ancient civilizations to the present time and offers clarity regarding the world's state of consciousness and what is needed for a smooth and easy transition into the 21st century.

THE ANCIENT SECRET OF THE FLOWER OF LIFE

VOLUME 2

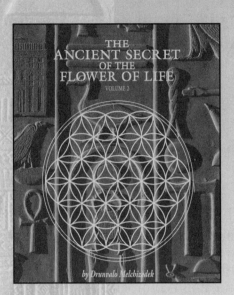

$25⁰⁰   Softcover 252 P.
ISBN 1-891824-21-X

- The Unfolding of the Third Informational System
- Whispers from Our Ancient Heritage
- Unveiling the Mer-ka-ba Meditation
- Using Your Mer-ka-ba
- Connecting to the Levels of Self
- Two Cosmic Experiments
- What We May Expect in the Forthcoming Dimensional Shift

The sacred Flower of Life pattern, the primary geometric generator of all physical form, is explored in even more depth in this volume, the second half of the famed Flower of Life workshop. The proportions of the human body, the nuances of human consciousness, the sizes and distances of the stars, planets and moons, even the creations of humankind, are all shown to reflect their origins in this beautiful and divine image. Through an intricate and detailed geometrical mapping, Drunvalo Melchizedek shows how the seemingly simple design of the Flower of Life contains the genesis of our entire third-dimensional existence.

From the pyramids and mysteries of Egypt to the new race of Indigo children, Drunvalo presents the sacred geometries of the Reality and the subtle energies that shape our world. We are led through a divinely inspired labyrinth of science and stories, logic and coincidence, on a path of remembering where we come from and the wonder and magic of who we are.

Finally, for the first time in print, Drunvalo shares the instructions for the Mer-Ka-Ba meditation, step-by-step techniques for the re-creation of the energy field of the evolved human, which is the key to ascension and the next dimensional world. If done from love, this ancient process of breathing prana opens up for us a world of tantalizing possibility in this dimension, from protective powers to the healing of oneself, of others and even of the planet.

Available from your favorite bookstore or:

LIGHT TECHNOLOGY PUBLISHING
PO Box 3540 • Flagstaff, AZ 86003
928-526-1345 • 800-450-0985 • FAX 928-714-1132
Or use our online bookstore: www.lighttechnology.com

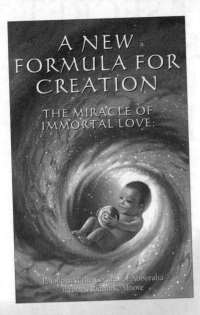

A NEW FORMULA FOR CREATION

THE MIRACLE OF IMMORTAL LOVE:

Raqui-Sha-Ma and Enak-Kee-Na

Laiolin and the Council of Abboraha through Judith K. Moore

"What do I think? Wow! It's definitely a mind-expanding experience. I can only imagine how it must have stretched Judith during the 'birthing' process. Perhaps the holographic message within this book will finally generate the 'critical mass' necessary to elevate human thinking above the egocentric mind control still so prevalent today. One way or another, a new age is dawning! This book admirably reminds us that that dawning extends far beyond just the refreshment of our patient little Mother Earth."

—Dr. Edwin M. Young

$16⁹⁵ Softcover 214 P.
ISBN 1-891824-57-0

Chapter Titles:

- Enak-Kee-Na Speaks
- Sacred Geometry and the Nature of Creation
- Expanded Understanding of DNA
- Raqui-Sha-Ma Hears Her Story
- Solstice 2001: The Time Portal Opens
- Opening the Seventh Seal
- Mastery of Transcendence: Sum Sat Na Godi
- Revelations Received During the Retreat
- The Lost Tablets of Abraham
- The Mystery of Abraham
- The Etheric Temple of Creation and the Distortion
- The Saturnian Empire
- The Enshroudment of Isha
- Isha, The Unified Field
- Demigods, Masters of Dimensions
- Masters of Dimensions Project the Distortion
- Reemergence of the House of David
- Cycles of Creation Complete
- Transitional Phase
- What of a Creation without Discordant Polarities?
- Dreams of Utopia: The New Paradigm
- Promise of Immortality
- Terra Gaia and the New Creation
- I AM ENAK-KEE-NA

. . . or use our online bookstore at www.lighttechnology.com

Lynn Buess's

Forever Numerology

Includes Master Numbers 11–99!

In *Forever Numerology*, Lynn Buess again takes a gigantic leap for numerology with extraordinary new insights and methods of interpretation. This volume will define new standards for years to come. You will be swept through transcendent realms of light and awareness, even as Buess's solid psychological base and down-to-earth reality keep you centered right here in the present moment.

Having practiced for decades as a psychotherapist, Buess has uncovered deeply repressed blocks and negative unconscious complexes in many of his clients. In this book, he works some of his insights for recognizing dysfunction into the interpretation of numerology in the hopes of awakening new seekers to the dark side of the self. Once you recognize this dark side, you have the possibility of working it out of your life. The interpretations and experiences presented in this book are given through the symbolic wisdom of numbers.

Truly, no complete volume can be written on any subject; however, the book you now hold comes closer than ever to portraying the evolution of consciousness through the symbology of numbers. It will be of help in your journey through life and in your search for the meaning of numbers.

Chapter Titles:

- Condensed History
- Cosmology and Consciousness
- Numerology of Cosmology
- The Vibrational Aspects of 1 to 9 (with 0)
- Master Numbers
- The Wisdom in Your Name
- Your Chosen Life Path

- Destiny Number
- Stress Numbers
- Karma and Numerology
- Symbology of Letters
- Progressed Chart
- Numerology and Male-Female Polarity
- Releasing Negative Patterns

$**17**^{95}$ SOFTCOVER 290 P.
ISBN 1-891824-65-1

available through
LIGHT TECHNOLOGY PUBLISHING
PO Box 3540 • Flagstaff, AZ 86003

Phone: 928-526-1345 or 1-800-450-0985 • Fax 800-393-7017 or 928-714-1132
... or use our online bookstore at www.lighttechnology.com

New From Light Technology!

THE GENTLE WAY

A SELF-HELP GUIDE FOR THOSE WHO BELIEVE IN ANGELS

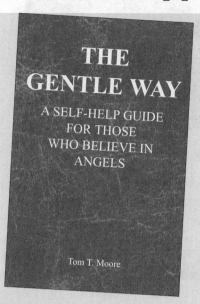

THE GENTLE WAY

A SELF-HELP GUIDE FOR THOSE WHO BELIEVE IN ANGELS

Tom T. Moore

Let me explain what I believe you'll achieve from reading this self-help book:

This book will put you back in touch with your guardian angel or strengthen and expand the connection that perhaps you already have. It will strengthen your spiritual beliefs. You will have more fun and less stress in your life. You will greatly lower the "fear factor" in everyday living. In lowering the fear factor, this book will give you the confidence that you can travel in safety wherever you go, whether it is to work and back home, to the store, across the country or around the world. It will assist you in achieving whatever goals you have set for yourself in your life. This book will assist in finding just the right job for you. It will even help you find that special person to share your life. It will assist you in handling those major challenges we all experience in life. This book will even inspire you to learn more about our world and universe. How can I promise all these benefits? It's because I have been using these concepts for over ten years, and I can report these successes from *direct knowledge and experience*. But this is a self-help guide, so that means it requires active participation on your part. What you are going to read in this book is *unique information* that you have *never seen before!* This book is for all faiths and beliefs with the only requirement being a basic belief in angels.

—Tom T. Moore

CHAPTER TITLES:

- ANGELS
- HOW I BEGAN
- EASY STEPS
- HOME LIFE
- THE CORPORATE ENVIRONMENT
- SMALL BUSINESSES
- POLITICS
- TRAVEL

- BINGO, CASINOS AND CARD GAMES
- REQUESTING BENEVOLENT OUT-COMES IN DANGEROUS PLACES
- THE RADIANT EFFECT
- LIVING PRAYERS
- "I HOPE" REQUESTS

$**14**^{95} Softcover
ISBN 1-891824-60-0

available through
LIGHT TECHNOLOGY
PUBLISHING
PO Box 3540 • Flagstaff, AZ 86003

THE LITTLE ANGEL BOOKS
by Leia Stinnett

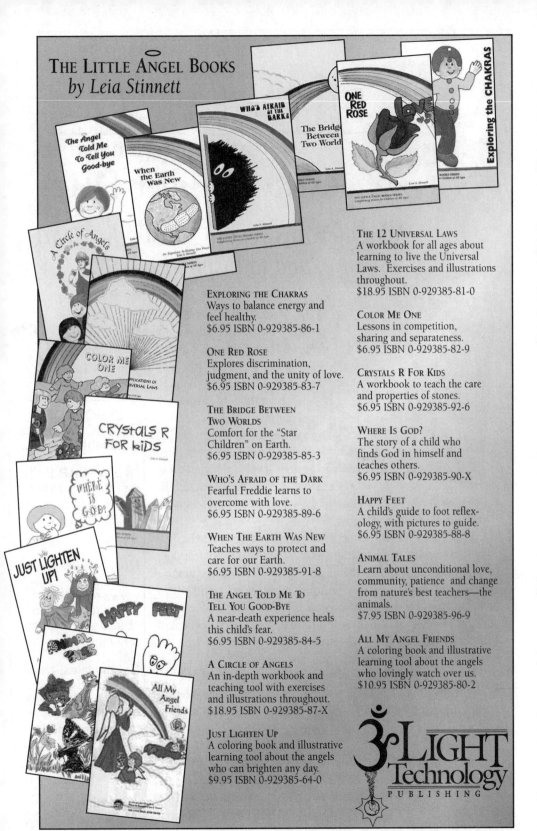

EXPLORING THE CHAKRAS
Ways to balance energy and
feel healthy.
$6.95 ISBN 0-929385-86-1

ONE RED ROSE
Explores discrimination,
judgment, and the unity of love.
$6.95 ISBN 0-929385-83-7

**THE BRIDGE BETWEEN
TWO WORLDS**
Comfort for the "Star
Children" on Earth.
$6.95 ISBN 0-929385-85-3

WHO'S AFRAID OF THE DARK
Fearful Freddie learns to
overcome with love.
$6.95 ISBN 0-929385-89-6

WHEN THE EARTH WAS NEW
Teaches ways to protect and
care for our Earth.
$6.95 ISBN 0-929385-91-8

**THE ANGEL TOLD ME TO
TELL YOU GOOD-BYE**
A near-death experience heals
this child's fear.
$6.95 ISBN 0-929385-84-5

A CIRCLE OF ANGELS
An in-depth workbook and
teaching tool with exercises
and illustrations throughout.
$18.95 ISBN 0-929385-87-X

JUST LIGHTEN UP
A coloring book and illustrative
learning tool about the angels
who can brighten any day.
$9.95 ISBN 0-929385-64-0

THE 12 UNIVERSAL LAWS
A workbook for all ages about
learning to live the Universal
Laws. Exercises and illustrations
throughout.
$18.95 ISBN 0-929385-81-0

COLOR ME ONE
Lessons in competition,
sharing and separateness.
$6.95 ISBN 0-929385-82-9

CRYSTALS R FOR KIDS
A workbook to teach the care
and properties of stones.
$6.95 ISBN 0-929385-92-6

WHERE IS GOD?
The story of a child who
finds God in himself and
teaches others.
$6.95 ISBN 0-929385-90-X

HAPPY FEET
A child's guide to foot reflex-
ology, with pictures to guide.
$6.95 ISBN 0-929385-88-8

ANIMAL TALES
Learn about unconditional love,
community, patience and change
from nature's best teachers—the
animals.
$7.95 ISBN 0-929385-96-9

ALL MY ANGEL FRIENDS
A coloring book and illustrative
learning tool about the angels
who lovingly watch over us.
$10.95 ISBN 0-929385-80-2

3° LIGHT
Technology
PUBLISHING

SEDONA

Journal of EMERGENCE!

Rated Number One!

We Offer Answers to Satisfy the Heart and to Inspire Lives!

The *Sedona Journal of Emergence!* is the one monthly magazine readers never throw away. It features Predictables that discuss what's happening right now, this day, this month, and how you can make the most of the potentials created by the acceleration of frequency in your life on every level— physical, mental, emotional, spiritual—and on the integrated levels of wholeness that are becoming possibilities now. It even offers your very own personal horoscope for each week of the month.

The *Sedona Journal* also contains the latest channeled information on what to do, as humans and the Earth move from the third to the fourth dimension, and reveals how these energies affect you and the Earth. No other monthly magazine offers the quantity and quality of guidance by other-dimensional beings to not only help you through these unprecedented times but to help you make sense of and understand what all of this opening and expansion means to you!

The *Sedona Journal* is filled with practical articles and features on healing, ETs, UFOs, flower essences, minerals, dreams, the tarot, numerology, the new children, reincarnation and more!

ELECTRONIC SUBSCRIPTIONS available for SJE!

$43⁰⁰/YEAR for 12 issues anywhere on the planet!
$77⁰⁰/YEAR for 24 issues!

Must be puchased online at: www.sedonajournal.com for you to obtain a user name and password.

Get the latest channeling and astrology 2 weeks before it is available on the newsstand.

Get SPECIAL UPDATES of channeled material before they're available on the newsstand with ELECTRONIC SUBSCRIPTIONS!

ORDER NOW TO RECEIVE SPECTACULAR SAVINGS

¡yes! Send Me:

Printed and Mailed Subcriptions

PRIORITY	1ST CLASS	2ND CLASS
☐ 2 yrs (24 issues)...$169	☐ 2 yrs... $139	☐ 2 yrs... $77
☐ 1 yr (12 issues)... $86	☐ 1 yr.... $76	☐ 1 yr.... $43

USA

AIR	SURFACE
☐ 2 yrs (24 issues).... $143	☐ 2 yrs.......... $99
☐ 1 yr (12 issues)...... $75	☐ 1 yr.......... $56

CANADA & MEXICO

U.S. dollars only

AIR	SURFACE
☐ 2 yrs (24 issues)...... $255	☐ 2 yrs......... $116
☐ 1 yr (12 issues)........$136	☐ 1 yr......... $62

ALL COUNTRIES
Except USA, Canada & Mexico

U.S. dollars only

Electronic Subscriptions

U.S. dollars only   ☐ 1 yr.... $43   ☐ 2 yr.... $77

Get the entire Journal online by subscription — and get it 2 weeks before it goes on the newsstand.

SAVE expensive overseas freight or postage on your Sedona Journal subscription!

My Name _____

Address _____

City _____ State: _____ Zip: _____

Phone _____

Email _____

Gift Recipient Name _____

Address _____

City _____ State: _____ Zip: _____

Personalized Gift Card from _____

METHOD OF PAYMENT:

☐ CHECK #   ☐ M.O.

☐ VISA   ☐ MASTERCARD   ☐ NOVUS   ☐ AMEX

CARD NO. _____

EXPIRATION DATE _____

SIGNATURE _____

ORDER NOW!

TO RECEIVE SPECTACULAR SAVINGS OFF OF THE COVER PRICE!

$5.95

SAVE $65.80 OFF THE COVER PRICE!

Electronic Subsriptions
Your e-subscription also entitles you to special channeled updates before they are available on our front page.

E-SUBSCRIBE NOW! ONLY $43.00 FOR ONE YEAR ANYWHERE ON THE PLANET. $77.00 FOR TWO YEARS.
Act now and get the Number One Rated Metaphysical Monthly online— with Source Information to help you through these incredibly challenging times.

Easy Order 24 Hours a Day

1 Order ONLINE!
http://www.sedonajournal.com

2 Order by MAIL
Send To:
Light Technology Publishing
PO Box 3870
Flagstaff, AZ 86003

3 Order by PHONE
800-450-0985
928-526-1345

4 Order by FAX
800-393-7017
928-714-1132

FREE SHIPPING for orders $100⁰⁰ or more.

excluding bookstores
USA only

Order ONLINE!
www.lighttechnology.com

Email:
customersrv@lighttechnology.net

Order by Mail
Send To:
Light Technology Publishing
PO Box 3540
Flagstaff, AZ 86003

Order by Phone
800-450-0985
928-526-1345

Order by Fax
800-393-7017
928-714-1132

*Available from your
favorite bookstore or:*

EASY ORDER 24 HOURS A DAY

LIGHT Technology PUBLISHING — ONLINE BOOKSTORE
www.lighttechnology.com

- Shopping Cart with Secure Transactions
- Want In-Depth Information on Books Listed?
  Find Excerpts and Detailed Tables of Contents in
  Our Book Market
- Sedona General Store
- Use Our Great Links to Other Sites

SEDONA Journal of EMERGENCE!
The #1 Monthly Spiritual Journal

www.sedonajournal.com

- Read Excerpts of Monthly Channeling and
  Predictions in Advance of Issue Date
- Subscribe or Renew Your Subscription
- Arrange Advertising in the Journal
- Change Your Address When You Move
- Order Back Issues
- Use Our Email Links to Contact Us or
  Send in Submissions
- Electronic subscription available—
  $43/12 issues

STARCHILD PRESS
A DIVISION OF
LIGHT TECHNOLOGY PUBLISHING

Angel books of spiritual teaching

- Metaphysical Lessons and Stories to Delight
  Children of All Ages
- Workbooks for Teachers of New Age Children
- Full Color Books with Great Art and Good Stories
- Coloring Books